THE SYNOPTIC GOSPELS
SET FREE

Studies in
Judaism and Christianity

*Exploration of Issues in the
Contemporary Dialogue Between
Christians and Jews*

Editor in Chief for
Stimulus Books
Lawrence Boadt

Editors
Lawrence Boadt, CSP
Rabbi Leon Klenicki
Kevin A. Lynch, CSP
Rev. Dennis McManus
Dr. Ann Riggs
Rabbi Leonard Schoolman
Dr. Elena Procario-Foley
Michael Kerrigan, CSP

A STIMULUS BOOK

THE SYNOPTIC GOSPELS SET FREE

Preaching without Anti-Judaism

Daniel J. Harrington, SJ

Foreword by Yehezkel Landau

A STIMULUS BOOK

PAULIST PRESS ◆ NEW YORK ◆ MAHWAH, NJ

In Memory of Krister Stendahl (1921–2008)

This book is to be used in conjunction with the *Lectionary for the Mass: for use in the dioceses of the United States of America*, Second Typical Edition Volume 1: Sundays, Solemnities, Feasts of the Lord, and the Saints. National Conference of Catholic Bishops, The Liturgical Press, Collegeville, MN, © copyright 1998, 1997, 1970 by the Confraternity of Christian Doctrine, Washington, D.C. All rights reserved. Copyright 1998 by The Order of Saint Benedict, Inc., Collegeville, MN. All rights reserved.

Other Scripture quotations contained herein are from:

Daily Roman Missal: Revised New American Bible, copyright © 1970, 1986, 1992, 1998, 2001, Confraternity of Christian Doctrine, Washington, D.C. Published in one volume by Midwest Theological Forum, Chicago, Illinois; Scepter Publishers, New York; Our Sunday Visitor, Huntington, Indiana. All rights reserved.

The *New Revised Standard Version: Catholic Edition* Copyright © 1989 and 1993, by the Division of Christian Education of the National Council of the Churches of Christ in the United States of America. Used by permission. All rights reserved.

Cover design by Sharyn Banks
Book design by Lynn Else and Theresa M. Sparacio

Cover art courtesy of Art Resource, NY, by permission:

"The Lion of Saint Mark the Evangelist" by Donata Veneziano; photo by Cameraphoto Arte, Venice / Art Resource, NY. "Saint Luke the Evangelist;" photo by A. De Gregorio © DeA Picture Library / Art Resource, NY. "Saint Matthew, Evangelist;" photo by Alinari/Regione Umbria / Art Resource, NY.

Library of Congress Cataloging-in-Publication Data

Harrington, Daniel J.
    The Synoptic Gospels set free : preaching without anti-Judaism /Daniel J. Harrington.
        p. cm.
    "A Stimulus book."
    ISBN 978-0-8091-4583-6 (alk. paper)
    1. Bible. N.T. Gospels—Criticism, interpretation, etc. 2. Antisemitism. 3. Christianity and other religions—Judaism. 4. Judaism—Relations—Christianity. I. Title.
    BS2555.52.H325 2008
    226'.083058924—dc22

                                                                    2008038479

Published by Paulist Press
997 Macarthur Boulevard
Mahwah, New Jersey 07430

www.paulistpress.com

Printed and bound in the United States of America

Contents

The Gospel of Mark

The Gospel of Luke

Foreword

Fr. Daniel Harrington has written a masterful overview of the Synoptic Gospels, one that demonstrates uncommon expertise and sensitivity in three areas crucial for Jewish-Christian relations in our time: *first,* the linguistic and historical contexts for statements attributed to Jesus and for the overarching narratives of the Evangelists; *second*, the contemporaneous developments in Jewish tradition (especially the *Mishnah,* Wisdom Literature, and the Dead Sea Scrolls of the Qumran community); and *third,* the two-thousand-year history of Jewish suffering at the hands of Christians, exacerbated by polemical and triumphalistic interpretations of gospel passages, especially the passion narratives.

Fr. Harrington writes in a clear and accessible style. His book is an exemplary work of biblical scholarship, reflecting the revolution in Catholic thought ushered in by the Second Vatican Council and *Nostra Aetate*, the historic statement on the Church's relations with other religions, notably Judaism. At the same time, Fr. Harrington's volume is a first-rate pedagogical resource, enhanced by the provocative questions at the end of each section. These questions invite the reader to engage the gospel messages personally and seriously, listening deeply to their different voices. The result is a mutually respectful conversation spanning two millennia. Harrington's gift as an exegete and writer is to make personalities in the first century of the Common Era (Jesus, his disciples, his Jewish adversaries, the Romans, other non-Jews, and even the Essenes) speak to us, Christians and Jews in the twenty-first century. Harrington compellingly, and successfully, argues that the key theological issues which the New Testament protagonists and writers were passionately debating are still alive for *us* as faithful students of scripture, both the Hebrew Bible and the New Testament. What does the covenant between the Lord of History and the people of Israel call us to do as we prepare for the messianic kingdom of God? Whose vision of redemption is closer to the fulfillment of biblical prophecies and promises? Is the New Testament notion of a suffering and crucified messiah in accordance with earlier Jewish teachings about a Davidic king and redeemer?

Jews and Christians can find common ground through engaging such questions together. Harrington's book is an invitation to do just that, and he is a helpful teacher and guide. He asks us to be mutually respectful and sensitive, to view each other as faithful partners rather than antagonistic competitors for God's favor and blessing.

What makes Fr. Harrington a trustworthy teacher for Jews is, above all, his acknowledgment that too many gospel texts are what he calls "neuralgic," carrying a painful and haunting legacy of demonization when they were taken out of their intra-Jewish context by a Gentile Church and used as murderous weapons against Jews over many centuries. To redeem this tragic history requires honesty and *teshuvah* or *metanoia* of the sort exemplified by Fr. Harrington. It also requires a new attitude and perspective on the part of Jews, so they can see their spiritual brother Jesus in a new light: not as an apostate or renegade, but as a Torah-observant wisdom teacher, healer, and prophetic messenger—with God-given powers akin to those of Elijah and Elisha—as well as a first-century Galilean rabbi expounding a radical, but still Jewish, understanding of the law of love at the heart of the Torah.[1]

Jesus' unconventional view of *Halakhah* (normative Jewish praxis) is most often conveyed in "debates for the sake of heaven" (a rabbinic term) with other, more mainstream communal leaders of his time, identified as the scribes and Pharisees. Harrington refutes the negative stereotype of the "legalistic" Pharisees and argues that Jesus shared a spiritual agenda with these learned teachers but was not one of them (unlike Paul, who started his career as a traditional Pharisee). It is hard to know where Jesus really stood in relation to his Jewish peers, because the New Testament writers painted a harshly polemical picture of his disputes with some of them, and because Rabbinic Judaism was still in a relatively early stage of development in the first century of the Common Era. I tend to agree with Rabbi Harvey Falk[2] that Jesus can be placed within the broad Pharisaic spectrum, although at a radical edge (examining, for example, his teachings about healing and feeding people on the Sabbath). As Rabbi Zalman Schachter-Shalomi has portrayed him,[3] Jesus might also be viewed as a kind of first-century Hasidic *rebbe* or *tzaddik,* who used homiletic stories to reach beyond the intellect to the listener's heart.

My own "Christian *rebbe,*" or mentor in New Testament studies, was Krister Stendahl, dean and New Testament professor at Harvard Divinity School when I pursued graduate studies there. He spoke about two principal *kerygmata,* or proclamations of faith, in the New Testament: the preresurrection kerygma *of* Jesus focusing on the eschatalogically present kingdom of God, and the postresurrection kerygma *about* Jesus as saving Lord.[4] In the two-millennia-long confrontation pitting Christians against Jews as supersessionist victors, the second kerygma eclipsed the first.

In our own time, as we work together to redeem and transform Jewish-Christian relations, we have the first chance ever to address the first kerygma anticipating the messianic kingdom, as a shared testimony of faith and hope. As both our traditions affirm, statements of faith need to be translated into actions that demonstrate love of God and love of neighbor. The ideal aggregate of such concrete actions is a messianic ethic or lifestyle of the kind that Jesus of Nazareth lived and taught. When Jews pray the *Kaddish* or *Aleinu* prayer, looking forward to the kingdom of God, it is the same redeemed future that Christians (and Muslims) anticipate, whoever the Redeemer will turn out to be.

Fr. Harrington presents the Synoptic Gospels as Jewish theological literature, not simply homiletical teachings aimed at making our lives more virtuous. Those teachings reveal something profound about God, *our* God, the God we often call Father or Parent or Beloved—the Creator, Sustainer, and Redeemer who loves us all and has sent messengers to bring us closer to the spark of holiness within each of us. The greatest prospective benefit of Harrington's beautiful book is its potential to help bridge the historic chasm between Judaism and Christianity, which has not only bred *inter*-faith division and suspicion, but has also caused tragic *intra*-faith consequences on both sides of the divide, splitting us off from sacred parts of ourselves. Unlike our ancestors, Jews and Christians today—joined on occasion by Muslims—can share careful and caring study of the Gospels, along with the *Tanakh* (and the Qur'an), aided by wise teachers of Fr. Harrington's caliber. Such creative learning opportunities in "intertextuality" promise to spark new insights that can enrich our faith and heal our society, so that future generations will be spared the animosity, suffering, vulnerability, and fear that our forefathers and foremothers knew.

Yehezkel Landau,
Faculty Associate in Interfaith Relations
Hartford Seminary

NOTES

1. Jewish historians of our time have offered their own positive reappraisals of Jesus the Jew, among them Joseph Klausner, Geza Vermes, and David Flusser.

2. Harvey Falk, *Jesus the Pharisee: A New Look at the Jewishness of Jesus* (Eugene, OR: Wipf & Stock Publishers, 2003).

3. See Zalman Schachter-Shalomi, *Paradigm Shift,* ed. Ellen Singer (Northvale, NJ / London: Jason Aronson, Inc., 1993), 33–37, for a multilayered Jewish Christology that envisions Jesus as a "Messiah son of *Joseph*," rather than David; as an embodiment of living Torah in the role of the "Nazarener Rebbe," with disciples akin to Hasidim of our own time; and as a mystical teacher who reveals the "sacred heart" of God and other esoteric dimensions of the Divine. Reb Zalman stresses humility as the central requirement of faith: We all need to admit that our theological formulations are tentative and, at best, inadequate attempts to convey the ultimate Logos.

4. Krister Stendahl, "One Canon Is Enough," in *Meanings: The Bible as Document and as Guide* (Philadelphia: Fortress Press, 1984), 55–68.

Introduction: Freeing the Word

The controversy over Mel Gibson's film, *The Passion of the Christ*, several years ago generated important questions: "Is Gibson an anti-Semite?" "Is the film anti-Jewish?" and "Are the Gospels anti-Jewish?" That last question is, to my mind, the most significant since it touches the core documents of Christianity.

My response to that third question has always been something like this: The Gospels in themselves are *not* anti-Jewish. But certain Gospel texts have fostered anti-Judaism, and so one can say that the Gospels may have an anti-Jewish potential. I regard the Gospels as Jewish books in the sense that their authors were Jews by birth, that their main characters were first-century Jews, that their narratives are set in the land of Israel, and that they are unintelligible apart from what we Christians now call the Old Testament and first-century Judaism.

At the same time, I recognize that the anti-Jewish potential of certain Gospel texts has been actualized in ways that embarrass and shame me as a Christian. For example, the cry of the Jerusalem crowd according to Matthew 27:25 ("his blood be on us and on our children," New Revised Standard Version, hereafter NRSV) has been used to accuse Jews of being Christ-killers and a deicide people. The negative examples can be greatly multiplied. But in this book my goal is to approach in a positive and constructive way those Synoptic Gospel texts that seem most troublesome in relationships between Jews and Christians today. I want to show that when read in their first-century Jewish context, problematic passages often turn out to be more intelligible and less likely to foster anti-Judaism.

My thesis is that one effective way to free the Synoptic Gospels (Matthew, Mark, and Luke) from their anti-Jewish potential is to read them in their first-century Jewish context. The paradox is one often met in historical studies, that is, historical research often has the effect of liberating us from our real or imagined past. My hope is that when

1

Christians and Jews recognize in these Gospels how much common ground there is between them, they will discover new and constructive ways of walking together into a new and better future.

This volume presents introductions to the Gospels of Matthew, Mark, and Luke, respectively, which situate each text in the context of first-century Judaism. Then it offers brief essays on fifteen passages in each Gospel that are either problematic or significant for better relations between Christians and Jews. I have correlated these selections with the three-year Sunday lectionary used in Roman Catholic churches and many mainline Protestant churches. These texts get the most public exposure in liturgies, and so need especially to be placed in their historical and theological contexts. Moreover, many religious education programs and Bible study groups use the Gospel passages from the lectionary as their starting points. For fuller treatments of these and other Synoptic Gospel texts, please consult the books listed in the For Further Study section at the end of this volume.

This book is intended primarily for Christian preachers and religious educators, as well as others with a special interest in Scripture. I will be especially pleased if it is used in Bible study groups, particularly ones that involve both Christians and Jews. Each essay concludes with three questions for reflection and discussion. In quoting biblical texts, I have generally followed the Revised New American Bible, the version used in most Catholic churches in the United States. It can also be used with the New Jerusalem Bible, the New Revised Standard Version, and other translations.

In dealing with the Gospels I am guided by the approach outlined in Vatican II's *Dei verbum,* according to which the Gospels are viewed as the product of a complex process of tradition involving three major stages: Jesus, the early church, and the evangelists. Here the focus of attention is the third stage, that is, what the evangelists made out of Jesus and his teachings and actions, and how they integrated the various traditions about Jesus into their Gospels.

These Gospels are called Synoptic because they offer a common view of Jesus in their wording, structure, and theology. Regarding the relationships among them I assume the two-source theory as the simplest and most efficient explanation. According to that hypothesis Mark was the first Gospel, and Matthew and Luke independently used it and a collection of Jesus' sayings commonly designated as Q and other special material designated as M (for Matthew) and L (for Luke).

This volume is a companion to George Smiga's *The Gospel of John Set Free: Preaching without Anti-Judaism* (2008), also published by Paulist Press. That work treats in detail the most important and problematic Johannine passages for Christian-Jewish relations. It also provides a good deal of recent official Catholic documentation on matters pertaining to biblical interpretation and Christian-Jewish relations. I have not repeated his work here, and I recommend that his book be read and used alongside mine.

It has been my privilege for more than forty years to devote myself to studying, teaching, and writing about Second Temple Jewish texts and the New Testament. This volume has allowed me to bring together my two academic passions. My hope is that these introductions and expositions will help to free these Gospel texts from their potential for fostering anti-Judaism precisely by showing their roots in first-century Judaism. I am grateful to Rev. Lawrence Boadt and Rabbi Leon Klenicki for their encouragement in bringing this project to completion.

The Gospel of
Matthew

Part One: Introduction

Matthew is sometimes called the most Jewish Gospel. It makes abundant use of Old Testament quotations and allusions. Its theology is expressed in thoroughly biblical categories. Its author and original audience seem to have been of Jewish origin. And it originated in a crisis that affected all Jews in the late first century CE. Nevertheless, Matthew's Gospel is sometimes described as anti-Jewish. Its critics accuse it of being the source of negative stereotypes of Jews, blaming the whole Jewish people for Jesus' death, and evacuating the Jewish tradition of ongoing significance. To deal with this question we need to place Matthew's Gospel in its Jewish historical context.

WHO, WHEN, WHERE?

The title of this Gospel as "According to Matthew" seems to have been added to manuscripts in the second century CE. Nowhere in the main text does the author identify himself or claim to have been an eyewitness. However, this Gospel has been traditionally associated with Matthew the tax collector (9:9) who became one of the twelve apostles (10:3). What exactly this figure contributed to the actual composition of the Gospel is not clear. He may simply have been an admired person in the community where the Gospel was written or circulated, or he may have been responsible for some of the source material incorporated in the text. While technically the work is anonymous, it is customary to call the writer who was responsible for the present form of the Gospel Matthew.

The evangelist was certainly a Jew. He knew Israel's Scriptures well and was eager to show how Jesus fulfilled them. He was also aware of and engaged in Jewish debates about various legal matters (grounds for divorce, ritual purity, Sabbath observance, etc.) that were controversial among Jewish teachers in the first century CE.

Moreover, he and his fellow Christian Jews were involved in an ideological and theological struggle over which movement best preserved and represented the heritage of Israel after the capture of Jerusalem and the destruction of its temple in 70 CE. His audience seems to have been predominantly Christian Jews like himself. Matthew tried both to confirm them in their Christian Judaism and to encourage them to join in the mission to non-Jews (see 28:19).

On the basis of possible allusions to Matthew's Gospel in early patristic writings it is customary to set the latest possible date of composition at 100 CE. And the apparent references to Jerusalem's destruction by the Romans in Matthew 21:41, 22:7, and 27:25 establish 70 CE as the earliest possible date. Most scholars today place its composition around 85 or 90 CE and regard it as a revised and expanded version of Mark's Gospel.

The place of the Gospel's composition is generally assigned to a large city in the eastern Mediterranean, most likely in Palestine or Syria. The city must have had a large Jewish population that could accommodate Matthew's Christian Jewish community and its Jewish rivals who controlled "their synagogues." Moreover, the city must have been a place where Greek was spoken and written widely, since the Gospel was composed in Greek. The most popular candidate among modern scholars is Antioch in Syria. Other possibilities include Caesarea Maritima in Palestine, Tyre or Sidon in Phoenicia, and Pella in the Decapolis in Transjordan.

WHY, WHAT, HOW?

Mark's Gospel seems to have been composed in Rome around 70 CE. Matthew had access to that Gospel, plus the Sayings Source Q and other oral and/or written traditions designated as M. In producing his second edition of Mark's Gospel, Matthew served as a careful editor by correcting minor mistakes, omitting what he regarded as extraneous details, and including more teachings of Jesus.

In writing his Gospel Matthew also responded to the crisis facing all Jews after 70 CE. The three great pillars of ancient Judaism were the Jerusalem Temple, the land of Israel, and the Mosaic Law. But the Temple had been destroyed, and the land was even more firmly under Roman military and political control. The question facing all Jews at that time was: How will the Jewish heritage continue, and who will carry it on?

There were several answers to that question. The militant Zealots promoted an insurgency against the Romans and worked toward a Second Jewish Revolt in 132–135 CE (the Bar Kokhba Revolt). The apocalyptists represented in works like 4 Ezra and 2 Baruch hoped for a future divine intervention. The early rabbis worked at developing a new form of Judaism focused on the exact observance of the Torah and the traditions associated with it. And Christian Jews like Matthew regarded Jesus as the authoritative interpreter of the Torah and the fulfillment of Israel's hopes for a Davidic Messiah. According to Matthew, the best way to preserve the heritage of Israel was to follow the teaching and example of Jesus of Nazareth, and to celebrate him as the Son of David, Messiah, Son of man, Son of God, and Lord.

Matthew's Gospel is a narrative about Jesus of Nazareth—his birth, his adult activity as a teacher and healer, and his death. While the Gospel looks like a biography and would have been considered as such in antiquity, it is really a form of preaching (kerygma) about a person who early Christians believed had been raised from the dead and now lives on with God and yet is somehow still among us as Emmanuel ("God with us").

In writing his Gospel the evangelist incorporated most of Mark's Gospel and used it as his narrative framework. Besides adding an infancy narrative in chapters 1—2, Matthew created an alternating sequence of narratives and discourses (mainly from Q and M material), and appended to Mark's passion narrative accounts of appearances by the risen Jesus to his followers. The five great speeches represent the most distinctive feature of Matthew's narrative. They are the Sermon on the Mount (chaps. 5—7), the missionary discourse (10), the parables of the kingdom (13), the community discourse (18), and the eschatological discourse (24—25). While originally composed for a Christian Jewish community perhaps in Antioch, Matthew's Gospel quickly circulated among other Christian communities and soon became the most important and influential Gospel, largely because it contains so many of Jesus' teachings.

The evangelist whom we call Matthew adopts the stance of an omniscient narrator informing interested readers about the life and teachings of Jesus of Nazareth. The chief character is Jesus, and he is portrayed in relation to his followers (the twelve and other disciples), his opponents (King Herod, the scribes and Pharisees, the chief priests and elders), and the crowds (the bulk of the people). All these characters live in the land of Israel in the early years of what we call the first century CE.

Nevertheless, Matthew's Gospel was not simply an objective report about characters and events some fifty years in the past. It was also part of a drama unfolding in the evangelist's own time in 85–90 CE. The drama concerned the struggle over Israel's heritage in the new situation created for all Jews with the destruction of the Jerusalem Temple. In that Jewish historical context Matthew's Gospel had a polemical edge to it, since the evangelist was also making the case for the superiority of his brand of Christian Judaism. When taken out of that specific intra-Jewish context, Matthew's Gospel can encourage anti-Judaism and so become a dangerous text.

MAJOR MATTHEAN THEMES

God: As a Christian Jewish theologian, Matthew presupposes the biblical picture of the God of Israel. This God created the universe and keeps it in existence, chose Israel as his special people, revealed to them his will (in the Torah), remains faithful to them despite their infidelities, and treats them with justice and mercy. Like other Christians, Matthew identifies this God as the Father of Jesus and portrays Jesus as the Son of God. As the Son of God par excellence, Jesus serves as the preeminent representative of God and so can be called Emmanuel, or "God with us" (1:23; see 28:20).

Kingdom of Heaven: Like other Jews of his time, Matthew out of reverence avoids using the name of God too frequently and often employs *heaven* as a substitute ("the kingdom of heaven is like..."). Matthew makes his own the Jewish understanding of the kingdom of God in both its classic biblical sense and its later apocalyptic form. He assumes that "the LORD reigns" over the world already, as many psalms proclaim. He also looks forward to the day when God's reign will be even more completely manifest ("thy kingdom come"). While orienting his readers toward the future fullness of God's kingdom, he portrays Jesus as the present embodiment and manifestation of God's kingdom. He wants his readers to recognize how Jesus has made

God's reign present in his healing and teaching activities, and especially through his resurrection from the dead. He orients them toward the full coming of God's kingdom, and counsels patience and watchfulness while anticipating its definitive arrival.

Jesus: Besides presenting Jesus as a wise teacher and powerful healer, Matthew takes over and develops honorific titles applied by early Christians to Jesus. The three main titles emphasized by Matthew are Son of God, Messiah, and Son of man. Each has a rich biblical background. Jesus' special relationship of intimacy with God as Father is acknowledged at his baptism (3:17) and transfiguration (17:5) when a voice from heaven identifies him as the Son of God (see Ps 2; Hos 11:1). The Greek word *Christos* ("anointed") is the equivalent of the Hebrew term *Messiah* (after the pattern of David the shepherd-king), and it functions in Matthew and elsewhere in the New Testament as practically the surname of Jesus. And he is the Son of man in keeping with the different nuances of that term: the one who identifies with other humans (see Ezekiel), who moves inexorably toward his passion and death (passion predictions), and who is expected to come again as the eschatological judge (see Dan 7; 1 Enoch 37−71; Matt 25:31–46). Finally, Matthew is especially fond of pointing out how Jesus fulfills the Scriptures in his person and actions. Especially prominent are the fulfillment quotations, which are prefaced by notices that in him the Scriptures are being fulfilled. This Gospel is also full of biblical allusions and echoes, all contributing to the impression that Jesus really is Emmanuel and does everything in accord with his Father's will.

Disciples: The closest followers of Jesus (the twelve) are portrayed more positively by Matthew than they are by Mark. However, during Jesus' lifetime they display what Matthew calls "little faith," which is better than no faith at all but is not yet perfect faith. The disciples take Jesus as their one teacher, do what he does in proclaiming God's kingdom and healing others, follow the Mosaic Law as interpreted by Jesus, and after Easter are commissioned to make disciples of all nations.

Ethics: Matthew supplies plenty of ethical content, especially in the five speeches and in the Sermon on the Mount in particular. The emphasis is not so much on right and wrong as it is on the formation of Christian character. The main concerns are one's identity as a follower of Jesus, the goal of human life (happiness with God in the kingdom of God), and the values and practices that will facilitate reaching that goal.

IS MATTHEW'S GOSPEL ANTI-JEWISH?

At first glance that question may seem nonsensical. Matthew was Jewish by birth, knew and respected the Jewish Scriptures, placed Jesus in his Jewish context, engaged in debates about Jewish legal issues, and portrayed Jesus as the fulfillment of Jewish hopes.

The charge that Matthew was anti-Jewish stems largely from the controversy in which he was involved around 85–90 CE. One of the evangelist's purposes in writing his Gospel seems to have been to contend that the Jewish heritage is best carried on by Christian Jews like himself who took Jesus of Nazareth as the authoritative interpreter of the Torah and the goal of Israel's hopes.

In making his case Matthew sharpened many early traditions and used them against his Jewish rivals. He caricatured the scribes and Pharisees and branded them as "hypocrites." He referred in a sneering way to "their synagogues." He constructed a polemical attack ("Woe to you") on the scribes and Pharisees in chapter 23 and heightened the responsibility of the Jewish officials for Jesus' death. He had "all the people" take upon themselves the responsibility for Jesus' death and suggested that the destruction of Jerusalem in 70 CE was just punishment for the execution of Jesus.

The Greco-Roman world in which Matthew wrote was not a place for polite religious and philosophical dialogue. For example, the Jewish group behind the Dead Sea scrolls (most likely the Essenes) said vicious things about a rival Jewish group (probably the Pharisees) whom they dismissed as "seekers after smooth things." In that historical context polemical language such as appears in Matthew's Gospel is understandable, though not necessarily admirable or worthy of imitation today.

The polemical parts of Matthew's Gospel are best understood as reflections of a family quarrel within late first-century Judaism over who best carries on the religious heritage of Israel. The problem comes when they are taken out of that context and applied to Jews today or throughout history. When Christianity became largely Gentile from the second century onward, the inner-Jewish context of

Matthew's polemics was lost and often turned against Jews in the local setting. Thus Matthew's Gospel became a dangerous text most obviously for Jews (because they suffered persecution) and also for Christians (because they ignored the Jewishness of Jesus and the Jewish roots of their faith).

Is Matthew's Gospel anti-Jewish? When read with an eye toward its original historical context, neither the Gospel nor the evangelist deserves that description. However, Christians today need to be aware of the anti-Jewish potential of this Gospel in perpetrating negative stereotypes about Jews and providing religious validation for anti-Jewish speech and activities. The expositions of key Matthean texts that follow seek to illustrate the positive value of approaching them as Jewish texts and to caution Christian teachers and preachers about material that might contribute to anti-Judaism.

Part Two: Lectionary Commentary

1
Matthew 1:1—2:23:
The Infancy Narrative
Cycles A, B, and C:
The Christmas Season

The familiar Christmas story combines elements from the two quite different infancy narratives in Matthew 1—2 and Luke 1—2. They agree on several points, and both emphasize Jesus' roots in Israel. But Matthew focuses on Jesus' place in Israel's past, whereas Luke concentrates on the Jewish characters around Jesus. Joseph is the main character in Matthew's story, while John the Baptist and Mary are especially prominent for Luke. The tone of Luke 1—2 is joyful and celebratory, whereas Matthew 1—2 is full of conflict and foreboding. While the full Christmas story may be deeply ingrained in us, it is enlightening and important for teachers and preachers to respect the integrity of each New Testament infancy narrative.

Matthew 1 answers the question, "Who is Jesus?" It establishes Jesus' identity as the Son of David and the Son of God in the context of Jewish history and the Jewish Scriptures. In effect, Jesus embodies the heritage of his people Israel.

Matthew's infancy narrative begins with the genealogy of Jesus in 1:1–17 (compare Luke 3:23–38). Following the linear format found in the Hebrew Bible (see Ruth 4:18–22; 1 Chr 2—3), it traces the Jewish ancestry of Jesus from Abraham through David and the Exile generation to Joseph and Mary. It divides the ancestors into three groups of fourteen men, though the pattern is interrupted by the

14

appearance of four unusual women (Tamar, Rahab, Ruth, and Bathsheba). The Matthean genealogy establishes Jesus as the Son of David and thus serves as a bridge to the Old Testament and a witness to Jesus' continuity with his people's history.

The account of Jesus' conception and birth (1:18–25) explains how Jesus the Son of David was also—and especially—the Son of God, and how in turn the Son of God became the Son of David. When Joseph discovers that his fiancée Mary is pregnant, he suspects her of adultery. As an observant Jew, Joseph agonizes over whether to expose her publicly to the penalty for adulterous behavior (see Deut 22:23–27) or simply send her away quietly. As happens frequently in the Old Testament, Joseph's dilemma is resolved by means of an angel and a dream, both understood as messengers from God. He is informed that Mary's pregnancy is through the agency of the Holy Spirit in fulfillment of the prophecy in Isaiah 7:14 that a virgin would conceive and bear a son to be named Emmanuel ("God with us" in Hebrew). Jesus the Son of God through the Holy Spirit thus becomes a legal Son of David through his putative father, Joseph.

Matthew 2 concerns the whereabouts of the infant Jesus. It explains how and why he went from Bethlehem in Judea to Nazareth in Galilee by way of Egypt. Its five episodes occur in different places and are explained with reference to different biblical texts. It portrays Jesus after the pattern of Moses in Exodus 1—2.

The first episode (2:1–6) occurs in Jerusalem and deals with the Messiah's place of birth. When the Magi (perhaps pagan priests from Persia or astronomers from Babylon) come to Jerusalem and inquire about the birthplace of "the king of the Jews," King Herod ascertains from Jewish priests and scribes that on the basis of Micah 5:1–2 and 2 Samuel 5:2 the new Davidic Messiah will be born in Bethlehem. Just as the Egyptian Pharaoh tried to kill Moses and the other Hebrew male children, so Herod who ruled in Israel from 37 to 4 BCE and his supporters in Jerusalem were disturbed by rumors of a Davidic descendant who might shepherd his people Israel.

The second episode (2:7–12) takes place in Bethlehem and alludes to Balaam's prophecy in Numbers 24:17: "A star shall advance from Jacob, / and a staff shall arise from Israel" (New American Bible, hereafter NAB). Whereas Herod pretends to want to pay homage to the child (2:2, 8) but really wants to kill him, the Gentile Magi do pay homage to the newborn child with sincerity

(2:11) and offer him precious gifts (see Isa 60:6 and Ps 72:10). When the Magi are told in a dream to avoid meeting with Herod again (lest the child's location be revealed), the evil king finds himself even more threatened and frustrated. Herod's own credentials as a Jew were suspect, and he ruled at the pleasure of the Roman emperor Augustus. To hear from Gentile visitors that "the king of the Jews" (2:2) had been born in Bethlehem (David's city) would make Herod very nervous about his own future tenure as king of the Jews.

The third episode (2:13–15) concerns the flight of the Holy Family into Egypt (frequently a place of refuge for Jews in biblical times) and climaxes with the quotation of Hosea 11:1: "Out of Egypt I called my son" (NRSV). Again, as in 1:20, Joseph is directed by an angel in a dream. Just as Pharaoh tried to have Moses killed (see Exod 2:15), so Herod wants to have the child Jesus killed (2:13). The quotation of Hosea 11:1, which originally referred to Israel collectively as the son of God, is now applied individually to Jesus and is used to develop further the theme of Jesus as the embodiment of Israel's heritage.

The fourth episode (2:16–18) describes the slaughter of the innocents in Bethlehem and environs, and interprets it as the fulfillment of Jeremiah 31:15. Herod's command to kill all the boys two years old and under echoes Pharaoh's command to throw all the Hebrew boys into the Nile River (Exod 1:22).

The final episode (2:19–23) explains why Joseph brought Jesus to Nazareth in Galilee. As in 1:20 and 2:13, Joseph is told by an angel in a dream to avoid returning to Judea because Herod's son Archelaus was ruling there after Herod's death in 4 BCE. In Genesis 37–50, of course, the patriarch Joseph is the dreamer par excellence. The child Jesus' arrival in Nazareth is also presented as the fulfillment of biblical prophecy. Whether the reference ("He shall be called a Nazorean," NAB) is to Judges 13:5, Isaiah 11:1, or another text remains debated. The point here and elsewhere in Matthew 2 is that the movements of the Holy Family fulfill Israel's Scriptures.

Matthew's infancy narrative is so full of biblical quotations, allusions, and echoes that some scholars regard them as midrash, that is, imaginative compositions based on Scripture rather than factual reports of historical events. Instead of delving into that debate here (which cannot be resolved anyhow), it is more fruitful for teachers and preachers to attend to what the evangelist seems most intent on trying to communicate: the Jewish identity of Jesus.

Matthew also wants to suggest that as Jesus was as an adult, so he was as a child. Through the infancy narrative the evangelist foreshadows themes that will reappear in the passion-resurrection narrative in chapters 26—28: opposition from the leaders of his people (Matt 2:1–23 = 26:3–5), the title "King of the Jews" (2:2 = 27:37), the mission to "all nations" (2:1–12 = 28:19), and the promise to be Emmanuel (1:23 = 28:20).

For Reflection and Discussion:

1. In what ways does Matthew situate the birth and infancy of Jesus within Judaism?
2. How would you describe the tone or mood of Matthew's infancy narrative in comparison with Luke's account?
3. What effect does Matthew's emphasis on the Jewishness of Jesus have on you as a reader of the Gospels today?

2
Matthew 3:13–17:
The Baptism of Jesus
Cycle A:
The Baptism of the Lord

With chapter 3 Matthew's narrative moves forward rapidly from Jesus' infancy to his public ministry as an adult. The bridge figure is John the Baptist. Although John exercised his own ministry, gathered disciples, and drew large crowds, Matthew and the other evangelists are careful to subordinate him to Jesus.

According to Luke 1:80, John prepared for his ministry in "the wilderness," presumably the Judean Desert where the Dead Sea scrolls were found in 1947 and afterward. That area was host to various Jewish religious movements in the first century. Whether John belonged to or had contact with the Essene community at Qumran is not certain. However, that group did take as one its biblical slogans Isaiah 40:3 ("in the wilderness prepare the way of the LORD," NRSV), the very text that the Synoptic evangelists associate with John.

According to Matthew 3:2, John preached the same message that Jesus preached: "Repent, for the kingdom of heaven has come near" (4:17, NRSV). John sought to prepare the people for the coming kingdom by his ritual of baptism. To underscore the prophetic character of his ministry, he dressed in "clothing of camel's hair with a leather belt around his waist" so as to evoke memories of the prophet Elijah (2 Kgs 1:8). The sample of John's preaching given in Matthew 3:7–10 is directed at the Pharisees and Sadducees, and warns them

18

(and all Israel with them) to repent of their sins and change their ways in the face of "the wrath to come," that is, the divine judgment that will accompany the full coming of God's kingdom. That John attracted large crowds is confirmed by the Jewish historian Flavius Josephus, who suggests that John was executed because Herod Antipas (one of Herod the Great's sons) became alarmed at John's popularity (see *Jewish Antiquities* 18:116–19).

John's ritual of baptism had precedents and parallels in the Jewish tradition. Priests who served in the Jerusalem Temple undertook various ritual washings, as did other Israelites in their ritual baths *(miqwa'ot)*. The Essenes at Qumran seem to have constructed an elaborate system of water channels so that they could perform their ritual purifications. Women converting to Judaism underwent the ritual bath known as proselyte baptism. And early Christians made baptism "in the name of Jesus" in their sacrament of initiation.

John exercised his baptism ministry at the Jordan River, traditionally the eastern border of the land of Israel. He took a rite that had some familiarity among the Jewish people and developed it into a symbolic preparation for the coming kingdom of God. What was distinctive about John's baptism was that it was received just *once* and *not* repeatedly, symbolized moral conversion ("repent"), and prepared the recipient for the divine judgment.

Matthew and the other evangelists present John as preparing the way for Jesus. They also insist that Jesus was superior to John. Luke's infancy narrative is elaborately structured to make the point that even from infancy John was great but Jesus was even greater. In Matthew 3:11–12 John admits that Jesus and his baptism are more important than he and his baptism are — so much so that John is not worthy to carry Jesus' sandals (something that a slave or servant would do). Whereas John's baptism is with water, Jesus' baptism will be with "the Holy Spirit and fire."

That Jesus was baptized by John is attested in all the Gospels and is among the most certain facts about Jesus' life. However, this fact caused embarrassment for some early Christians. If Jesus was so superior to John, why did he undergo John's baptism? Moreover, if John's baptism signified repentance and moral conversion, why did Jesus the Son of God and Messiah need that baptism?

This embarrassment is confronted in Matthew 3:14–15, a passage found only in this Gospel. In a short dialogue John protests that

Jesus should be baptizing him and not vice versa. Jesus responds, "Allow it now, for thus it is fitting for us to fulfill all righteousness" (NAB). Here and elsewhere in Matthew (see 1:19), *righteousness* seems to mean God's will or the divine plan. It includes but is not limited to Torah observance. The baptism is portrayed as providing the occasion to learn more about Jesus' identity and vocation.

The momentous character of the revelation at the baptism is underlined by the use of three biblical symbols: the opening of the heavens (Ezek 1:1), the Spirit's dove-like descent (Gen 1:2), and the voice from heaven (like the rabbinic *bat qol*). These three symbols suggest that the barriers between heaven and earth have broken down, and we are to learn something very important about Jesus.

What the voice says ("This is my beloved Son, with whom I am well pleased," NAB) is thoroughly biblical. Jesus is revealed to be the Son of God (Ps 2:7 = the Davidic king identified as the Son of God), the beloved one (Isaac = Gen 22:2), and the Servant of the Lord with whom God is pleased (Isa 42:1; 44:2). Matthew intends for us to imagine this revelation as a public event, and through it Jesus (and Matthew's readers) comes to know more clearly who he is and what he is expected to do. The temptation narrative that follows in 4:1–11 will demonstrate what kind of Son of God Jesus is.

There are obvious connections between John's baptism of Jesus and Christian baptism. However, Christian baptism is basically participation in the life, death, and resurrection of Jesus (the paschal mystery) and initiation into the Christian community. Matthew's account of Jesus' own baptism by John is more concerned with Jesus' identity and his preparation for public ministry. That baptism occurs in a thoroughly Jewish context, and his significance is conveyed by a pastiche of Old Testament images and phrases.

For Reflection and Discussion:

1. What elements in Jesus' baptism mark it as a Jewish event?
2. Why might some early Christians have been embarrassed by Jesus' baptism?
3. What aspects of Jesus' identity and vocation are revealed at his baptism?

3
Matthew 4:1–11:
The Testing of God's Son
Cycle A:
First Sunday of Lent

The Gospel episode commonly known as the "temptation of Jesus" appears in two forms, one that is very short (Mark 1:12–13) and another that is quite long (Matt 4:1–11 and Luke 4:1–13). The longer form (whose two versions are almost identical) seems to have come from the Sayings Source Q, though it stands out by its length and literary form (biblical debate) from the short sayings generally assigned to Q. Its several biblical quotations reflect the use of the Greek Bible (the Septuagint). I suggest that the longer version is better entitled the "testing of God's Son," and that it can be understood only with reference to Deuteronomy 6—8.

In that Old Testament passage Moses addresses the people of Israel in order to prepare them to enter the promised land of Canaan. The premises of Moses' speech are God's love for and choice of Israel as his special people (Deut 7:6–7) and God's relationship with Israel in the form of a covenant. Moses insists that the people learn from the negative example of the wilderness generation and not repeat their mistakes when they enter the land. He describes those experiences as a "test" by which God could find out whether it was Israel's intention to keep God's covenantal stipulations (Deut 8:2). He places the warnings in terms of the father-son relationship: "So you must realize that the LORD, your God, disciplines you even as a man disciplines his son" (Deut 8:5, NAB). Moses hopes that, whereas the wilderness generation failed the test, the new generation of Israelites entering the promised land will pass God's test.

After a narrative introduction (4:1–2), the Matthean version of the testing of God's Son consists of three dialogues between Jesus and the devil (4:3–4, 5–7, 8–10) and a narrative conclusion (4:11). Each dialogue has the devil offering a test to Jesus and Jesus responding to the test with a quotation from Deuteronomy 6—8. In each case Jesus passes the test and refuses to test God in return.

It is important for teachers and preachers to avoid language that contrasts biblical Israel and Jesus as the "new (or true) Israel." While there is a contrast of Jesus with the earlier wilderness generation (see also Heb 3:7—4:10), Jesus stands with Israel in hearing and accepting the challenges posed by Moses in Deuteronomy 6—8. Early Christian claims about Jesus' divine sonship are closely connected with his solidarity with the Israel addressed by Moses (see Hos 11:1/Matt 2:15).

The narrative introduction identifies the main characters (Jesus and the devil) and provides a rich biblical background for the debate. While the reader is to imagine a setting in the Judean Desert, the more important point is that the wilderness was the place where the wilderness generation was tested and failed (see Deut 8:2). Here the devil takes the role of Satan as the "tester" as in Job 1—2, Zechariah 3:1–2, and 1 Chronicles 21:1. The reference to Jesus fasting for forty days and forty nights recalls the forty-day fasts by Moses (Deut 9:18) and Elijah (1 Kgs 19:8) as well as the forty years during which Israel was tested in the wilderness.

The form of the debate in 4:3–10 is similar to the disputes among the rabbis found in later Jewish literature in which the disputants engage the topic and their colleagues by quoting biblical texts and reasoning from them. The assumption is that the biblical texts are authoritative and capable of illumining or even settling the debate.

The first and second rounds in the debate are prefaced by challenges by the "tempter," "If you are the Son of God" (4:3, 6, NAB). The same challenge is presupposed in the third round, though it is not made explicit (4:9). The point of the debates is to determine what kind of Son of God Jesus really is.

The first test (4:3–4) concerns Jesus' willingness to turn stones into bread in order to satisfy his physical needs after his long fast. Jesus responds by quoting Deuteronomy 8:3: "One does not live by bread alone, / but by every word that comes forth from the mouth of God" (NAB). The response recalls Deuteronomy 2:7, where Moses reminds the people that God fed them for forty years in the wilderness with manna.

The second test (4:5–7) concerns Jesus' willingness to presume on God's protection by throwing himself down from some high point in the Temple complex with the expectation that angels will save him from harm. Here the devil also quotes Scripture (Ps 91:11–12) in the hope of convincing Jesus to take up his suggestion. Jesus responds by quoting Deuteronomy 6:16: "You shall not put the Lord, your God, to the test" (NAB).

The third test (4:8–10) concerns Jesus' willingness to accept power over all the kingdoms of the earth in return for worshipping Satan. Jesus responds by quoting Deuteronomy 6:13: "The Lord, your God, shall you worship / and him alone shall you serve" (NAB). The debate ends abruptly in 4:11 with Satan departing and angels ministering to Jesus.

The "temptation" narrative is traditionally read on the first Sunday of Lent. The mentions of Jesus' forty-day fast and his resisting the three tests pertaining to food, fame, and power make it an appropriate selection. However, these themes, attractive and important as they are, can distract from the christological focus of the Matthean/Lukan version. Lent is primarily about the paschal mystery and only secondarily about us. What is especially significant about this account is that it identifies Jesus as the Son of God in relation to his people Israel. Jesus emerges victorious from the tests because he relies on the word of God as expressed in Deuteronomy 6–8.

For Reflection and Discussion:

1. What major themes emerge from your reading of Deuteronomy 6–8?
2. In light of the testing narrative, how would you describe Jesus' relationship to Israel?
3. How do Israel's Scriptures function in the testing story? What authority do they have?

4
Matthew 5:38–48:
Nonretaliation and Love of Enemies
Cycle A:
Seventh Sunday in Ordinary Time

When asked about what distinguishes Christianity from Judaism, Christians often point to Jesus' teachings about nonretaliation and love of enemies. But those claims are frequently belied by the practice of Christians, and they also neglect the fact that Jesus was a Jewish teacher rooted in the Jewish tradition and concerned always to go to the root of the Torah.

The word *Torah* derives from the Hebrew root *yarah,* which means "teach, instruct." Today it generally refers to the first five books of the Hebrew Bible and in particular to the 613 laws within them. For observant Jews the Torah is divine revelation, God's plan for the life of God's people, the will of God for them.

The Torah places the laws in the historical-theological context of God's election of Israel as a special people with the call of Abraham, the liberation of Israel from slavery under Moses, and the covenantal relationship given structure at Mount Sinai. The customary translation of Torah as "law" reflects the ancient Greek rendering of it as *nomos*. While not incorrect, this identification can mislead people today into dismissing Judaism as legalistic and into neglecting the profound narrative and theological context in which the laws now appear.

The first great speech in Matthew's Gospel (chaps. 5—7) is commonly known as the Sermon on the Mount. Matthew portrays

Jesus as delivering this discourse on a mountain, thus evoking the memory of Moses at Sinai (see Exod 19—24). This setting has encouraged interpreters to describe Jesus as the "new Moses" and the context as the "new law." Without denying the importance of the figure of Moses in Matthew's Gospel, it is better to understand the Sermon on the Mount as a wisdom instruction (see Prov 1—9 and 22—24, the Book of Sirach, etc.) concerned primarily with forming the character of those who wish to follow the way of Jesus.

In the first part of the sermon (5:3–20) Jesus sets forth the values and attitudes proper to aspirants to God's kingdom in a series of beatitudes, stresses the social importance of those who share and practice them ("salt of the earth" and "light of the world"), and states that he has come *not* to *abolish* but to *fulfill* the Law and the Prophets. Next in the antitheses in 5:21–48 he challenges his followers not to be satisfied with keeping the letter of the Law but rather to go to its roots and deeper intentions. Then in 6:1–18 he indicates how his followers should practice three essential elements in Jewish piety: almsgiving, prayer, and fasting. Next in 6:19—7:12 Jesus treats various topics in short, unconnected units (treasures, the healthy eye, serving two masters, etc.), as is customary in Jewish wisdom instructions. He concludes in 7:13–27 with exhortations to enter the narrow gate, bear good fruit, and build on solid foundations, thus reflecting the Jewish emphasis on practical wisdom.

An antithesis is a contrast or opposition. The six antitheses in Matthew 5:21–48 present an Old Testament teaching ("You have heard that it was said," NAB) alongside a statement by Jesus ("But I say to you," NAB). The six short units concern murder, adultery, divorce, oaths, retaliation, and enemies. In their content the teachings of Jesus are not so much oppositions or contradictions as they are exhortations to go to the root of the biblical commands and to make sure that they are not infringed.

The two most challenging of the six antitheses concern nonretaliation and love of enemies. The law of retaliation *(lex talionis)* appears in Exodus 21:24, Leviticus 24:20, and Deuteronomy 19:21. The Old Testament principle of "an eye for an eye" was intended to keep the cycle of revenge within some boundaries and to avoid a continuing escalation of violence. Its biblical formulations affirm personal responsibility for one's actions, equality of persons before the Law, and just proportion between crimes and their punishments.

Without explicitly abolishing the law of retaliation, Jesus urges his followers to forgo responding to violence with violence and in this way to try to break the never-ending cycle of violence. The four extreme examples that follow not only illustrate nonviolent resistance but also show how violence can be effectively met with goodness. The hope of these teachings is to win over the perpetrators of violence to the way of nonviolence.

The sixth and last antithesis concerns love of enemies. Here the biblical starting point is one of Jesus' favorite biblical texts: "You shall love your neighbor" (Lev 19:18, NAB). The second part of the quotation about hating one's enemies in fact does not appear in the Hebrew Bible, though there are statements like it in the Dead Sea scrolls.

Of course, Jesus does not *prohibit* loving one's neighbor! Instead, he widens the scope of the term *neighbor* to include all humans as the children of God. Here Jesus makes the example of God the ultimate criterion for dealing with one's enemies. Loving one's close neighbors and friends (relatives, benefactors, powerful persons, etc.) is easy enough and can be practiced out of enlightened self-interest by practically anyone, even tax collectors (suspected of thievery and disloyalty) and non-Jews. But if we try to adopt God's perspective rather than our all too human approaches to justice, then we can begin to face up to Jesus' difficult challenge to love even our enemies.

In teaching and preaching on texts in the Sermon on the Mount and especially on the antitheses, it is important always to keep in mind Jesus' own thesis statement in Matthew 5:17: "I have come not to abolish but to fulfill" (NAB). If we take that statement seriously, we cannot interpret the six antitheses as abolishing the biblical passages quoted by Jesus in the six antitheses. In some cases Jesus urges his followers to go to the root of matters like murder and adultery by avoiding anger and lust, respectively. In this he agrees with the rabbinic dictum attributed to the men of the great assembly: "Make a fence for the Torah" (*m. Abot* 1:1).

It is also important in dealing with these texts to avoid reinforcing stereotypes about Jewish legalism and perpetuating contrasts between Jewish legalism and the Christian ethic of love. In the Sermon on the Mount (as in the Old Testament and other Jewish texts) Law and love go together and reinforce one another.

For Reflection and Discussion:

1. When asked, how do you describe the difference between Judaism and Christianity?
2. How do you understand nonviolent resistance? Can it be a successful political strategy?
3. Have you ever seriously tried to take God's perspective in dealing with enemies? What happened?

5
Matthew 11:25–30:
Jesus the Wisdom of God
Cycle A:
Thirteenth Sunday in
Ordinary Time

The quest for wisdom is deeply rooted in human nature. It was a major concern in the ancient Near East, especially in Egypt and Mesopotamia. The Jewish adaptation of the international wisdom movement is best illustrated in the Book of Proverbs, and is subjected to critique in the Books of Job and Ecclesiastes (also known as Qoheleth). The Book of Sirach (also known as Ecclesiasticus) is the product of a school in Jerusalem run by Jesus Ben Sira in the early second century BCE. The Book of Wisdom (also known as the Wisdom of Solomon), composed in Alexandria in the first century BCE, attempts to integrate traditional Jewish religious concerns and Greek philosophical concepts. Whereas Sirach is the largest compilation of ancient Jewish wisdom teachings (fifty-one chapters), Wisdom is a book about (not surprisingly) wisdom and its importance. The latter two books are canonical for Catholics and Orthodox Christians, but not canonical for Jews and Protestants.

Jesus of Nazareth can be identified as a wisdom teacher. He used the literary forms that Jewish wisdom teachers used: beatitudes, instructions, admonitions, numerical proverbs, and so on. He dealt with topics that Jewish wisdom teachers treated: social relations, money, marriage, family concerns, and so on. He gathered disciples and taught them how to live righteously and to find happiness.

In the Jewish wisdom writings it is possible to discern an attempt at answering two great questions: "What is wisdom?" and "Where is wisdom?" In Proverbs 8:22–36 Wisdom is portrayed as a female figure who was present at creation as God's companion and assistant. Sirach 24 locates Wisdom's dwelling place in the Jerusalem Temple and identifies her with the Torah. According to 1 Enoch 42, Wisdom searched for a home on earth, and, on finding none, returned to heaven. Now she is accessible through dreams, visions, and heavenly trips. The Book of Wisdom equates Wisdom with the Stoic world-soul, the principle that permeates and animates all of creation. Thus Wisdom is everywhere. In these texts one can find the roots of rabbinic Judaism (Sirach), Jewish gnosticism and mysticism (1 Enoch), and Hellenistic Judaism (Wisdom).

The New Testament letter to the Colossians quotes a very early Christian hymn in 1:15–20 that celebrates Jesus as the Wisdom of God in both the order of creation and the order of redemption. The locus of Wisdom then is the body of Christ, which is identified at least in part as the church. For other identifications of Jesus as Wisdom, see John 1:1–18 and Hebrews 1:1–4.

As the wisdom texts found among the Dead Sea scrolls show, there were also tendencies in Jewish wisdom circles around Jesus' time to regard the most important wisdom to be the product of divine revelation and to identify the content of this wisdom with the mysteries pertaining to the kingdom of God. These two trends plus the fascination with the figure of Wisdom provide necessary background for Jesus' self-disclosure as the recipient of divine revelation from his heavenly Father in Matthew 11:25–30.

The Matthean passage consists of what were very likely once three independent sayings, all concerned with the general theme of revelation. The first saying (11:25–26) describes the childlike rather than the learned as the recipients of Jesus' revelation. Then in 11:27 Jesus identifies himself as the privileged recipient of revelation from his Father. Finally, in 11:28–30 Jesus invites prospective recipient of his revelation to come to his school and promises them rest in return. The text appears in a context (Matt 11 — 12) that features misunderstanding of Jesus and opposition to him, and its positive statements stand out in that context.

The first saying (11:25–26) is a thanksgiving in a form familiar from the Book of Psalms. A later collection of *Thanksgiving Hymns* (*Hodayot* in Hebrew) was found among the Dead Sea scrolls and ranks among the most important of those documents. In a thanksgiving the speaker makes a public statement to the effect that God has protected him from harm or revealed something of great significance. Here Jesus points to his Father ("I give praise to you") for having allowed the childlike (simple, good-hearted persons) to receive his teachings about God and the coming kingdom while religious professionals like the scribes and Pharisees fail to understand and accept it. He addresses God as both "Father" (an expression of personal intimacy) and "Lord of heaven and earth," thus preserving the typical Jewish tension between the immanence and the transcendence of God. He attributes the varied receptions of his teaching and especially the embrace of it by some unlikely ("childlike") persons to God's "gracious will" or favor. That tax collectors, sinners, and other marginal persons among the Jewish people more readily accepted Jesus and his teaching than the scribes and Pharisees is one of the best-attested facts about Jesus' life.

The second unit (11:27) should be read against the background of the Jewish controversy about the figure of Wisdom and the two questions, "What is Wisdom?" and "Where is Wisdom?" While Wisdom was understood to have been with God at creation (Proverbs) or now to be in heaven (1 Enoch) or in the Jerusalem Temple (Sirach) or everywhere (Wisdom), this New Testament saying indicates that God's wisdom is present in the person of Jesus. As in John's Gospel, Jesus is both the revealer and the revelation of God. Here the relationship between God and Jesus is described in terms of the Father and the Son. It is likely that Matthew's readers understood that relationship as having at least some associations with Israel's role as God's special people ("Out of Egypt I called my son," see Hos 11:1; Matt 2:15, NAB).

The third unit (11:28–30) returns to the theme of the recipients of Jesus' revelation. Found only in Matthew, it takes the form of an invitation to come to Jesus' school and contains many parallels with (if not influences from) Ben Sira's invitation in Sirach 51:23–28. The schoolmaster Jesus Ben Sira invites the "uneducated" to come to his "house of instruction" *(bet midrash)* in Jerusalem. He calls on prospective students to put their necks under Wisdom's "yoke" (a harness imposed on beasts of burden) but promises that his yoke will be easy and his burden will be light. And just as Ben Sira did (see also Jer 6:16), so Jesus the wisdom teacher promises that the result will be rest, that is, the peace that comes from right relationship with God and other persons.

Matthew 11:25–30 is rich in theological themes: Jesus as both a wisdom teacher and the Wisdom of God, thanksgiving as public acknowledgment of what God has done, the reception of the gospel by unlikely persons, true knowledge as revelation mediated through Jesus, and finding rest in the wisdom of Jesus. This passage helps to explain why early Christians celebrated their Jewish wisdom teacher as the Wisdom of God and found the dwelling place of Wisdom in the body of Christ (see Col 1:15–20).

For Reflection and Discussion:

1. Why might childlike persons have been more receptive to Jesus and his teachings than scribes and Pharisees?
2. Does the figure of Wisdom fully explain the significance of Jesus? Does "Son" add anything?
3. What makes the schools of Jesus Ben Sira and Jesus of Nazareth so attractive? Would you like to attend such a school?

6
Matthew 13:24–43:
Parables of God's Kingdom
Cycle A:
Sixteenth Sunday in Ordinary Time

According to Matthew 4:17, the major theme of Jesus' preaching was the kingdom of God: "Repent, for the kingdom of heaven is at hand" (NAB). Out of Jewish reverence for the divine name, Matthew often prefers the expression "the kingdom of heaven." The kingdom of God refers to God's future display of power and judgment, and the final establishment of God's rule over all creation. Then all peoples and indeed all creation will recognize and acknowledge the God of Israel as the only God and Lord.

The idea of God's kingship is deeply rooted in the Hebrew Bible, especially in the psalms that proclaim God's reign (see 29, 47, 82, 93, 96—99). In early Judaism and the New Testament the fullness of the kingdom is regarded as future and eschatological (pertaining to the end-times), though there are present manifestations or dimensions of it. The hope is that when the Day of the Lord comes, God's will shall be done on earth as it is in heaven. What we call the Lord's Prayer (Matt 6:9–13) is a prayer for the full coming of God's kingdom.

The third discourse in the series of Jesus' five major speeches in Matthew's Gospel (13:1–52) consists mainly of parables about the kingdom of heaven. A parable is a narrative taken from nature or everyday life that is somehow unusual or surprising and points to another (higher) level. The purpose of parables is to make the listener or reader think actively about the ultimate topic raised in the story. The word *parable* derives from a Greek verb *(paraballo)* that means to place one thing beside another. It is analogical thinking. That is why many parables are introduced by the phrase "the kingdom of God (or heaven) is like..." To grasp what the kingdom is like, one must read the whole parable, not just the first few words.

The kingdom of heaven as proclaimed by Jesus is God's kingdom (and therefore transcendent, or beyond full human comprehension) and eschatological (and therefore future in its fullness). The kingdom by its nature cannot be exhausted by a prose definition. Its very nature demands the use of images and analogies with things we know from everyday life. Therefore, Jesus communicated his vision of the kingdom chiefly through analogies or by parables.

In the church's lectionary for Year A the parables in Matthew 13 are spread over three consecutive Sundays. Their two main themes are the overwhelming value of God's kingdom and the mixed reception that Jesus' proclamation of it received. The selection for the Fifteenth Sunday in Ordinary Time treats the parable of the sower and its interpretation as an explanation for the mixed reception. The parables read on the Sixteenth and Seventeenth Sundays in Ordinary Time deal with both themes. Here we will focus on the second set of parables, while drawing on material from the first and third sets.

The parables in Matthew 13 reflect the everyday lives of people in Galilee in the first century (and to a large extent, today also). Galilee has relatively fertile soil, and so farming was (and is) a major occupation. And so there are parables about a sower of seeds (13:3–23), weeds sown among wheat (13:24–30, 36–43), and a mustard seed growing into a large bush (13:31–32). The Sea of Galilee was (and is) an important place for fishing, and so there is a parable about the nets used by professional fishermen like Jesus' first disciples (13:47–50). The remaining parables about baking bread (13:33), finding buried treasure (13:44), and buying and selling pearls (13:45–46) all fit well in the Galilean context of Jesus' public ministry. With his parables Jesus the wise teacher meets his audience on their own ground and leads them to reflect on the kingdom of God. Many scholars contend that in the parables of the kingdom we come very close to hearing the voice of Jesus (even if they have been translated from Aramaic into Greek).

The three most elaborate parables in Matthew 13 concern the mixed reception of Jesus' preaching. The theme is introduced in the parable of the sower and its allegorical interpretation (13:3–23). There the emphasis is on the magnificent harvest produced by the good soil in which the seed has been sown and (in the allegorical interpretation) on the reasons why the good seed (Jesus' preaching) sown by the good sower (Jesus) fails to yield an abundant harvest.

The parable of the weeds sown among the wheat (13:24–30) and its allegorical interpretation (13:36–43) also concern the mixed reception of Jesus' preaching. But here the issue is the attitude that Jesus' followers ought to show toward those who refuse his good news about God's kingdom. That attitude should be one of patience and tolerance in the present, out of the conviction that God will serve as a just judge in the fullness of the kingdom. The image of the harvest as a metaphor for the last judgment is well known from the Hebrew Bible (Joel 3:13; Hos 6:11; Jer 51:33; etc.; see also Rev 14:15–16). The allegorical interpretation in 13:36–43 makes even more explicit what is already clear from the parable itself.

The same dynamic is at work in the parable of the fishing net and its allegorical interpretation in 13:47–50. Here the catch of fish and the sorting out of good (edible) from bad fish provides the image of the divine judgment. The suggestion is that God will preside at the last judgment and then will separate good from bad persons. In the meantime the proper attitude is one of patience and tolerance. These parables leave no opening or encouragement for forced conversions or violence against infidels in the name of religion.

The mysterious character and surpassing value of the kingdom of God is brought out by two pairs of short parables. The first pair (13:31–33) concerns the mustard seed and the yeast. In both cases there is a small beginning (a tiny mustard seed and a small amount of yeast) and a very large product (a huge bush and enough bread to feed a hundred persons). Between the small beginnings and the grand results there is a mysterious process that goes on beyond ordinary comprehension. Likewise, while Jesus' preaching and other activities may seem to be only a very small beginning, the final result will be superabundant. Meanwhile, something mysterious and important (the person of Jesus) is occurring in the present.

The second pair of short parables (13:44–46) stresses the ultimate value of God's kingdom and the total commitment that it inspires and deserves. Both the treasure buried in the field (13:44) and the very valuable pearl (13:45–46) demand swift and decisive action on the finder's part. The value of each is so great and obvious that the finder "sells all that he has" (NAB) in order to gain possession of it. And its possession brings the greatest joy of all. Likewise, recognizing the supreme value of God's kingdom as proclaimed by Jesus can and does lead those who find it to dedicate themselves totally to that cause.

For Reflection and Discussion:

1. What does the expression "kingdom of God" mean to you?
2. Why was the parable an especially appropriate and effective vehicle for Jesus' teachings about God's kingdom?
3. What do Jesus' parables teach about God's kingdom in the present and in the future?

7
Matthew 14:13–21:
Jesus Feeds Five Thousand
Cycle A:
Eighteenth Sunday in
Ordinary Time

At two points in Matthew's narrative (14:13–21 and 15:32–39) Jesus feeds large crowds of people with very little food. In giving the two accounts, one featuring five thousand persons and the second featuring four thousand persons, Matthew follows Mark (see 6:35–44 and 8:1–10). Similar accounts appear in Luke 9:12–17 and John 6:1–15. This episode is firmly rooted and well attested in various strands of the tradition about Jesus.

Scholars have often argued about the historical basis of the tradition. Did Jesus *really* feed all those people with so little food? Did he do it *twice*? Or did he simply convince persons in the crowd to share whatever food they brought along with them? Or does the narrative reflect some event in between and on a smaller scale? Rather than arguing about the issues of historicity or speculating about the historical kernel, I suggest that we look instead at the Jewish background and symbolic significance of Matthew's account as it now stands.

The first feeding story in Matthew's Gospel (14:13–21) is occasioned by the enthusiasm of the crowds who had heard Jesus teach and saw him heal those in need. Since the crowds were in an isolated place and without food, Jesus' disciples suggest that he dismiss them and so allow them to obtain food in nearby villages. But Jesus rejects their suggestion and instead orders the disciples to begin feeding the crowds. When the disciples protest that they have only five loaves and two fishes, Jesus nevertheless finds a way to feed the crowds and in the process the disciples serve as the distributors of the food. The result is that all the crowd (five thousand men, "not counting women and children") eat and are satisfied, and there are twelve wicker baskets of leftovers.

In rewriting Mark 6:35–44, Matthew smoothes out some awkward features (as he does throughout his Gospel), portrays the disciples in a more positive light (they understand better and participate more actively in the feeding), and magnifies the scope of the healing (by adding the note about women and children).

The biblical prototype for the New Testament feeding stories appears in 2 Kings 4:42–44. There the prophet Elisha tells his servant to place twenty loaves of barley bread and some fresh ears of grain before a crowd of one hundred men. The servant resists at first but then follows the prophet's order. The result is that all were fed, and there were some leftovers. There are some obvious parallels between 2 Kings 4:42–44 and Matthew 14:13–21: the small amount of food available, the skepticism and protests of Elisha's servant and of Jesus' disciples, their success in feeding a large crowd, and the surprising amount of leftovers. The much larger numbers of the crowd and of the leftovers in Matthew's account suggest the superiority of Jesus to Elisha.

Several features indicate that Matthew followed Mark in focusing the first feeding miracle on Jews and the second on Gentiles. At least, the first feeding takes place in "a deserted place," thus evoking God's feeding of Israel in the wilderness with manna from heaven. Moreover, the fact that there are twelve baskets of leftovers indicates a connection with the twelve tribes of Israel. And the Greek word for *basket (kophinos)* was especially associated by the Roman satirist Juvenal with the kind of wicker baskets in which Jews carried their food. If we recognize the Jewish context of this feeding miracle, we can therefore assume that when Jesus said the blessing, he would have recited something like the traditional Jewish blessing before meals: "Blessed are you, O Lord our God, king of the universe, who brings forth bread from the earth." Finally by placing Jesus' banquet for God's people directly after Herod Antipas's banquet for his courtiers at which Herod's immoral actions lead to the execution of John the Baptist (see Matt 14:1–12), Matthew contrasts the two presiders. One (Herod) gives death, and the other (Jesus) gives life.

One of the well-documented features of Jesus' public ministry was his practice of sharing meals with various kinds of persons, including marginal figures such as tax collectors and sinners. Thus he continues the universal human custom of shared meals as occasions for displaying friendship and hospitality, as well as opportunities to share wisdom. The practice appears in the Bible in meals celebrating the "cutting" of a covenant (see Exod 24) and in association with sacrifices in the Jerusalem Temple. The Dead Sea scrolls show that the Jewish community (Essenes) behind those texts regarded their communal meals as preparations for or anticipations of the banquet that will take place when God's kingdom comes in its fullness. And various biblical and Jewish apocalyptic texts portray the kingdom of God in terms of a festive banquet. This tradition is presupposed in Jesus' saying in Matthew 8:11: "Many will come from the east and the west, and will recline with Abraham, Isaac, and Jacob at the banquet in the kingdom of heaven" (NAB). See also the parable in Matthew 22:1–10, where the kingdom of heaven is compared to "a king who gave a wedding feast for his son" (NAB).

The way in which Jesus' action at the feeding of the five thousand is described ("he said the blessing, broke the loaves, and gave them to his disciples") links this episode with Jesus' Last Supper (see Matt 26:26) and with the early Christian celebration of the Lord's Supper or Eucharist (see 1 Cor 11:23–26). In doing so it also connects Jesus' action here backward with the biblical tradition of shared meals (covenants, sacrifices, etc.) and forward to the fullness of life in God's kingdom. Attention to the various dimensions of Jesus' custom of shared meals can greatly enhance our appreciation of the Jewish background of the Christian sacrament of the Eucharist and its character as an expression of hope for the full coming of God's kingdom.

For Reflection and Discussion:

1. What significance do meals have for you? What distinguishes an ordinary meal from a banquet?
2. Why and how did Jesus use meals as a means of teaching about the kingdom of God?
3. How do you understand the sacrament of the Eucharist?

8
Matthew 15:21–28:
The Canaanite Woman's Faith
Cycle A:
Twentieth Sunday in Ordinary Time

We all are God's children, and so we all are equal before God. This statement can be described as a humanistic version of religious universalism. Whatever validity it has (and I do not want to argue its merits or demerits here), it is not exactly what we find in the Jewish and the Christian Bibles. The Bible regards Israel as a people especially chosen by God that throughout its history has had a special (covenantal) relationship with God and has been the recipient of certain promises from God. The God of the Bible is the God of Israel, not some distant deity or vague Great Spirit or Unmoved Mover. Members of other nations can become children of God by becoming part of Israel as God's chosen people. This is the Jewish version of biblical universalism.

The God of Jesus is the God of Israel. Non-Jews (Gentiles) can call upon and experience this God through Jesus the Jew as the representative par excellence of the Jewish people. So Christians believe. The roots of Christianity are in Judaism. Gentile Christians have been grafted onto Israel as God's olive tree (see Rom 11:17, 24). This is the Christian development of the Jewish version of biblical universalism.

Matthew's version of the healing of the daughter of a non-Jewish woman (15:21–28) can provide the occasion for reflecting on biblical universalism and its significance for Christian-Jewish relations. This text also allows us to glimpse some of Matthew's editorial techniques and theological concerns as a transmitter and an interpreter of early Christian traditions, in this case the narrative of the healing of the Syrophoenician woman's daughter in Mark 7:24–30.

Matthew's most obvious change concerns the woman's ethnic origin. While Mark identifies her as "a Greek, a Syrophoenician by birth" (NAB), Matthew calls her "a Canaanite woman" (NAB). The Canaanites were the pagan inhabitants of the Holy Land before the arrival of the ancient Israelites under Joshua. Matthew's designation of her in this way makes it clear from the start that she is a non-Jew, of a type historically hostile to Jews. Matthew also describes Jesus' geographical movements in an even more obscure way than Mark did, thus making it dubious whether Jesus actually entered "the region of Tyre and Sidon" (outside the Holy Land). One could imagine from Matthew's account alone that the woman approached Jesus on his turf, rather than the opposite. Recall that in Matthew 10:6 Jesus instructed his disciples to go only to "the lost sheep of the house of Israel" (see also 9:36; 18:12). Also, if we only possessed Matthew's account, we could easily imagine that the daughter was accompanying the Canaanite woman, and was not left at home (and so requiring a healing at a distance).

In the body of the story Matthew heightens the element of dialogue. Instead of restricting the debate to the climax as in Mark 7:27–29, Matthew has the disciples' direct address to Jesus and his reply in verses 23–24 and has the Canaanite woman address Jesus three times (vv. 22, 25, 27) and has Jesus answer her directly (vv. 24, 28). This expansion of the use of dialogue is a technique that Matthew uses frequently in his retelling of the Markan miracle stories (see chaps. 8—9). It serves to underline the element of "praying faith" that he regarded as essential to such narratives.

The theme of prayer is also heightened by the Canaanite woman's addresses to Jesus as the "Son of David" (v. 22, perhaps evoking Solomon's reputation as a powerful healer) and as "Lord" (vv. 22, 25, 27), which in the Matthean context means more than "Sir." Moreover, the woman pays "homage" to Jesus as the Magi did in 2:1–12 and as the eleven disciples will do in 28:17. Finally, Matthew makes explicit why the woman's daughter was healed from her demonic possession: "O woman, great is your faith!" (NAB).

The conversation between the Canaanite woman and Jesus revolves around his comment, "It is not right to take the food of the children and throw it to the dogs" (15:26, NAB). On the surface today, that may sound quite offensive. The assumption seems to be that the "children" are Israelites and the "dogs" are Gentiles. In this context it appears as a rationale for Jesus restricting his earthly mission and that of his first disciples to "the lost sheep of the house of Israel" (see 10:6, NAB). The woman's riposte, or response, about dogs eating the scraps from their master's table seems to change Jesus' attitude to the point that he uses his healing powers to drive out the demon from the woman's daughter. This is the only instance in the Gospels where Jesus seems to lose a debate and change his mind. And this happens as the result of a clever response from a Gentile woman!

Through his conversation with the Canaanite woman, Jesus comes to see some place for Gentiles in God's plan of salvation. Of course, this idea has been foreshadowed by the appearance of the pagan Magi in 2:1–12 and will be made an explicit part of the disciples' mission by the risen Jesus in 28:19 ("make disciples of all nations," NAB).

In the biblical vision of universalism the non-Jewish nations will come to God through Israel. For example, Isaiah 2:2–4 and Micah 4:1–3 present visions of "all nations" streaming toward the Jerusalem Temple and of the word of the Lord going forth from Mount Zion. This view is taken up and developed especially in the postexilic parts of the Book of Isaiah (chaps. 40—66), where Israel is portrayed as "a light to the nations" (42:6; 49:6) and where all the nations are said to come to Israel's light, who is God (60:2).

While the Books of Ezra and Nehemiah display a more restrictive approach to Israel's relationship with non-Jews, the Isaianic position is represented in a most striking way in Zechariah 8:20–23. There the peoples of the earth are said to come to Jerusalem to seek the favor of the Lord. The scene is captured most beautifully in the oracle that accompanies the picture: "In those days ten men of every nationality, speaking different tongues, shall take hold, yes, take hold of every Jew by the edge of his garment and say, 'Let us go with you, for we have heard that God is with you'" (Zech 8:23, NAB). Matthew and other early Christians (see Rom 9—11) believed that Jesus was such a Jew, and that through him membership in God's people has been opened up to "all the nations." This is the biblical universalism at the heart of Matthew's Gospel.

For Reflection and Discussion:

1. On the basis of a close comparison of Mark 7:24–30 and Matthew 15:21–28, how would you describe Matthew as an editor?
2. What is the effect of Matthew's emphasizing the prayer dimension of the episode?
3. How would you explain the biblical concept of universalism to a Hindu?

9
Matthew 18:15–20:
Reconciliation to the Community
Cycle A:
Twenty-Third Sunday in
Ordinary Time

In recent years Catholics have come to refer to the sacrament that most of them used to call *confession* or *penance* by the term *reconciliation* (though the official title remains "the sacrament of penance"). This change in nomenclature better expresses the goal of the ritual, that is, to bring straying members back into right relationship with God and with the Christian community. Catholics need to recognize that the theme of reconciliation has deep roots in the Hebrew Bible, first-century Jewish life, and the New Testament. Matthew 18:15–20 can help us in understanding better how early Christians dealt with sinners within their own community and how they sought to bring them back to full communal participation.

As the fourth of the five great speeches of Jesus in the Gospel, Matthew 18:1–35 provides pastoral advice for Christian community life. After defining true greatness in 18:1–5 as accepting the kingdom of heaven as a child accepts everything (as a gift), Jesus in 18:6–9 warns against putting obstacles in the spiritual path of "these little ones" and against allowing any part of the body (both physical and communal) to destroy the whole body. Then in the parable of the straying sheep, he urges that every effort be made to reconcile errant members with the community again. In 18:15–20 he outlines a process by which such reconciliations might be carried out. Finally with the parable of the unforgiving servant in 18:21–35 he illustrates that there should be no limits to our willingness to forgive (just as there are no limits to divine mercy and forgiveness).

The process of reconciliation outlined in 18:15–17 includes three steps. The occasion for using it arises "if your brother sins." Some manuscripts add "against you," probably under the influence of its presence in 18:21. But the best manuscripts lack this precision, and thus allow a wider scope of ways by which the sinner might stray and so need to be reconciled. At each step in the process the goal is to reconcile the errant member to the community.

The first step involves one Christian confronting another in private. Here there seems to be an echo of Leviticus 19:17 and its directive to reason with or reprove one's neighbor lest you incur sin because of him. The second step involves reproving the straying neighbor in the presence of one or two witnesses. Here the echo is from Deuteronomy 19:15: "a judicial fact shall be established only on the testimony of two or three witnesses" (NAB).

The third step involves telling the "church," either in a formal assembly of the whole community or in approaching its board of elders. This is one of only two uses of the word *church (ekklesia)* in the Gospels. The word is, of course, very common in Acts and the epistles. In Matthew's community it may have been a way of delineating his group from "their synagogues," one of the evangelist's ways of referring to his Jewish rivals. It is likely, however, that the Matthean community had a board of elders, as the synagogues of the time had.

If all three steps fail to bring about the straying member's reconciliation, then he should be treated "as a Gentile and tax collector." This is a peculiar expression, since thus far in Matthew's narrative several Gentiles (8:5–11; 15:21–28) and tax collectors (9:9–13; 11:19) have actually shown faith in Jesus. However, in a Christian Jewish milieu, it was probably an idiom for those outside "our" community. At any rate, this stern judgment sounds very much like a decree of excommunication as in 1 Corinthians 5:1–13. In both cases the intent of the excommunication may have been to shock the offender into recognizing the seriousness of his sin and thus to move him toward reconciliation.

There is good parallel to the Matthean community's practice of reconciliation in the Dead Sea scrolls. The work known as *The Rule of the Community*, a kind of handbook for the director of a Jewish religious community (probably Essenes) something like a Christian monastery or retreat facility, directs that a member should rebuke an errant fellow member "on the very same day lest he incur guilt because of him." It goes on to state that no one should "accuse his companion before the congregation without having admonished him in the presence of witnesses" (5:26–6:1). The same document specifies severe penalties for various offenses (apparently to shock the perpetrator into recognition), with excommunication as a last resort.

Whether the Matthean community borrowed this procedure from the Essenes or the two groups developed it independently cannot be decided with certainty. In both cases, however, the goal seems to have been to make the sinner conscious of his sin and own it, and then to bring the straying member back into full communion with the group.

The sayings about binding and loosing (18:18) and about two or three gathered in the name of Jesus (18:19–20) may well have originated separately from the sayings in 18:15–17. They have certainly been interpreted in various ways throughout the centuries. But in their present Matthean context they provide impressive theological foundations for the process of reconciliation. According to 18:18, God stands behind the decisions of the community (see also 16:19), and, according to 18:19–20, Jesus abides in the community gathered in his name. The idea of the divine presence dwelling among the rabbis appears in *m. Abot* 3:2 ("When two are sitting and the words of Torah pass between them, the Presence is with them") and 3:3 ("when two who eat at a single table and talk about the teaching of Torah while at that table they are as if they eat at the table of the Omnipresent").

Over the centuries the church has developed new and different ways of reconciling errant members to God and the Christian community. Jews, of course, observe the Day of Atonement as a major point on their religious calendars. There is no reason for either Christians or Jews to reproduce the specific procedures employed in the Matthean or Qumran communities. Nevertheless, the noble goals behind those procedures remain in force: to help members to recognize and acknowledge their sins, and to restore straying members to right relationship with God and their religious community.

For Reflection and Discussion:

1. How do you understand the sacrament of reconciliation? What do you expect from it?
2. People today often use something like the three-step process of reconciliation in what we call an intervention. Have you ever been involved in such an action?
3. What do you understand by the image of two or three gathered together in Jesus' name?

10
Matthew 21:33–46:
The Parable of the Vineyard
Cycle A:
Twenty-Seventh Sunday in
Ordinary Time

To supersede means to take the place of something or someone. For example, the new computer program supersedes the old one, or the new toaster supersedes the old one. The older model usually ends up in the trash bin or its equivalent. In theology and especially in Christian-Jewish relations, the term *supersessionism* is very important. In this context it describes the Christian theological view according to which the church has replaced Israel as the people of God and so Israel no longer has significance in God's plan for salvation.

One of the key texts in the debate about Christian supersessionism is the parable of the vineyard in Matthew 21:33–46. And one of the key verses comes at the end of the parable: "Therefore, I say to you, the kingdom of God will be taken away from you and given to a people that will produce its fruit" (21:43, NAB). I hope to show that when this Gospel text is read against its biblical background and in the context of first-century Judaism, it appears that the supersessionist interpretation of it misses the mark.

The biblical background is clearly Isaiah 5:1–7, which in the Sunday lectionary is paired with Matthew's parable of the vineyard. In Isaiah's parable "the vineyard of the LORD of hosts is the house of

Israel" (5:7, NAB). The owner of the vineyard (God) did all the necessary preparations to ensure an abundant harvest from his vineyard. But "what it yielded was wild grapes" (NAB). God then asks what more he could have done on his vineyard's behalf, and so he decides to destroy it. In the Book of Isaiah the parable of the vineyard is a warning to Judah that unless it mends its ways, God will let it be destroyed by the Assyrians. Note that what is destroyed here is the vineyard itself (that is, Israel, or at least Jerusalem).

A version of Isaiah's parable appears in Mark 12:1–12. The very first words ("a man planted a vineyard, put a hedge around it, dug a wine press, and built a tower," NAB) echo the language of Isaiah 5:1–7 and prepare us to expect something like it. The Markan parable, however, seems more concerned with the emissaries sent by the owner and the vicious treatment that they receive from the tenant farmers. The reader quickly recognizes that the owner is God and the servants are the prophets (who often received harsh treatment from their people). The last emissary is the owner's son. The owner expects that his son will be respected by the tenant farmers and so will be able to collect the produce owed to him. However, the son is seized by them, beaten, and killed, and his corpse is thrown outside the vineyard. In response the owner determines to "put the tenants to death, and give the vineyard to others" (NAB). Mark concludes the parable by noting that "the crowd" realized that the parable was addressed to them, and that Jesus hurried away out of concern for his own safety.

Those who read the Gospels of Mark and Matthew would have been familiar with the economic system presupposed in the parable of the vineyard. Absentee landowners in the Greco-Roman world let out their land to sharecroppers who worked the land in exchange for a fee or a percentage of the produce. The bulk of the profits went to the landowner, who at appropriate times sent his agents to collect what was owed to him. The tenant farmers' plan to inherit the vineyard was illegal and ultimately foolish as long as the landowner was alive. However, they seem to have imagined that with the son's death the owner might yield the property to them.

In the context of Mark's Gospel, the parable of the vineyard is a kind of allegory of salvation history. The vineyard is Israel as God's people, the owner is God, the servants are the prophets, and the son is Jesus. The murder of the son points forward to the crucifixion of Jesus and (perhaps) the destruction of Jerusalem by the Romans in 70 CE. Note that the vineyard itself is not destroyed.

Matthew in 21:33–46 takes over much of the language of Mark's parable (and Isaiah's parable too) and adopts Mark's salvation-historical perspective. As was his editorial practice, Matthew smoothes out some rough stylistic edges and adapts the parable to his own historical situation. Matthew has the owner send two batches of servants (prophets) and describes their bad treatment (beating, killing, and stoning) only once. With regard to the abuse visited upon the son, Matthew notes that the tenant farmers first threw him out of the vineyard and then killed him. Thus, he seems to be conforming the order of events to what happened to Jesus, who was first taken outside the walls of the Jerusalem and then executed (see Matt 27:33; Heb 13:12).

Matthew's most substantive change comes at the end, where he notes that the audience that took exception to Jesus' parable was not the crowd but rather "the chief priests and Pharisees" (21:45, NAB). The lectionary obscures this fact by omitting 21:44–46 and shifting the mention of the audience to the beginning of the parable: "Jesus said to the chief priests and the elders of the people" (NAB). Of course, the chief priests and Pharisees are Jesus' (and Matthew's) rivals throughout the Gospel.

The major difference between Isaiah's parable of the vineyard and those told in the Gospels of Mark and Matthew concerns the fate of the vineyard. Whereas in Isaiah's parable the vineyard is destroyed, in the Gospels' version the vineyard is preserved but there is a change in the tenant farmers (leadership). Matthew describes the new leaders as a "people" *(ethnos)* that will produce fruit. Here *ethnos* need not mean nation or even less the Gentile church. In this Matthean context *ethnos* refers to those who take Jesus as the authoritative interpreter of the Torah and to the largely Christian Jewish church as the continuation of Israel's heritage after 70 CE.

Whatever supersession there may be in Matthew 21:33–46 concerns not Israel's identity as the people of God but rather the leadership of the people of God. Following Mark's lead, Matthew insists that the vineyard (Israel) is preserved. What changes are the leaders. And in Matthew's situation the proper leaders after 70 CE are not the chief priests and the Pharisees but rather Christian Jews like Matthew and his community. If supersession means that Israel has been replaced as God's people and that Israel is no longer significant in God's plan of salvation, what we find in Matthew's Gospel is not really supersessionism.

For Reflection and Discussion:

1. What happens with the vineyard (Israel) in each of the three versions of the parable of the vineyard?
2. How do you understand supersessionism? Do you find it in the New Testament?
3. What problems might supersessionism pose in Christian-Jewish dialogue today?

11
Matthew 22:1–14:
The Parable of the Royal Wedding Feast
Cycle A:
Twenty-Eighth Sunday in Ordinary Time

The destruction of Jerusalem in 70 CE was a momentous event in Israel's history. A minor rebellion that began in 66 CE soon turned into a full-scale Jewish revolt against their Roman occupiers. It was Roman policy to put down such revolts quickly and brutally, and so the Roman general Vespasian was put in charge of restoring order in Judea. The rebel leaders converged in Jerusalem, which was relatively well fortified. Thus a long siege ensued. Before Vespasian could conquer the city, he was recalled to Rome and became the emperor. He put his own son Titus (who eventually succeeded Vespasian as emperor) in charge of the siege of Jerusalem in 70 CE, and Titus succeeded in destroying the city and its Temple. Thus what had been the religious and cultural center of the Jewish people was in Roman hands, and all Jews were faced with challenge of carrying on the heritage of Israel without their Temple and Holy City.

Who was responsible for Jerusalem's destruction in 70 CE? Some religious Jews traced it to the sins of the people and their leaders, much as their ancestors did after the destruction of the First Temple in 587 BCE. The Jewish historian Flavius Josephus blamed it

on the factionalism that divided the Jewish people and on the leaders
of those factions. Josephus had once served as a general among the
Jewish rebels in Galilee. However, he became frustrated by and quar-
reled with other Jewish leaders, and went over to the Roman side. He
eventually made his way to Rome and served as kind of researcher
and propagandist for the Flavian emperors. He wrote a detailed
account of the rebellion *(Jewish War)* and a twenty-book account of
the history of the Jewish people up to the late first century CE *(Jewish
Antiquities)*. In describing the destruction of Jerusalem in 70 CE
Josephus portrayed Vespasian and Titus positively, as noble and even
reluctant victors, while he described the leaders of the various Jewish
factions in a very negative way.

That statement occurs in Matthew's parable of the royal wed-
Matthew seems to have composed his Gospel around the same
time as Josephus was producing his writings. Jesus as the main figure
in Matthew's narrative had died some forty years before the destruction of the Jerusalem Temple. And so we would not expect to find
explicit references to the events of 70 CE in Matthew's narrative
about Jesus. Nevertheless, there are some hints that Matthew was
aware of Jerusalem's destruction in 70 CE, and that he, like Josephus,
was intent on blaming the alleged leaders of the Jewish people for it.
Perhaps the clearest indication of this appears in Matthew 22:7: "The
king was enraged and sent his troops, destroyed those murderers, and
burned their city" (NAB).

That statement occurs in Matthew's parable of the royal wedding feast in 22:1–10. To appreciate Matthew's perspective, it is necessary to look at the parallel banquet parable in Luke 14:16–24.
Luke's version is very likely close to what appeared in the Sayings
Source Q. It tells about a man who invited many to a banquet. When
the time came, he sent his servant to summon the invited guests. But the
guests offered various excuses and refused to come. One had bought a
field, another had purchased farm animals, and a third had recently
married. When the host heard about this, he was angry and bade his
servant to bring in "the poor and the crippled, the blind and the
lame." On learning that there was still room, he commanded the servant to bring in anyone he could find, but swore that the original
invitees would never participate in his banquet. In the context of
Jesus' ministry, the parable highlighted the need to accept Jesus'
invitation to God's kingdom, defended his practice of ministering to

marginal persons, and warned the religious professionals (scribes and Pharisees) not to disregard or reject Jesus' preaching.

If we assume that Luke gives us the earlier Q form of the text (that is generally a correct assumption), then by comparing Matthew's version we can see an aggressive editor at work. The audience for Matthew's version ("them") is apparently the same as that for the previous parable ("the chief priests and Pharisees"). The banquet has become a royal wedding feast honoring the king's son. When the servants (the prophets) are sent to summon the invited guests, they are given flimsy excuses, and are abused and even killed. The king is so angry that he sends his army against their city and has them and their city destroyed (22:7). Then he instructs his servants to issue a general invitation to his banquet since those who were originally invited were no longer available.

If Matthew rewrote the parable in light of the events of 70 CE (as seems likely), then he was interpreting the destruction of Jerusalem as due to the failure of the Jewish religious establishment (the chief priests and the Pharisees, not the whole people) to accept Jesus' invitation to enter the kingdom of heaven. This move does present a problem, since it suggests that the Roman conquerors were instruments of God for punishing Jerusalem and its leaders. However, the biblical prophets frequently designated their people's conquerors (Assyrians, Babylonians, Persians, etc.) as instruments of God's wrath (though with the assumption that they too would eventually be punished).

Matthew's parable of the royal wedding feast has a rich biblical background. The theme of the invitation to Wisdom's banquet is prominent in Proverbs 1—9, with its climax in the contrasting banquets hosted by Lady Wisdom and Lady Folly. Matthew identified Jesus as the Wisdom of God in 11:25–30, and so rejecting his invitation means rejecting Wisdom. Moreover, Matthew's upgrading of the banquet into a royal wedding feast in honor of the king's son combines the motifs of God's kingdom as a banquet and Jesus' identity as the Son of God and Israel's Messiah/Son of David.

Matthew seems also to have added a second parable (22:11–14) to the first. It concerns a man who because he is not dressed properly is tossed out. This is a strange and obscure text. In the Matthean context, however, the point seems to be that it is not enough to merely come to the wedding feast. One must behave accordingly. If not, one runs the risk of being expelled.

Matthew 22:1–14 contains many themes for preachers and teachers. It is important, however, that they avoid interpreting Matthew as rejecting Israel per se and viewing the church as Israel's replacement (supersessionism). Throughout his Gospel Matthew (like Josephus) makes it clear that his quarrel was with Israel's alleged leaders and not with the people as a whole. In fact, Matthew was convinced that Israel's heritage as God's people was best preserved by those who accept Jesus' invitation to his royal wedding feast in God's kingdom and try to act in accord with Jesus' own teachings.

For Reflection and Discussion:

1. Compare the two versions of the parable of the banquet. What is the same and what is different?
2. What do you make out of the short parable in Matthew 22:11–14?
3. What problems might Matthew's version of the parable of the royal wedding feast pose in conversations between Jews and Christians?

12
Matthew 23:1–12:
Scribes and Pharisees
Cycle A:
Thirty-First Sunday in
Ordinary Time

We know that the worst feuds are often family feuds and the worst wars are often civil wars. Even among religious people there are Catholics who get along famously with Jews and Muslims but detest certain other Christians or even other Catholics. One reason is that we care most deeply about issues that are close to us and part of our everyday life, whereas we frequently show more tolerance to outsiders with whom we have little in common and where little is at stake.

It is hard to classify Jesus within first-century Judaism. The noted Catholic biblical scholar John P. Meier characterizes Jesus as "a marginal Jew." The Essenes are never mentioned in the Gospels, and the Sadducees are present only rarely. The most prominent Jewish group is the Pharisees. Jesus frequently enters into debate with them over issues that were apparently important to both of them. While it is unlikely that Jesus was ever a Pharisee (though Paul was), we can say that Jesus at least shared an agenda with the Pharisees and that of all the contemporary Jewish groups he was closest to them.

The evangelist Matthew also seems to have had a close (though tense) relationship with the Pharisees. After 70 CE the group that emerged eventually as the rabbinic movement certainly included some Pharisees and took over many Pharisaic concerns and teachings. In fact, the term *Pharisees* in Matthew's Gospel is a kind of symbol or cipher for his Jewish rivals who controlled "their synagogues."

Matthew seems to have constructed his infamous chapter 23 out of Jesus' brief denunciation of the scribes in Mark 12:38–40 and some Q materials preserved in Luke 11:37–52. The result is infamous for the aggressive and even virulent tone in which the scribes and Pharisees are attacked. Many Jews and Christians contend that Matthew's criticisms have been the source of negative stereotypes about Jews and Judaism, and have poisoned relationships between Christians and Jews over the centuries. This chapter is a dangerous text and has often functioned as a stumbling block to progress in Christian-Jewish dialogue.

The objects of Jesus' criticisms in Matthew 23 are the scribes and the Pharisees. The scribes were persons able to read and write in a society in which literacy was relatively rare. They wrote and copied legal documents and contracts. They were conversant with the Torah, which for Jews at this time functioned as their law code. The author of the Book of Sirach ran a school for potential scribes in Jerusalem in the early second century BCE, and there he trained young men to serve as intellectual and political counselors. The scribes were both lawyers and theologians, and contributed greatly to the early rabbinic movement with their love of learning, knowledge of the Torah, and penchant for argument.

The Pharisees were a Jewish religious movement active in the land of Israel between the second century BCE and the first century CE. They differed from the Sadducees in their beliefs in free will, life after death, and postmortem rewards and punishments. They were the progressives among Jewish groups, often adapting biblical commandments to the needs and realities of their time. Before 70 CE they showed special interest in ritual purity, tithing, and Sabbath observance. In their rulings and debates they called on various biblical books and oral traditions outside the Bible. They held fellowship meals and cultivated a kind of "priesthood of all believers" spirituality. They sought to apply biblical commandments intended only for priests in the Temple to all Israel and thus hoped to make Israel into a truly holy people.

The negative tone of Matthew 23 may seem excessive or even scandalous to modern readers. However, we should bear in mind that in the Greco-Roman world and in the Jewish parts of it there was little room for academic politeness. Philosophers and preachers often said very harsh things about their rivals and opponents. For example, the Jews behind the Dead Sea scrolls (Essenes) referred to the Pharisees as "seekers after smooth things" (because they made things too easy) and criticized them vigorously even to the point of not respecting their identity as Jews. Or read Paul's letters, and see the harsh things being said by his rival Christian Jewish missionaries about Paul and by him about them. Whether we like it or not, Matthew's critique of the scribes and the Pharisees fits well in the contentious atmosphere of the Mediterranean world of the first century CE.

In chapter 23 Matthew has Jesus first acknowledge the teaching authority of the scribes and Pharisees with the image of their occupying the "chair of Moses." He tells them to accept their teachings but not follow their example. His chief criticism concerns hypocrisy. He charges that "they preach but they do not practice" (NAB). The Matthean Jesus also contends that they perform their religious actions mainly to gain a reputation for holiness. The "burdens" that they impose probably refer to their traditions and their program to make all Israel into a priestly people. The term *phylacteries* refers to small boxes containing Scripture texts, while the *fringes* are tassels on their outer garments or prayer shawls. These would have been signs of serious religious observance.

Another contentious issue was the rivals' increasing use of honorific titles for their teachers. Those titles included Rabbi, Father, and Master. While these titles began to flourish in the early rabbinic movement, the Matthean community seems to have rejected them out of the conviction that they had only one teacher (Jesus) and one master, the Messiah.

The series of seven woes that follow in 23:13–36 accuses the scribes and Pharisees of shutting off access to the kingdom of heaven, making "converts" worse than they were beforehand, engaging in hypocritical casuistry, neglecting the weightier issues of the Law, being more concerned with externals than with internal dispositions, trying to appear righteous without being so, and building monuments to the prophets of old while killing off the prophets of their own time.

In dealing with Matthew 23 teachers need to supply information about the historical context and to warn against perpetuating ugly stereotypes about Jews and Judaism. Without turning a homily into a history class, preachers should give some historical context and show that what is criticized in Matthew 23 are the traps and temptations into which religious professionals in all religions can and do fall. There is nothing said about the scribes and Pharisees that cannot also be said about Christian ministers and theologians in the past and the present.

For Reflection and Discussion:

1. In what sense does Matthew 23 bear witness to a family feud?
2. How do you react to the heated rhetoric in this text?
3. Have clergy or teachers from your denomination fallen into the abuses denounced in Matthew 23?

13
Matthew 25:31–46:
The Last Judgment
Cycle A:
Christ the King

Jesus and the early Christians agreed with the Pharisees that there is life after death, and that individuals will be rewarded or punished by God according to their deeds during their life on earth. The climax of Jesus' public ministry, according to Matthew, comes at the end of his fifth and last great speech (the eschatological discourse in chaps. 24—25) and before the passion narrative (chaps. 26—27). That climax is the Last Judgment scene in Matthew 25:31–46, one of the most beloved and most challenging texts in the New Testament. The text is read in Catholic churches on the last Sunday in Ordinary Time, in late November, just before the beginning of the Advent season.

The Matthean Last Judgment scene follows three parables about the delay of the coming of the Son of man. These parables counsel constant watchfulness and faithful dedication to one's assigned tasks in the present as the best preparation for the coming of the Son of man (the risen Jesus) in glory. Here the Son of man figure is based on the "one like a son of man" (NAB) in Daniel 7 (who in that context is most likely Michael the archangel). Early Christians, however, identified this Son of man with the risen Jesus, whom they expected would return in glory.

In Matthew 25:31–46 (NAB) the Son of man presides at the Last Judgment, rewarding some and condemning others on the basis of their works. After introducing the judge and those to be judged ("all

59

the nations"), the text has the Son of man address the "blessed" and explains why they are invited to share in his "blessedness." It is because they had done acts of mercy to "these least brothers of mine." The process is repeated with those who are condemned. There is a sentence and the reason for it, a request for clarification, and an explanation. Here the reason for their condemnation is their failure to perform acts of mercy for "one of these least ones." The final verse summarizes the process: The wicked go off to eternal punishment, while the righteous go off to eternal life.

Jewish literature from the Book of Daniel onward, especially the apocalyptic writings, provides many judgment scenes. What makes Matthew's judgment scene Christian is the identification of the judge ("the Son of Man," NAB) as the risen Jesus. In the Synoptic Gospels the title "Son of man" appears in three contexts. In some sayings Jesus uses it to refer to himself, thus expressing his solidarity with humankind. In the three predictions of his passion and resurrection Jesus refers to himself as the Son of man. And in other passages, especially near the end of the Gospels, Jesus appears as the glorious end-time figure whose portrayal is clearly influenced by Daniel 7 and other Jewish apocalyptic texts. The judge in Matthew's Last Judgment scene is clearly meant to be identified as the risen Jesus.

Who is being judged? At the beginning of the narrative they are identified as "all the nations" (NAB). The Greek phrase is *panta ta ethne*. Does it include Jews? Elsewhere in Matthew's Gospel *ethnos* and similar expressions refer to Gentiles, that is, non-Jews (see 4:15; 6:32; 10:5, 18; 12:18, 21; 20:19, 25; 21:43; 24:7, 9, 14; 28:19). Here the phrase "all the nations" seems to suggest that those being judged are *not* Jews. This assumption is confirmed by an earlier saying in Matthew 19:28, where Jesus promises that those who have followed him (the twelve apostles) will sit on twelve thrones judging the twelve tribes of Israel. The idea of separate judgments for Israel and for the Gentiles appears in Paul's letter to the Romans (2:9–10) and in various Jewish apocalyptic texts (1 Enoch 91:14; 4 Ezra 13:33–49; 2 Baruch 72:4–6).

By what criteria will "all the nations" be judged? The answer is, by their deeds of compassion toward "the least." "The least" are clearly those in greatest human need. They are the hungry, thirsty, strangers, naked, sick, and imprisoned. Whether they are Christians only (as "these least brothers of mine" might suggest) or all needy persons without distinction, is much debated among scholars. But the basic point is that acts of mercy toward those most in need of it will constitute the criteria by which "all the nations" will be judged.

Why are these acts of mercy so important? Because doing them for the needy one is effectively doing them for Jesus, the now glorious Son of man who is to preside at the Last Judgment. Here is where the three uses of the title come together. Having suffered in solidarity with humankind, the glorious Son of man remains in solidarity with all humans who suffer. By his total identification with humankind, it is the Son of man who is being ultimately served by the good deeds done by the righteous, whereas the wicked fail to take the opportunity to do so. Matthew's Gospel begins by identifying Jesus as Emmanuel ("God is with us") and ends with the risen Jesus' promise to be with his followers always until the end of this age.

The Matthean Last Judgment scene concerns the criteria by which non-Jews and non-Christians will be judged after their deaths. Those criteria concern the doing (or failing to do) acts of kindness toward those most in need. Of course, the text is written from a (narrow) Christian perspective. When read in this way, it deals with an issue of very great concern today: Christian theological thinking about the salvation of non-Christians (and non-Jews).

Both Judaism and Christianity stress to their adherents the positive value of good works. Both are practice-oriented religions in which beliefs are supposed to issue in good actions. And we expect to be judged by God according to our actions. If good works are so important for non-Christians (and non-Jews) to perform (as Matthew's Last Judgment scene suggests), how much more can they be expected from Christians and Jews! And if Gentiles are to be rewarded for good deeds done to strangers and needy persons, so also Christians and Jews can expect to be rewarded for doing likewise.

For Reflection and Discussion:

1. What might qualify Jesus to serve as the judge at the Last Judgment?
2. What are some implications of this text for developing a Christian theology of other religions?
3. How might the Matthean judgment scene serve as a stimulus for Christians and Jews to dedicate themselves anew to acts of mercy to those in need (social justice)?

14
Matthew 26:1—27:66:
The Passion Narrative
Cycle A:
Passion (or Palm) Sunday

The Sunday before Easter is known as both Palm Sunday and Passion Sunday. It is called Palm Sunday because it commemorates Jesus' entrance into Jerusalem when the crowd put palm branches on the road to greet him (see Matt 21:8). It is called Passion Sunday because it inaugurates Passion Week, and on that day the whole passion narrative from one of the Synoptic Gospels is read or chanted. In Year A of the lectionary cycle the text is Matthew 26—27, in Year B it is Mark 14—15, and in Year C it is Luke 22—23. John 18—19 is read on Good Friday.

The New Testament passion narratives are sometimes accused of being anti-Jewish or at least capable of arousing anti-Jewish sentiments, since the Jewish leaders and the crowds are often portrayed negatively. Because the reading is very long, whatever homily is given may be short and may fail to address the anti-Jewish potential of these texts. Christians need to learn especially that whatever Jewish responsibility there was for Jesus' death, it involved only a few Jews long ago and far away. There is no historical or theological rationale for blaming Jesus' death on all Jews either today or throughout history.

Matthew's passion narrative is a slightly revised version of Mark 14—15. According to their common outline (also followed by Luke), the Jewish leaders plotted with Judas to kill Jesus. Jesus celebrated Passover with his disciples, was arrested in Gethsemane, was tried first before the Jewish Sanhedrin (or council) and then by Pilate, was crucified, and died rather quickly. His corpse was brought to a new tomb owned by Joseph of Arimathea. His male disciples abandoned Jesus, while a few female followers (most prominently, Mary Magdalene) saw him die, observed his burial, and planned to go to the tomb on Easter Sunday.

Matthew edited Mark's passion narrative as he did throughout his Gospel—by smoothing out Mark's rough Greek, by omitting what he regarded as unnecessary details, and by adding traditions that were apparently not known by Mark. In retelling Mark's story, Matthew increased the biblical quotations, allusions, and echoes to indicate further how the events of Jesus' passion and death took place "according to the Scriptures." He also portrayed Jesus as even more foreseeing and more in control of the events as they unfolded. And he heightened the responsibility of the Jewish leaders and the crowd under their direction for Jesus' death while playing down the responsibility of the Roman authorities.

By way of addition Matthew included an explanation for why Jesus did not resist arrest (26:52–54), an account of Judas' suicide (27:3–10), a report about a dream by Pilate's wife regarding Jesus' innocence (27:19), a scene in which Pilate acknowledges Jesus' innocence (27:24–26), a series of portents associated with Jesus' death (27:51–53), and information about a group of soldiers formed to guard Jesus' tomb so that his body could not be stolen (27:62–66). Whether these additional passages came from one or several sources, and whether those sources were written or oral, is much debated among scholars.

Here the focus will be on two issues in Matthew's passion narrative that are very important in Christian-Jewish dialogue: the figure of Judas and the words attributed to the Jewish people at Jesus' trial ("his blood be upon us and upon our children," NAB). The nature of the Last Supper (Passover meal or not?), the legal responsibilities for Jesus' death, and his last words are treated in the section on Mark's passion narrative in Part Two.

Judas: Matthew follows Mark in describing the plot between him and the chief priests and elders to betray Jesus. Judas's motive for betraying Jesus has often been a matter of speculation. Matthew blames it on his greed, while suggesting also that through him the Scriptures were being fulfilled.

Only Matthew specifies the exact sum of thirty pieces of silver, which was the value placed on a slave in Exodus 21:32. In Zechariah 11:12–13 thirty pieces of silver is the wage of the shepherd who casts them back into the treasury. The latter text prepares for Matthew's account of Judas's suicide in 27:3–10. (A quite different account appears in Acts 1:18–19.) According to Matthew, Judas changed his mind and tried to return the money to the chief priests. When they refused to accept it, Judas despaired and hanged himself. The chief priests in turn put the money toward the purchase of a field in which to bury indigents on the grounds that it was "blood money."

Judas's betrayal of Jesus remains a mystery and a scandal. How someone who had heard Jesus teach and seen him healing people in need could have betrayed Jesus is hard to explain. Although the betrayal was an embarrassment for early Christians, they never denied it, presumably because it was so well known. Some have argued that Judas was not really a historical figure at all but rather a projection of early Christian contempt for Jews and Judaism. But Judas was a common name, and his betrayal of Jesus was hardly something that Christians would have invented. At any rate, there remains a danger among readers today of turning Judas into a source of stereotypes of Jewish greed and treachery. But Judas is more a problem for Christians than he is for Jews.

The People's Cry: The trial of Jesus before Pilate reaches its climax when "the whole people" cry out, "His blood be upon us and upon our children" (Matt 27:25, NAB). This text has sometimes been interpreted as a self-curse on the Jewish people that doomed them to a life of wandering and persecution. It has also been taken as the basis of the charge of deicide, in the sense that Jews are held guilty of having killed the divine being Jesus. Such attitudes were explicitly condemned in Vatican Council II's document on the relation of the Catholic Church to other religions *(Nostra aetate)*. But the Matthean exegetical problem remains. What did this text (found only in Matthew's Gospel) mean for the evangelist and his community?

If (as seems likely) Matthew and most of his Christian community were Jews by birth, Matthew 27:25 can hardly imply a blanket condemnation of all Jews in the first century and still less throughout the centuries. In Matthew's narrative it refers most obviously to the relatively small crowd gathered in Jerusalem one spring morning in 30 CE that witnessed the trial of Jesus before the Roman prefect, Pontius Pilate. Whatever protestations of innocence that Pilate made, the ultimate legal responsibility lay with him. In Matthew's own late first-century context the self-curse of the crowd may have extended to the leaders (and their followers) during the Jewish revolt of 66–73 CE. These were the ones on whom Matthew blamed the destruction of Jerusalem and its temple. The idea would be that in the generation after Jesus' death in 30 CE the self-curse uttered by those few Jews who were party to Jesus' condemnation came to rest upon and be fulfilled in their "children" in the next generation in 70 CE.

For Reflection and Discussion:

1. From your reading of Matthew's passion narrative how would you apportion the responsibilities for Jesus' death?
2. Have you ever heard anyone take Judas as a symbol for the Jewish people? How did you react?
3. Have you ever heard anyone describe Jews as a "deicide people" or its equivalents? How did you react?

15
Matthew 28:16–20:
The Great Commission
Cycle A:
Trinity Sunday

In the church's calendar Trinity Sunday is the Sunday after Pentecost. In Cycle A in the Sunday lectionary the Gospel reading for Trinity Sunday is the very last passage in Matthew's Gospel (28:16–20). This text is chosen primarily because it refers to baptizing "in the name of the Father, and of the Son, and of the Holy Spirit" (28:19, NAB). These words very likely reflect the baptismal formula used in Matthew's community and elsewhere in early Christian circles. This passage is also a neat summary of what Matthew teaches about Jesus and those follow him.

Matthew 28 consists of an empty tomb story (28:1–8), an appearance story (28:9–10), a report about the guard at Jesus' tomb (28:11–15), and an appearance of the risen Jesus to his disciples in Galilee (28:16–20). For a full discussion of the empty tomb and related issues, see the treatment of Mark 16:1–8 in this volume, and for a full discussion of an appearances near Jerusalem and related issues, see the treatment of Luke 24:13–35.

In rewriting Mark's empty tomb narrative, Matthew simplified the names of the women ("Mary Magdalene and the other Mary," NAB) and identified the "young" man as an angel. He also developed the ideas of guards present at the tomb (see 27:62–66) and explained why they did not put up a struggle (they fainted out of fear). Finally, instead of leaving the women in fear and silence (as in Mark 16:8), Matthew makes it clear that they were overjoyed and proclaimed the resurrection of Jesus to his disciples.

On their way (28:9–10) the women meet the risen Jesus and pay him "homage"—a theme introduced in the Magi story of the infancy narrative back in 2:1–12. Jesus in turn tells them to tell the disciples to meet him in Galilee, thus fulfilling his own prophecy at the Last Supper (see 26:32).

The soldiers guarding the tomb appear only in Matthew (see 26:62–66, 28:4, 28:11–15). Their function in the Matthean narrative is to refute the claim that Jesus' disciples stole his body and then falsely proclaimed that he had been raised from the dead. Whether the presence of the guard at Jesus' tomb was a historical fact or a later apologetic device that arose in early Christian circles or from the evangelist is debated among scholars.

The climactic appearance of the risen Jesus to his eleven disciples in Galilee consists of the appearance itself (28:16–18a) and the declaration and commission by Jesus (28:18b–20). The audience for the appearance is the eleven disciples (the twelve minus Judas) who had accompanied Jesus through most of his public career. Much of Jesus' public ministry took place in Galilee, and it served as the location for the various manifestations of his teaching ability and mighty deeds. Just as a mountain had been the site of his first great speech (5:1–2), so a mountain in Galilee is the place of his final commission to his followers. At his sudden appearance some of the eleven paid him "homage" (see 2:1–12), while others apparently doubted that it was really him. As the risen Jesus came closer to them and spoke, it seems that their doubts passed away.

The commission itself (28:18b–20) can be divided into three parts: Jesus' revelation of his own power and authority, the mission charge to his disciples, and his promise to be present and to help them. In introducing himself the risen Jesus adopts the persona of the glorious Son of man after the pattern set in Daniel 7:13–14. This biblical passage seems to have inspired the statements about Jesus' power and authority ("he received dominion, glory, and kingship," NAB), along with the references to "all the nations" ("nations and peoples of every language serve him") and to his abiding presence with his followers ("his dominion is an everlasting dominion").

The Great Commission imparted by Jesus brings together many of the honorific titles applied to Jesus throughout Matthew's Gospel. As we have seen, all of them have rich backgrounds in the Old Testament and in the Judaism of Jesus' time. Now the risen Jesus is worthy to be approached and to be the object of "homage" as the King of the Jews/Son of David/Messiah. As the Son of man he affirms that all authority has been given to him by his heavenly Father. As the Son of God he directs that "all the nations" be baptized in his name. As the only Teacher he commissions his disciples to carry on his activity and spread it throughout the Mediterranean world. As Emmanuel (see 1:22–23) he promises to be with his followers until the end of the present age.

The disciples who throughout Jesus' public ministry were sometimes characterized as having only "little faith" now encounter the risen Lord in his glory. And they are entrusted with the task of carrying on Jesus' mission by making more disciples, baptizing them, and teaching them. Just as the Gentile Magi came to the land of Israel at the time of Jesus' birth to seek out the King of the Jews, so after his death and resurrection the risen Messiah sends out his disciples to all the nations. The prophetic vision of all the nations coming to Mount Zion (see Isa 2:2–4; Mic 4:1–3) is reversed, and through the agency of Jesus the Jew from Nazareth the good news rooted in Scripture and in God's own people goes forth to all the world.

If the expression "all the nations" *(panta ta ethne)* in Matthew 28:19 means what it seems to mean elsewhere in the Gospel (see 24:9, 14; 25:32), then the Great Commission may have had special relevance for the Matthean community. As a largely (if not exclusively) ethnic Jewish community, the commission to make disciples of "all the nations" may well have given them added impetus to seek new members not only from ethnic Israel but also from among Gentiles (as Paul and others had already done). The evangelist Matthew would have understood this mission as bringing the spiritual treasures and religious heritage of Israel to all kinds of people. In order to understand his Gospel, both Jews and Gentiles would have to learn much about and to make their own the Scriptures of Israel and the Judaism of Jesus' time.

For Reflection and Discussion:

1. In what respects is Matthew 28:16–20 a good summary of the whole Gospel?
2. In what ways might Matthew's Gospel be a help toward better dialogue between Jews and Christians today?
3. In what ways might Matthew's Gospel be an obstacle to better dialogue between Jews and Christians today?

The Gospel of
Mark

Part One: Introduction

Among the four Gospels, Mark has probably received the least attention in Christian-Jewish dialogue. The Gospels of Matthew and John have attracted the most attention because they seem to reflect conflicts between Jesus and his disciples on the one hand and "the scribes and Pharisees" (Matthew) or "the Jews" (John) on the other hand, which are most likely reflections of the conflicts between some Christian Jews and some other Jews in the late first century CE. Luke's attitudes toward Jews and Judaism are sufficiently subtle and ambiguous to have elicited learned scholarly tomes arguing either that Luke is the father of Christian anti-Semitism, or that he stood deeply within Jewish traditions and is a witness for Jewish Christianity after 70 CE. Perhaps more attention to the topic of Mark and Judaism might provide a fresh start for more positive and constructive conversations between Jews and Christians on Jesus and the Gospels.

My thesis is that Mark's Gospel is a Jewish book, one that was not anti-Jewish in intent but rather was written by a Christian Jew who believed that in portraying Jesus' public ministry in the land of Israel he was advancing the legacy of Israel. Of course, Mark's Gospel contains some theological affirmations that were not accepted by most Jews in the first century or thereafter. And I admit that, when taken out of its historical context, Mark's Gospel is potentially anti-Jewish and may well have been used in the service of anti-Judaism through the centuries. That, in fact, is precisely my point.

My point is that when read within its first-century Jewish and Christian context Mark's Gospel is a Jewish book with regard to its narrative framework, authorship, use of Jewish Scriptures, christological titles, apocalyptic thinking, and portrayals of Jews.

After laying out the general framework for viewing Mark's Gospel as a Jewish book, I will treat fifteen key passages in Mark's Gospel that appear in Cycle B of the Sunday lectionary of Scripture readings used in Roman Catholic and mainline Protestant churches.

These expositions call attention to Jewish backgrounds and Jewish elements in Mark's portrayal of Jesus, and try to show how an appreciation of first-century Judaism can illumine the content of these texts. They also warn against certain false moves in interpretation and attitudes that can promote negative or prejudiced views about Jews. For full treatments of these texts and the whole of Mark's Gospel, see John R. Donahue and Daniel J. Harrington, *The Gospel of Mark* (Sacra Pagina 2; Collegeville, MN: Liturgical Press, 2002).

A JEWISH NARRATIVE

Mark's narrative about Jesus of Nazareth is set in the land of Israel and follows a geographical-theological outline. In it Galilee serves as a place of the manifestation of Jesus' authority as a teacher and healer as well as the site of growing misunderstanding and rejection (1:1—8:21), the journey from Galilee to Judea is the occasion for Jesus to teach about his identity and about discipleship (8:22—10:52), and Jerusalem is the place of his final rejection and death, as well as his resurrection from the dead (11:1—16:8). Jesus is clearly a Jewish teacher, his disciples are Jews, and most of the people with whom he comes into contact are Jews. In this sense it is a Jewish narrative. (Mark 16:9–20 is generally regarded as a second-century addition to make up for Mark's lack of accounts about appearances of the risen Jesus.)

A JEWISH AUTHOR

The Gospel of Mark is technically an anonymous composition. The title "According to Mark" found in many Greek manuscripts seems not to have been part of the original text but rather was a later addition based on the early Christian tradition of ascribing this Gospel to Mark. Nowhere in the text itself does the author identify himself or claim to have been an eyewitness to or a participant in the events described in the Gospel.

Who then was Mark, and on what grounds was this Gospel assigned to him as its author? Mark was a common name in the Greco-Roman world of the first century. There are, however, references to an individual named Mark in the Pauline epistles as one of Paul's co-workers (see Phlm 24; 2 Tim 4:11) and as "the cousin of

Barnabas" (Col 4:10). There are also three references apparently to this same figure as John Mark in the Acts of the Apostles. According to Acts 12:12, the house of Mary "the mother of John who is called Mark" (NAB) was a place where early Christians in Jerusalem came to pray. In Acts 12:25 Barnabas and Saul/Paul returned to Jerusalem with "John called Mark" (NRSV). And in Acts 15:37–39 "John, who was called Mark" (NAB), was the occasion for a split between Paul and Barnabas, and their decision to go their separate ways. All these references suggest that Mark was a Jew from Jerusalem who became a Christian and engaged in missionary activity with his cousin Barnabas and with Paul.

This Mark also seems to have had an association with Peter. In the personal greetings at the end of 1 Peter, we read: "The chosen one at Babylon sends you greeting, as does Mark, my son" (5:13, NAB). It appears that the "chosen one" refers to the church, and that "Babylon" was a code-name for Rome (see Rev 14:8; 17:5; 18:2). This text links Mark to Peter and to Rome.

The earliest patristic testimony about the authorship of Mark's Gospel comes from "the Elder" as quoted by Papias as quoted in turn by Eusebius in his *Ecclesiastical History* 3.39.15: "Mark, having become the interpreter of Peter, wrote down accurately whatever he remembered of what was said or done by the Lord, but not in order." This description is full of problems. But at least it does assume that Mark as Peter's interpreter *(hermeneutes)* was fluent in Aramaic (and Hebrew?) and in Greek (and Latin?). The tradition that Mark was Peter's interpreter is repeated by many early Christian writers. The description suggests that this Mark was the Jewish Christian from Jerusalem referred to in the Pauline letters and in Acts.

My intention here is not to insist upon the correctness of the traditional ascription of this Gospel to Mark (and through him to Peter). My real point is to emphasize that the early Christian tradition assumed that the author of this Gospel was indeed a Jew and to that extent his work may be called a Jewish Gospel.

As the expositions of Gospel texts will show, the evangelist whom we call Mark knew a good deal about the land of Israel, Jewish customs, legal debates among various Jewish groups, and so forth. The author also assumed that his readers knew about such matters and were interested in them, and even sometimes provided parenthetical comments to help them understand better. He seems to have been open to Gentile members in the church (see 7:24–30; 8:1–10; 11:17; 15:39), perhaps for the reasons that Paul had given in his letter to the Romans a few years before.

It must admitted, however, that Mark made some mistakes about Jewish matters. For example, in 1:2 he ascribes to Isaiah a mixed quotation consisting of Exodus 23:20 and Malachi 3:1, and in 2:26 he says that Abiathar (rather than Ahimelech) was the high priest in the episode about David and the bread of the presence in 1 Samuel 21:1–7. And his parenthetical comment about "all Jews" observing the various Pharisaic purity rules in 7:3–4 is open to historical critique. Nevertheless, the New Testament and the patristic traditions about Mark as well as the content of the Gospel itself indicate that the early readers of the Gospel assumed that the evangelist was a Jew.

USE OF THE JEWISH SCRIPTURES

At many points in his narrative about Jesus, Mark appeals to biblical texts in a way that suggests that his readers know these texts and regard them as authoritative. In 1:2–3 Mark begins by citing "Isaiah the prophet" to explain the relationship between John the Baptist ("my messenger" and "a voice") and Jesus ("the Lord").

In Mark's account of Jesus' public ministry there are many explicit biblical quotations, especially from Isaiah, the psalms, and Daniel. For example, Jesus appeals to Isaiah 6:9–10 ("Keep listening, but do not comprehend; keep looking, but do not understand," NRSV) to explain why "those outside" (4:12) and even his own disciples (8:18) fail to grasp his preaching about the kingdom of God. In criticizing the Pharisees' attempt at surrounding the biblical purity laws with their own traditions, Mark in 7:6–7 has Jesus give a version of Isaiah 29:13: "These people draw near with their mouths and honor me with their lips, while their hearts are far from me" (NRSV). The crowd's acclamation of Jesus in 7:37 uses material from Isaiah 35:5–6: "He has done all things well. He makes the deaf hear and [the] mute speak" (NAB).

When Jesus enters Jerusalem on Palm Sunday, the crowd greets him with the words of Psalm 118:26: "Blessed is he who comes in the name of the LORD!" (NAB). His symbolic action in cleansing the Jerusalem Temple is explained in terms of an appeal to Isaiah 56:7

and Jeremiah 7:11: "Is it not written: / 'My house shall be called a house of prayer for all peoples'? / But you have made it a den of thieves" (NAB). The parable of the wicked tenants in 12:1–12 ends with a quotation of Psalm 118:22–23: "The stone that the builders rejected / has become the cornerstone; / by the Lord has this been done, and it is wonderful in our eyes" (NAB). In 12:35–37 Jesus offers an interpretation of Psalm 110:1 ("the Lord says to my Lord," NRSV) to show that the title Lord is superior to those of Messiah and Son of David. Many of the major terms and concepts in Jesus' apocalyptic discourse in Mark 13—the great tribulation, the abomination of desolation, the glorious Son of man, and the resurrection of the dead—come ultimately from the Book of Daniel.

In the Markan passion narrative the fulfillment of the Jewish Scriptures is a major motif. In 14:27 Jesus prophesies his desertion by his disciples when he quotes Zechariah 13:7: "strike the shepherd, / and the sheep will be dispersed" (NAB). At his arrest Jesus accepts rough treatment so "that the scriptures may be fulfilled" (14:49, NAB). In his trial before the Sanhedrin, Jesus identifies himself as the glorious Son of man in words taken from Daniel 7:13: "you will see the Son of Man / seated at the right hand of the Power / and coming with the clouds of heaven" (14:62, NAB). In Mark 15 the many quotations of and allusions to Isaiah 53 and Psalm 22 place the suffering and death of Jesus in the biblical traditions of the Suffering Servant and the Suffering Righteous One, respectively.

JEWISH TITLES FOR JESUS

The three most prominent titles for Jesus in Mark's Gospel are Messiah, Son of God, and Son of man. Already traditional in early Christian circles, these titles had rich backgrounds in the Jewish Scriptures and in early Jewish writings. They serve to locate Jesus in a Jewish context and presume some familiarity on the part of Mark's first readers. In Mark, all three titles are interpreted in light of the mystery of the cross.

Messiah is the Hebrew word for "Anointed One." Its Greek equivalent is *Christos*. In the Jewish Scriptures priests, prophets, and kings are anointed ones. In New Testament times there was no uniform Jewish doctrine of the Messiah, and much depends on the context in which the term appears. In 1:1 Mark refers to "Jesus Christ." In 9:41 Jesus speaks about those who "belong to Christ"; in 12:35–37 he relates "Messiah" and "Son of David"; and in 13:21 he warns about those who might be saying, "Look, here is the Messiah!" The most important Markan occurrences of Messiah/Christ appear in the context of Jesus' suffering and death. When Peter in 8:29 confesses that Jesus is "the Messiah," Jesus in 8:31 issues his first passion prediction. At the trial before the Sanhedrin, the high priest inquires: "Are you the Messiah, the son of the Blessed One?" (14:61, NAB). And when Jesus is lifted up on the cross, the chief priests and scribes mock him by saying: "Let the Messiah, the King of Israel, come down" (15:32, NAB). These texts indicate that Mark uses Messiah/Christ often in the context of Jesus' suffering and death, and redefines the title with reference to the mystery of the cross.

"Son of God" is applied in the Jewish tradition to angels (Job 38:7), kings (Ps 2:7), Israel (Hos 11:1), and the Suffering Righteous One (Wis 2:18). This title is also part of the very first verse of Mark's Gospel in most manuscripts: "The beginning of the gospel of Jesus Christ the [Son of God]" (NAB). It is the title used by the voice from the heavens at Jesus' baptism (1:11) and his transfiguration (9:7). The "unclean spirits" or demons recognize Jesus as "the Son of God" (3:11, NAB) and as the "Son of the Most High God" (5:7, NAB). In the parable of the vineyard (12:1–12) the "beloved son" seems to be Jesus. In stating that no one knows "that day or hour" (13:32, NAB), Jesus appears to be speaking about himself as the son. When the chief priest asks whether Jesus is "the son of the Blessed One" (14:61, NAB), Jesus answers, "I am" (14:62, NAB). And at the moment when Jesus dies, the Roman centurion says, "Truly this man was the Son of God!" (15:39, NAB). As with Messiah/Christ, the title Son of God is being redefined in the light of the cross.

"Son of man" appears in Ezekiel as a designation for the prophet himself (see Ezek 2:1, 3, 6, 8; etc.), in Daniel 7:13 ("one like a son of man," NAB), and in 1 Enoch 48 as a glorious heavenly figure. In Mark there are several references to Jesus himself as "the Son of man" in a sense like that in Ezekiel (see Mark 2:10, 28; 14:21, 41). In other texts "Son of man" refers to a glorious eschatological figure (see 8:38; 13:26) as in Daniel 7 and 1 Enoch 48. But the most important and distinctive uses of "Son of man" in Mark appear in Jesus' predictions about his suffering, death, and resurrection (8:31, 9:31,

10:33–34). Mark 10:45 is another especially significant text: "For the Son of Man did not come to be served but to serve and to give his life as a ransom for many." As the Son of man, Jesus is a human, glorious, and suffering figure.

A JEWISH APOCALYPTIC DRAMA

The evangelist's summary of Jesus' preaching appears in Mark 1:15: "This is the time of fulfillment. The kingdom of God is at hand. Repent, and believe in the gospel" (NAB). This summary situates Mark's story of Jesus in an apocalyptic, or end-time/eschatological, context, and thus the unfolding of Mark's narrative is sometimes described as an apocalyptic drama. Its main topic is the kingdom of God, which refers to the moment when all creation will acknowledge God's sovereignty and proceed according to God's original plan. While the kingdom's fullness is still future, the teaching and healing activity of Jesus represent its anticipated or inaugurated dimension. Jesus' proclamation of the future and present dimensions of God's kingdom demands an appropriate response by way of conversion and faith in the good news that Jesus brings.

The testing of Jesus by Satan (1:12–13) alerts the reader to Mark's presentation of Jesus' ministry as a struggle against the cosmic forces of evil. An eschatological dualism familiar from the Dead Sea scrolls (the Prince of Light with the children of light versus the Prince of Darkness with the children of darkness; see the Qumran *Rule of the Community* 3—4) seems to have been an assumption that underlies Mark's narrative (as it did other Jewish and Christian works of the time). Jesus' first public activities in 1:21–45—his exorcisms and healings—are decisive moments in the struggle against the forces of the Evil One. The debate with the scribes in 3:20–30 makes clear that the origin of Jesus' power as a teacher and healer is from the Holy Spirit, and that he stands over against Satan (also known as Beelzebul and the Prince of Demons).

Jesus' parables about the kingdom of God in 4:1–34 teach that it is God's task to bring about the kingdom. There is a contrast between its small beginnings in the present (in Jesus' ministry) and its future fullness (at the eschaton). Something decisive is happening in Jesus' ministry. And Jesus' proclamation of God's kingdom demands an enthusiastic and fruitful response. Jesus' power as the herald of God's kingdom is then illustrated by his deeds in 4:35–5:43, when he shows himself to be the master of the storm at sea, the demons, sickness and the suffering it brings, and death. In Jewish and ancient Near Eastern traditions these chaotic forces appear to be under the dominion of Satan.

Having placed Jesus' ministry in the context of a cosmic and eschatological struggle against the forces of evil, Mark from chapter 6 onward presents Jesus as confronting misunderstanding and hostility from human opponents: the people of Nazareth (6:1–6), his own disciples in 8:14–21 and throughout the journey and passion narratives, and the Jerusalem leaders (the chief priests, elders, and scribes) from chapter 11 onward. The transfiguration account (9:2–8), however, provides an insight into the true nature of Jesus and an anticipation of his role as the glorious Son of man. And in Jesus' apocalyptic discourse (13:1–37) the climax of the scenario of end-time events is the manifestation of "'the Son of Man coming in the clouds' with great power and glory" (13:26, NAB). Since these events are to take place in "this generation" (13:30, NAB) and since their precise time remains unknown (13:32), the appropriate religious and ethical stance is constant vigilance (13:33–37).

In some Jewish circles in Jesus' time, the resurrection of the dead was expected to be an eschatological event (see Dan 12:1–3). In Mark 12:18–27 Jesus stands with the Pharisees against the Sadducees, and argues that resurrection is in the Torah (see Exod 3:6, 15–16) and within the power of God. According to 16:6, the reason that is given for why Jesus' tomb was found empty was that "he has been raised." In Mark's narrative Jesus is the first example or case of the resurrection of the dead. In the resurrection of Jesus a decisive event in the eschatological scenario has already taken place in "this generation."

PORTRAYALS OF JEWS

While Mark's Jesus is a Jewish teacher and healer, Mark also presents his hero as superior to other Jewish teachers and healers, and as possessing significance for non-Jews too (see 7:24—8:10). During his Galilean ministry, Jesus engages fellow Jews in debate (2:1—3:6), and his success results in a plot against him by Pharisees and Herodians (3:6). During his ministry in Jerusalem, Jesus has more controversies with representatives of various Jewish groups (11:27 — 12:44), and here too gains the envy and hostility of the chief priests, elders, and scribes. While these Jewish officials appear to take the initiative in getting Jesus arrested and condemned to death, it is the Roman prefect Pontius Pilate who is ultimately responsible for Jesus' execution.

From his entry into Jerusalem at the beginning of Mark 11, Jesus is especially critical of the Jerusalem Temple and those who are responsible for it. His action in the Temple complex in 11:15–19 is sandwiched between sections about the withered fig tree (11:12–14, 20–21). Jesus' symbolic action and his prophecy about the destruction of the Temple (13:2) are major issues in the trial before the Sanhedrin (14:58) and at the crucifixion (15:29). And those who plot Jesus' arrest and execution (most obviously the chief priests) stand to lose the most if Jesus' prophecies about the Temple should come to pass.

So the Markan Jesus has conflicts with other Jews and Jewish groups, and is critical of the Jerusalem Temple and the Jewish leaders associated with it. But these facts hardly set Jesus outside the boundaries of Judaism in the first century. As the Dead Sea scrolls have shown, Judaism in Jesus' time was both diverse and contentious, and there was strong opposition to the Jerusalem Temple and its officials from Jews other than Jesus.

There are, however, several little noticed texts in Mark's Gospel in which Jews who do not belong to Jesus' followers are treated with tolerance and respect. When an outsider (presumably a Jew) has success in casting out demons in Jesus' name, Jesus counsels his disciples to be tolerant on the grounds that "whoever is not against us is for us" (9:40, NAB). When a rich man inquires about what he must do to inherit eternal life, Jesus tells him to keep the commandments set forth in the Torah (10:19), as if that is enough to inherit eternal life. When a scribe agrees with Jesus about the centrality of the love commandment(s) in the Torah, Jesus pronounces him as being "not far from the kingdom of God" (12:34, NAB). In 12:38–44 the model of Jewish (and Christian) piety is not a scribe but rather a generous widow. And Mark offers no clear indication in 15:43–46 that he regards Joseph of Arimathea as a disciple of Jesus (though Matthew and John do). Rather, Mark gives the impression that Joseph tended to

Jesus' burial out of respect for the biblical commandment in Deuteronomy 21:22–23 to bury someone who had been hanged upon a tree on "that same day" (NAB)—in Jesus' case before the Sabbath began. These examples suggest that, in Mark's view, there were righteous Jews outside of Jesus' circle, and they express a certain openness toward Jews other than those who followed Jesus.

Mark's Gospel is generally regarded as the earliest Gospel, most likely written around 70 CE for a mixed Jewish Christian and Gentile Christian community in Rome that was facing persecution or the threat of it. However, it purports to tell about persons and events in the land of Israel around 30 CE. Its central character is a Jew named Jesus of Nazareth, and almost all its characters are Jews. It describes these persons and events in the context of Judaism in the first century CE.

The expositions that follow give particular attention to the Jewish context of Mark's Gospel. Besides providing the Jewish background information necessary for properly understanding the texts in their Jewish setting, they show how Mark's Jesus interacts with his Jewish contemporaries and point out where the Markan texts might be misinterpreted in anti-Jewish directions. Thus they try to illustrate why in a real sense Mark can be regarded as a Jewish text, and so, perhaps, can provide a bridge between Jews and Christians today concerning Jesus and Judaism.

Part Two: Lectionary Commentary

1
Mark 1:1–8:
Witnesses to Jesus
Cycle B:
Second Sunday of Advent

The very first verse in Mark's Gospel functions as the heading or title for the whole book. Just as John the Baptist's ministry marks the beginning of the story of Jesus, so the public career of Jesus marks the beginning of the saving event of Jesus' death and resurrection being proclaimed as "good news" throughout the Mediterranean world (see Rom 1:3–4). While the term *euangelion* ("good news," or "gospel") was associated with the Roman emperor, it is also rooted in the vocabulary of divine favor and redemption that is prominent in Isaiah 40–66 (see 52:7; 61:1–2).

Mark's good news concerns Jesus of Nazareth, who right at the start is called Christ (Anointed One, Messiah) and Son of God. Along with Son of man, these are the most common and important titles applied to Jesus in Mark's Gospel. Both have deep roots in the Hebrew Scriptures and in Jewish tradition. And in developing his portrait of Jesus as Messiah and Son of God, Mark will draw extensively on these Jewish sources. At the same time, the evangelist will redefine those titles to fit the person of Jesus. The basic question running through Mark's Gospel is, "What kind of Messiah and Son of God is Jesus?"

Mark's story of Jesus is prefaced by John the Baptist and his proclamation: "One mightier than I is coming after me" (1:7, NAB). Mark first presents the appearance of John the Baptist (and Jesus) as the fulfillment of the Hebrew Scriptures and thus fully in accord with God's will and plan. The quotation attributed to "Isaiah the prophet" in Mark 1:2–3 is in fact a combination of Exodus 23:20 and Malachi 3:1 in 1:2 and Isaiah 40:3 in 1:3. The attribution to Isaiah may signal at the start that, for Mark, Isaiah is the biblical prophet par excellence (since quotations of and allusions to Isaiah are sprinkled throughout this Gospel). Or it may be due to Mark's use of an anthology of biblical quotations *(testimonia)* like those found among the Dead Sea scrolls. Indeed, the Qumran community seems to have adopted Isaiah 40:3 as its motto and rationale: "And when these become members of the Community in Israel according to all these rules, they shall separate from the habitation of unjust men and shall go into the wilderness to prepare there the way of Him; as it is written, 'Prepare in the wilderness the way of the Lord, make straight in the desert a path for our God'" *(Rule of the Community* 8:12–14).

The biblical texts in 1:2–3 are read in the context of the Christ event (that is, Jesus' life, death, and resurrection). So in 1:2 "my messenger" is John the Baptist, and his task is to be the precursor of the Messiah, the one who goes before and prepares the way. Likewise, in 1:3 the "Lord" is Jesus, and John's task of preaching in the desert and smoothing the way of Jesus evokes the memory of Israel's return to the Holy Land from exile in Babylon in the sixth century BCE (as seen in Isa 40 — 55).

This apparently tendentious use of the Hebrew Scriptures by Mark (and, in fact, all the New Testament writers) would have been quite acceptable among Jews in the first century. For example, the Dead Sea scrolls known as the Pesharim interpret the Prophets and Psalms in the light of their community's life and history as the interpretive key to the Scriptures. So also the early Christians took Jesus (and whatever was related to him) as their interpretive key. While respecting the authority of the Hebrew Scriptures, Mark was also convinced that they became fully intelligible in light of the Christ event (Jesus' life, death, and resurrection).

In 1:4–8 Mark presents Jesus as the herald pointing toward the coming of Jesus. The "desert" (1:4) where John appeared was undoubtedly the Judean Desert, the general area in which the Dead Sea scrolls were found. If there was any direct connection between Jesus and the Qumran group, the most likely candidate is John the Baptist (see Luke 1:80). That John achieved great popularity in preaching his baptism of repentance for the forgiveness of sins is confirmed by the Jewish historian Josephus (see *Jewish Antiquities* 18:116–19), who says that Herod Antipas had John killed because he feared an uprising under John's influence.

The lifestyle (1:6) that John adopted ("clothed in camel's hair, with a leather belt around his waist," NAB) was deliberately reminiscent of prophet Elijah (see 2 Kgs 1:8 and Mark 9:13). And his diet ("locusts and wild honey") not only showed his dependence upon God but also was acceptable under Jewish food laws (Lev 11:20–23; Deut 32:13).

Mark's version of John's message contrasts John and Jesus with reference to their persons (1:7) and their baptisms (1:8). In the Markan context at least, John first identifies Jesus as "one mightier than I" (see 1:22, 27; 3:27, NAB). John serves as the precursor to the coming kingdom of God (like Elijah in Mal 3:23/4:6) and claims to be unworthy even to act as the servant of Jesus the Messiah. Then John compares his own baptism "with water" and Jesus' baptism "with the holy Spirit." In the background of this comparison seems to be God's promise in Ezekiel 36:25–26: "I will sprinkle clean water upon you to cleanse you....I will give you a new heart and place a new spirit within you" (NAB).

All the elements in Mark 1:1–8—the Gospel's title, the biblical quotations, and the description of John the Baptist—place Mark's narrative of Jesus in the context of Judaism. For Mark, Jesus is the fulfillment of the Hebrew Scriptures and of Judaism. But fulfillment does not mean abolition (see Matt 5:17). Indeed, what most Christians call the Old Testament was the (only) Bible of the early church. Without those writings the story of Jesus would make little or no sense. By reading and reflecting on the Jewish Scriptures and understanding Jesus in light of them, Christians today continue the theological process that began with Jesus and his first followers. Jesus cannot be separated from Judaism.

For Reflection and Discussion:

1. How do you evaluate the use of the Jewish Scriptures in Mark 1:2–3?
2. How does John the Baptist serve as a bridge between the Hebrew Bible and Jesus?
3. What do you think of when you read or hear the word *fulfillment* with regard to the Hebrew Scriptures and the Gospels?

2
Mark 1:14–20:
The Kingdom of God and Discipleship
Cycle B:
Third Sunday in Ordinary Time

In the Markan narrative about the baptism of Jesus by John (1:9–11), a voice from the heavens declares the identity of Jesus in terms based on Psalm 2:7 and Isaiah 42:1–2: "You are my beloved Son; with you I am well pleased" (NAB). In the Markan account about the testing or temptation (1:12–13), Jesus repeats successfully the "forty days" fasts undertaken by Moses (Deut 9:18) and Elijah (1 Kgs 19:8). Having shown what kind of Son of God he is, Jesus begins his public ministry of proclaiming God's kingdom (1:14–15) and calls disciples to be with him and to share in his mission (1:16–20).

Whereas Jesus' baptism by John and his testing were located at the Jordan River and in the Judean Desert, respectively, the bulk of Jesus' public ministry, according to Mark 1:14—8:21, took place in his home area of Galilee. The Holy Land is often described as "the Fifth Gospel." To visit Galilee and Judea and to see the sites associated with Jesus in the Gospels is an intellectually and spiritually rewarding experience and a great help toward reading and appreciating the four canonical Gospels. And few places on earth are as beautiful as the Sea of Galilee and its environs.

The heart of Jesus' preaching is captured in the statement: "The kingdom of God is at hand" (1:15, NAB). A good starting point toward understanding what Jesus meant can be found in the biblical psalms that proclaim "the LORD is king" (see Pss 93, 96, 97, 99). An important element in ancient Israel's faith was the conviction that the God of Israel (YHWH) is the Lord of all creation. The biblical kingship psalms confess and celebrate the kingship of Israel's God, and look forward to all creation joining in this confession.

In Jesus' time there was a growing conviction among many Jews that the fullness of God's reign was yet to come. They believed that when the fullness of God's reign does come, all creation will acknowledge Israel's God as Lord and will join in an eternal chorus of praise. Then will occur the resurrection of the dead, the Last Judgment, the giving of eternal rewards and punishments, and a new heaven and a new earth. This kingdom of God is future in its fullness and transcendent insofar as it is primarily God's undertaking.

For Jewish beliefs about the future kingdom of God, see the apocalypses found in Daniel, 1 Enoch, Assumption of Moses 10, 4 Ezra (= 2 Esdras 3 — 14), and 2 Baruch. See also Jesus' own prayer — the Lord's Prayer — in Matthew 6:9–13 and Luke 11:2–4, which is a Jewish prayer for the coming of God's kingdom in its fullness. The Jewish prayer known as the *Kaddish* and popularly regarded as a prayer for the dead is, in fact, a prayer for the coming of God's kingdom in its fullness: "Magnified and sanctified be his great name in the world which he has created according to his will. May he establish his kingdom during your life and during your days, and during the life of all the house of Israel, even speedily and at a near time."

Jesus shared the belief of his Jewish contemporaries that the fullness of God's kingdom is future. And so he taught his disciples to pray: "Thy kingdom come" (Matt 6:10; Luke 11:2, NAB). Nevertheless, according to Mark and the other evangelists, Jesus saw in his own time — indeed, in his own person and ministry — the beginning or inauguration of God's reign: "This is the time of fulfillment." According to Mark, the kingdom of God was already breaking in through Jesus' preaching and healing activity. So it is fair to describe Jesus as the presence of God's kingdom. Where Jesus is, there is the kingdom of God.

Recognition of the kingdom's future fullness and present reality demands a response: "Repent, and believe in the gospel." The proclamation of God's kingdom involves by way of response conversion (as with John's baptism) and faith in its most basic sense: the confidence that God is for us, the trust that God cares for us and guides our lives, and the conviction that God wants us to share eternal life with the risen Christ in the fullness of God's kingdom.

The first disciples whom Jesus called to follow him (1:16–20) were four Jewish fishermen—Peter and Andrew (1:16–18), and James and John (1:19–20)—at the Sea of Galilee. We should not imagine that these were lazy men sitting in shade with a piece of string tied to a stick. No, they were apparently hardworking and successful commercial fishermen (with nets, boats, and employees). Then as now, commercial fishing at the Sea of Galilee was a major industry. People could and did make a steady and comfortable income from it. The point is that Jesus' first disciples had good reasons for staying exactly where they were: familiar surroundings, solid business prospects, and family ties.

Instead, they left their homes and businesses to follow Jesus. Why did they do so? The strangeness of their action is further highlighted when we recall that the usual pattern in rabbinic Judaism was for disciples to seek out their prospective teacher. For example, in Mishnah *Abot*, 1:6, Joshua ben Perahiah says, "Set up a master for yourself, and get yourself a fellow disciple." Here, however, the teacher seeks out the disciples.

The story of Jesus' call of his first disciples (1:16–20) is told in a very indirect way. There is no indication that these first disciples had known or even met Jesus beforehand. The way in which Mark tells the story suggests that there was no preparation at all. Rather, Jesus bursts on the scene by the Sea of Galilee, and says to Peter and Andrew: "Come after me, and I will make you fishers of men" (1:17, NAB). And they come. Then he meets James and John, and calls them. And they come. The very indirectness, lack of preparation, and surprising response all serve to communicate a positive message about Jesus: How attractive and persuasive Jesus must have been to have such an effect! How dynamic his person and how powerful his presence must have been to convince four fishermen from Galilee to leave everything and follow him.

Everything that Jesus says and does, according to Mark's Gospel, is in the service of God's kingdom. And by his resurrection he anticipates the fullness of God's kingdom. Those who heed Jesus' call to follow him as disciples live in his presence, share his company, and participate in his work of teaching and healing. Thus they bear witness to the present and future dimensions of God's kingdom.

The kingdom of God is very much a Jewish concept, and the idea of a Jewish teacher with disciples is at the heart of the rabbinic movement. The first followers of Jesus were all Jews, and the early Jesus movement would have been regarded not as promoting a new religion but rather as attempting a reform of Judaism—indeed, a renewal movement within Judaism comparable to Pharisaism or Essenism.

For Reflection and Discussion:

1. What do you understand by the expression "kingdom of God"?
2. What might have motivated these Galilean fisherman to follow Jesus? How does Mark bring this out?
3. Do you by your activities build the kingdom of God on earth? Or can only God bring about the kingdom?

3
Mark 1:21–28:
Teaching and Healing on
the Sabbath
Cycle B:
Fourth Sunday in Ordinary Time

The two most prominent activities of Jesus according to Mark's account of his public life were teaching and healing. These two activities are featured in Mark 1:21–28, which in Mark's narrative is Jesus' first public action. One of the common literary devices used by the evangelist is intercalation, or the sandwich (ABA), technique. With this device Mark begins one story, tells a second story, and returns to the first story. For other examples see Mark 3:20–35; 5:21–43; 6:7–32; 11:12–26; 14:1–11; and 14:54–72. This device not only creates suspense but also interprets or contrasts one narrative by the other.

Mark 1:21–28 starts by recounting Jesus' teaching in the synagogue at Capernaum and the positive reaction to that teaching (1:21–22). Then it tells the story of Jesus performing an exorcism on a man with "an unclean spirit" (1:23–26, NAB). Finally it returns to Jesus' prowess as a teacher and the response of amazement that he evoked (1:27–28). The point of the ABA technique here is to say that the one who is powerful in word is also powerful in deed, and vice versa.

In Mark's narrative, Jesus' first public action takes place in the synagogue at Capernaum. The term *synagogue* (from the Greek word for "gathering, coming together") can refer to an assembly of people or to the building where their assembly takes place. For Jews in Jesus' time there was only one Temple (in Jerusalem) where sacrifices could be offered. But all over the Holy Land and in the Diaspora, Jews gathered in synagogues (or Jewish "gathering places") for study, prayer, and social activities. The remains of a synagogue from the second or third century CE have been found at Capernaum. And given the custom of the time, it is likely that the first-century synagogue was in the same place. However, it is not at all clear how elaborate a building the synagogue at Capernaum was in Jesus' time. It may have looked much like a private house.

According to Mark 1:21, Jesus entered the synagogue and taught there. While there is some dispute about the exact structure of the Sabbath synagogue service in Jesus' time, it very likely consisted of readings from the Hebrew Scriptures, an exposition of the biblical texts, prayers and petitions, and praises of God. It is plausible that a young Jewish teacher from Nazareth might be invited to read the biblical passages and offer comments on them. Neither priestly lineage nor rabbinic ordination was required for a person to do so in Jesus' time. However, the initial response of those gathered in the synagogue, according to 1:22 (see also 1:27), was astonishment, because "he taught them as one having authority and not as the scribes" (NAB).

The term *scribe* (*grammateus* in Greek, *sopher* in Hebrew) covers a wide range of activities, from basic reading and writing skills to intellectual and even political leadership. In Sirach 39:1–4, there is a marvelous description of the ideal scribe and his training: / "How different the man who devotes himself / to the study of the law of the Most High! / He explores the wisdom of the men of old / and occupies himself with the prophecies; / He treasures the discourses of famous men, / and goes to the heart of involved sayings; / He studies obscure parables, / and is busied with the hidden meanings of the sages. / He is in attendance on the great, / and has entrance to the ruler" (NAB).

In Jesus' time scribes wrote and interpreted legal contracts (deeds of sale, marriage contracts, divorce decrees, etc.). In a society in which the Torah served as the basis for the Jewish legal system, scribes were expected to be thoroughly familiar with the Law of Moses. And as the equivalent of our lawyers, it is likely that scribes collected anecdotes and sayings that served as precedents for or at least helps toward deciding legal matters. Scribes functioned as legal notaries, biblical scholars, lawyers, and theologians all in one.

The scribes were not a unified Jewish group or sect (like the Pharisees and the Sadducees). They were people who practiced a profession (like our lawyers). In Mark's Gospel they are associated with Jerusalem (3:22; 7:1, 5), and in the passion narrative the scribes along with the chief priests and elders become the primary Jewish instigators in moving forward the process that leads to Jesus' death (see 14:1, 43, 53; 15:1, 31; also 8:31; 10:33; 11:18). Their opposition to Jesus is in the long run far more fatal than the opposition of the Pharisees is.

The first example of Jesus' healing power (1:23–26) takes the form of an exorcism, the expulsion of an "unclean spirit." For other exorcisms in Mark's Gospel, see the narratives about the Gerasene demoniac (5:1–20), the daughter of the Syrophoenician woman (7:24–30), and the boy with an unclean spirit (9:14–29). However we in the twenty-first century might diagnose the man's condition and explain the healing of it by Jesus, people in Jesus' time regarded the man with an unclean spirit as ultimately under the power of Satan (see 1:12–13). In the Dead Sea scrolls Abraham and Daniel function as exorcists. And there is a Jewish tradition about Solomon, the son of David par excellence, as an exorcist. In Mark 1:24 the unclean spirit correctly identifies Jesus as "the Holy One of God" (NAB). And Jesus' success in banishing the unclean spirit means that he has supernatural or superhuman powers. Indeed, Jesus' display of power over the unclean spirit places all his healing activities in the context of the apocalyptic battle between the Prince of Light (probably Michael in the Dead Sea scrolls, Jesus in Mark) and the Prince of Darkness (Satan and his minions).

The first public actions in Jesus' ministry take place in the context of a Sabbath service held in a synagogue. He reads the Jewish Scriptures and offers interpretations of them. It is the Jewish onlookers in the synagogue, and not Jesus himself, who bear witness to his unusual method of teaching and to his power in word and deed.

For Reflection and Discussion:

1. Does it surprise you that Jesus' first public action in Mark's narrative occurs on a Sabbath in a synagogue?
2. What does it mean to you that Jesus (unlike the scribes) taught as one having "authority"? What authority did he have? Where did it come from?
3. How do the interlocking stories about Jesus as a teacher and a healer serve to interpret and confirm one another?

4
Mark 2:23—3:6:
Work on the Sabbath
Cycle B:
Ninth Sunday in Ordinary Time

In the Greco-Roman world of the New Testament, one of the practices that distinguished Jews from other peoples was their observance of the Sabbath—the seventh day of the week, or Saturday—as a day of rest from work. This practice was rooted theologically by Jews in the very fabric of creation according to the Priestly creation account: "on the seventh day God…rested" (Gen 2:1–3, NAB). It appears prominently among the Ten Commandments first in the context of creation (Exod 20:8–11, NAB) and then with reference to liberation from slavery in Egypt and to humanitarian concerns (Deut 5:12–15). According to Exodus 31:16–17, Sabbath observance also functions as a sign or reminder of God's covenant relationship with Israel: "as a perpetual covenant…an everlasting token."

In Mark's Gospel Jesus never rejects or even questions the Sabbath as an institution. In fact, Jesus goes to the synagogue on the Sabbath and participates in the services there (1:21; 3:1; 6:2). He waits until after sundown on the Sabbath to heal the sick (1:32). And his female followers wait until the Sabbath is over before visiting Jesus' tomb on Easter Sunday morning (16:1).

The two Sabbath controversies described in Mark 2:23–28 and 3:1–6, respectively, concern not the Sabbath itself as an institution but rather what constitutes work on the Sabbath. The definition of work

94

on the Sabbath was what especially occupied Jewish teachers in Jesus' day. A very strict approach to the definition of work on the Sabbath appears in a text found among the Dead Sea scrolls at Qumran and known as the *Damascus Document* in its section on Sabbath observance (10:14—11:18). For example, no one is to "speak any vain or idle word on the Sabbath day. He shall make no loan to his companion. He shall make no decision in matters of money and gain. He shall say nothing about work or labor to be done on the morrow. No man shall walk abroad to do business on the Sabbath" (10:17–20). The *Damascus Document* 11:13–14 even forbids on the Sabbath lifting out a beast that had fallen into a cistern or pit, a very strict ruling rejected by both Jesus and the Pharisees in Matthew 12:9–14.

Mishnah *Shabbat* 7:2 provides a list of thirty-nine actions—sowing, plowing, reaping, binding sheaves, threshing, and winnowing—which are regarded as work and so as prohibited on the Sabbath. This list may be viewed as the rabbinic end-product of debates among earlier Jewish teachers about what counted as work on the Sabbath. It is important to take Mark 2:23–28 and 3:1–6 as contributions to the ongoing Jewish debate in the context of first-century Judaism.

The issue in Mark 2:23–28 was whether the action of Jesus' disciples in plucking heads of grain (2:23–24) constituted work on the Sabbath. There was no doubt about their right under the Torah to take food from someone else's field: "When you go through your neighbor's grainfield, you may pluck some of the ears with your hand" (Deut 23:26, NAB). The question here concerned the timing—whether this action might be performed on the Sabbath. Jesus' Jewish opponents—in this case Pharisees—apparently regarded the disciples' action as reaping and therefore as work forbidden on the Sabbath.

Jesus defends his disciples' action and establishes his own position first in 2:25–26 by appealing to the precedent set by David in 1 Samuel 21:1–6, though close inspection of the biblical text reveals that the precedent is not exactly the same case. Then in 2:27 Jesus recalls the humanitarian dimension of Sabbath observance ("the sabbath was made for man," NAB) and in 2:28 seems to top off his argument by appealing to the Son of man's authority as "lord even of the sabbath" (NAB). So in his disciples' defense Jesus suggests that Deuteronomy 23:25, the precedent set by David, common sense, and

Sabbath humanitarianism all favor a freer attitude toward their action on the Sabbath.

In Mark 3:1–6 the issue is whether healing a man with a withered hand on the Sabbath is work and therefore is prohibited. The problem was that the man's physical condition was not a matter of life and death, and so could presumably have been put off until the Sabbath was over. The man's withered hand was a long-term, probably congenital, affliction. Why not wait?

The account in Mark 3:1–6 is a combination of a healing narrative and a debate. As a healing story it identifies the man's condition ("a withered hand," NAB) and recounts his immediate and complete healing by Jesus. The debate concerns whether it is lawful to perform such an action on the Sabbath. Here the motive of the opponents—the Pharisees—is portrayed as quite hostile: "so that they might accuse him" (3:2, NAB). Here Jesus' defense takes the form of a question: "Is it lawful to do good on the sabbath rather than to do evil, to save life rather than to destroy it?" (3:4, NAB). Even though the man's condition was not life-threatening, Jesus' healing of his hand on the Sabbath is here identified as doing good and saving life, and therefore allowable.

In both episodes the opponents are Pharisees. In 2:23–28 they seem to be hoping to catch Jesus and his disciples in some "unlawful" activity. In 3:1–6 their goal is said to be finding some reason for accusing Jesus, and Jesus recognizes their "hardness of heart" (NAB). And in 3:6 the Pharisees join forces with the Herodians "to put him to death" (NAB), the first indication that Jesus' ministry of teaching and healing will result in his own death.

Among all the Jewish groups, the Markan Jesus seems to be closest to the Pharisees. While Jesus was not a Pharisee (as Paul was), Jesus at least shared an agenda with the Pharisees on many issues, including defining what constitutes work on the Sabbath. The debate between them takes place within the parameters of Jewish opinions in the first century. On this matter, Jesus represents a more liberal attitude than that of the Pharisees. However, this is not always the case, as his strict teaching on marriage and divorce in Mark 10:2–12 shows.

Christian teachers and preachers need to be very cautious about dismissing the Pharisees as Jewish legalists. In fact, within the context of first-century Judaism, the Pharisees were generally the liberals or progressives on most matters. They tried to adapt the Torah to the real-life conditions of Jewish life in the first century. They did so to such an extent that the more rigorously observant Essenes (who gave us the Dead Sea scrolls) referred to the Pharisees as "seekers after smooth things," thus complaining that the Pharisees were making life too easy for their fellow Jews. Careless remarks about the Pharisees' alleged legalism and even the pejorative use of the adjective *pharisaic* can serve to reinforce dangerous anti-Jewish stereotypes, which in fact have no historical foundation.

For Discussion and Reflection:

1. How would you assess the respect toward the Sabbath observance shown by Jesus and his first followers?
2. What is the precise point of difference between Jesus and the Pharisees in each episode?
3. Does the idea of the Pharisees as liberals or progressives surprise you? What about Jesus sharing an agenda with them and being closest to them than to other Jewish groups?

5
Mark 3:20–35:
The Family of Jesus
Cycle B:
Tenth Sunday in Ordinary Time

As Jesus' public ministry continues in Galilee, he gains support from Jewish crowds all over the Holy Land and even beyond (3:7–12), and he appoints the twelve apostles as the inner core of his movement (3:13–19). The choice of the twelve, of course, clearly evokes the memory of the twelve tribes of ancient Israel and so places the Jesus movement in the context of Israel's history and heritage. While Jesus' popularity was growing, so also was the opposition to him, according to Mark.

Whereas in 3:6 the initial opposition consisted of Pharisees and Herodians, in 3:20–35 Jesus suffers opposition not only from the scribes from Jerusalem but also from his own family. This passage takes the form of an intercalation, or sandwich: A—Jesus' family opposes him (3:20–21); B—scribes from Jerusalem question the source of Jesus' power (3:22–30); A—Jesus defines his true family (3:31–35).

While surprising to modern readers, the opposition from Jesus' own family described in 3:20–21 very likely had some historical basis. In the Mediterranean world of the first century, family ties and honor and shame were important values. To bring honor on the family in the eyes of the wider society was a great achievement. But to bring shame on the family was a disgrace for all family members, and the family felt an obligation to repair the damage. Some members of Jesus' own family seem to have decided that he was out of his mind and so was bringing shame on their family. They needed to do something about him.

Opposition from Jesus' own family during his public ministry is not the kind of thing that early Christians or the evangelist Mark would have invented, since it reflected badly on their hero, Jesus of Nazareth. Moreover, after Jesus' death, members of Jesus' family (especially James) became prominent in the Jesus movement. In fact, a recently discovered ossuary (bone box) with an Aramaic inscription stating "James, son of Joseph, brother of Jesus" may (if it is authentic) once have contained his bones. We know from Josephus (*Jewish Antiquities* 20:200) that James died a martyr's death in 62 CE under the high priest Ananias.

Whether these were Jesus' full siblings born of Joseph and Mary, or Jesus' stepbrothers and stepsisters from Joseph's earlier marriage, or simply Jesus' "relatives" (the extended family), has been debated since patristic times. In the Markan context (see also 6:1–6) it suffices to say that Jesus was very likely opposed by some members of his family, whatever their precise relationship was.

In their skepticism about Jesus, the family members were joined by scribes from Jerusalem (3:22–30). These scribes were primarily concerned with the origin of Jesus' power as an exorcist and healer. Was it from God or from Satan? The scribes did not deny the fact of Jesus' power. They did, however, suspect that his power came from Satan. These Jerusalem scribes were religious and legal experts. To be suspected of being in league with Satan by them was a serious matter and needed a response.

The specific charges made by the scribes are presented in 3:22 ("He is possessed by Beelzebul" and "By the prince of demons he drives out demons," NAB) and in 3:30 ("He has an unclean spirit," NAB). In 3:23–26 Jesus argues against these charges by means of "parables," that is, similitudes or analogies. His point is that with his exorcisms and other healings Jesus is effectively driving out Satan (who was regarded as the source of possession and illness), and so he could hardly belong to the kingdom or household of Satan. Then in 3:27 Jesus compares his role as the "stronger" or "more powerful one" (see 1:7) to one who invades and plunders the house of "the strong man" (Satan, NAB). Finally, in 3:28–29 Jesus defines as "an everlasting sin" (NAB) what he calls blasphemy against the Holy Spirit—which in this context means attributing the work of Jesus and the Holy Spirit to Satan. This whole defense presupposes the framework of Jewish apocalyptic dualism and serves to locate Jesus on the side of God and not on the side of Satan. The origin of Jesus' power is with God, not with Satan.

In 3:31–35 the narrative returns to the opposition from Jesus' own family (as in 3:20–21). We are told that "his mother and his brothers" (NAB) had arrived (from Nazareth) on the scene (in Capernaum) and were demanding to see him. Their presence serves as the occasion for Jesus to redefine his true family: "Here are my mother and my brothers. [For] whoever does the will of God is my brother and sister and mother" (3:34b–35, NAB). The real family of Jesus was constituted not by his blood relatives or by the religious and legal experts of his own people (the scribes) but rather by those who earnestly seek to do the will of God.

This redefinition of family is sometimes called fictive kinship. In this way persons not related by blood come to regard one another as brothers and/or sisters on the basis of some spiritual or social ideal. The sociological term, however enlightening it may be, should not distract from the revolutionary character of Jesus' teaching about his true family as those who seek to do God's will. Now there is something more important than blood relationship, clan, tribe, or family. Now there is a new understanding of family that subordinates racial and social factors to the spiritual ideal of commitment to doing God's will. In Jesus' new family of those who seek to do God's will, it is possible for all to find meaning, companionship, and hope.

Mark's picture of Jesus' relatives in 3:20–21 and 3:31–35 seems to imply that his mother Mary was among his opponents. In rewriting Mark's Gospel, however, Luke portrays Mary in the infancy narrative (Luke 1—2) as the one who hears the word of God and acts upon it. Then he defines the true family of Jesus as "those who hear the word of God and act on it" (Luke 8:21, NAB; see 11:27–28), and thus presents Mary as the perfect disciple of Jesus insofar as she is totally committed to doing the will of God.

In the new family of Jesus as defined in Mark 3:31–35, there is no mention of fathers (see also 10:30: "brothers and sisters and mothers and children," NRSV). In the patriarchal family structure prevalent in first-century Judaism and indeed all over the Greco-Roman world it was assumed that the father had supreme power in the household *(paterfamilias)*. In the new family of Jesus, however, the real father is God. The divine paternity relativizes all human fatherhood and all patriarchal power exercised within the household.

In the Markan context the "unforgivable sin" turns out to be a failure in discernment. The scribes—the religious and legal professionals—emerge as incapable of discerning the action of God at work in Jesus' activity as a healer and an exorcist. However, it is too easy for Christian readers today to look back in light of what they have come to believe about Jesus and to judge harshly the apparent obtuseness of the scribes in Jesus' time. As we often say, "hindsight is 20-20." Rather, the scribes in this passage provide a salutary and sobering challenge to all religious professionals today—priests, ministers, rabbis, religious educators, and other ministers—that despite all our efforts and study we too often fail to discern where and when the Holy Spirit is at work among us.

For Reflection and Discussion:

1. Why might members of Jesus' own family have opposed him?
2. What is the logic of the various short parables in Mark 3:22–30?
3. Who qualifies to be a member of family of Jesus? What kind of family values does he represent?

6
Mark 4:35–41:
Who Is This?
Cycle B:
Twelfth Sunday in Ordinary Time

After the "day of parables" in Mark 4:1–34, the focus shifts from Jesus the teacher to Jesus the wonder-worker. The story of the stilling of the storm in Mark 4:35–41 is the first in a series of four miracle stories. It is followed by the exorcism of the evil spirits from the man from Gerasa who was under the power of a "legion" of demons (5:1–20), and by the healing of a woman with a chronic flow of blood (5:25–34) and by the restoration of a young girl—the daughter of Jairus—to life (5:21–24, 35–43). In this cycle of four miracle stories Jesus shows his power over nature (the storm), demons, chronic illness, and even death. All these stories evoke the question that ends the story of the stilling of the storm: "Who then is this whom even wind and sea obey?" (4:41, NAB).

Mark 4:35–41 leads us to imagine a sudden and fierce storm on the Sea of Galilee, the large lake near which Jesus exercised much of his public ministry. It was not unusual that Jesus and his disciples should be out in a boat on the lake. His first disciples were fishermen there. And it was not unusual that a squall or sudden storm should arise. Such storms are said to be fairly common on the Sea of Galilee. The panic of the disciples is reminiscent of the prophet Jonah's description of his near-drowning: "For you cast me into the deep, into the heart of the sea, / and the flood enveloped me; / all your breakers

102

and your billows passed over me" (Jonah 2:4, NAB). What is unusual is that Jesus the teacher should make the storm subside simply by saying, "Quiet! Be still!" (NAB). What is unusual is that the wind and sea should obey the command given by Jesus.

To understand better the significance of the wind and sea obeying the word of Jesus, it is helpful to look at the readings (Job 38:1, 8–11; Ps 107:23–31) that accompany Mark 4:35–41 in the church's lectionary for the Twelfth Sunday in Ordinary Time in Cycle B. The reading from Job 38 marks the beginning of God's speeches from the whirlwind. Here God finally responds to Job's very impatient search for an explanation of his suffering. The thrust of God's response is not to reply directly to Job's questions but rather to remind Job (and us) that humans do not have the whole picture, that our vision is too narrow, and that we measure things in all too human ways. In the following verses from Job 38:8–11, God appeals to his power in setting limits and imposing order on chaotic forces of the sea. According to Job 38:8–11, the wind and sea obey God: "And who shut within doors the sea, / when it burst forth from the womb; / When I made the clouds its garment / and thick darkness its swaddling bands? / When I set limits for it / and fastened the bar of its door, / And [I] said: Thus far shall you come but no farther, / and here shall your proud waves be stilled!" (NAB).

The selection from Psalm 107 concerns a storm at sea. Here the perspective is that of sailors in a boat in the midst of a terrible storm at sea (see also Jonah 1). The language used to describe the motion of the waves and the reactions of the sailors is vivid and picturesque: "They mounted up to heaven; they sank to the depths; / their hearts melted away in their plight" (Ps 107:26, Lectionary). You can almost feel the emotional ups-and-downs of the sailors moving in time with the waves. The only hope that the sailors have is to pray to God. And so they call out to God in their distress. And their prayer is answered: "He [God] hushed the storm to a gentle breeze, / and the billows of the sea were stilled" (Ps 107:29, Lectionary). The psalm text from here on is a thanksgiving for rescue from the storm. Whom do the wind and sea obey, according to Psalm 107? They obey God.

These two passages from the Hebrew Bible provide important context for grasping the theological point of Mark's account about Jesus stilling the storm. In the face of a violent and sudden storm that threatens to overwhelm Jesus and his disciples in the boat, Jesus returns the raging sea to its normal calmness and to its natural boundaries by his word alone: "Who then is this whom even wind and sea obey?" (4:41, NAB). This is clearly no ordinary or even extraordinary human being. Rather, this is a person in whom divine power is at work. This is someone who does what God does in stilling the storm. In this story, as elsewhere in the Gospels, there is an implicit claim to Jesus' divinity. Jesus does what only God can do. From stories like this, one can see how Christian belief in the divinity of Jesus arose.

The stilling of the storm is often referred to as a nature miracle. In it Jesus seems to transcend or overcome the laws of nature. People in biblical times had more fluid concepts about nature and its laws than most of us do today. For them the extraordinary deeds done by Moses, Joshua, Elijah, and Elisha were primarily signs of God's presence in the life and history of God's people. In the New Testament the miracles of Jesus are signs of the presence of God's kingdom and so part of his ministry of proclaiming God's kingdom in word and deed.

The nature miracle of the stilling of the storm in Mark 4:35–41 readily evokes biblical texts like Job 38 and Psalm 107. And so it is hard to know where the factual description of events ends and the biblical echoes begin. However one solves this critical problem, the purpose of the narrative as it now stands in Mark's Gospel is to elicit the same question from readers today as it did in the first century: "Who then is this whom even wind and sea obey?"

In this episode Jesus' disciples are portrayed as fearful and obtuse. When they awaken Jesus, they say: "Teacher, do you not care that we are perishing?" (4:38, NAB). And after calming the storm (in the manner of an exorcist), Jesus rebukes them for their lack of faith: "Why are you terrified? Do you not yet have faith?" (4:40, NAB). Even though the first disciples were called to be with Jesus and to share in his mission, Mark portrays them as repeatedly failing to understand Jesus (8:14–21) and in the end deserting Jesus at his arrest in Jerusalem (14:50). Here they fail to trust in Jesus' power to save them from a very dangerous situation. If Mark's own Gospel was composed against the background of actual or threatened Roman persecution (as early Christian tradition assumes and many modern interpreters think), it is likely that the account of Jesus' stilling the storm provided encouragement and hope to its first readers.

According to the Sunday lectionary, mainline Christians today read Mark (and the other Gospels) along with selections from the Old Testament. The first reading has usually been selected in light of the

Gospel text (as is clearly the case here with Job 38 and Mark 4:35–41), and the psalm serves as a bridge between the first reading and the Gospel passage. The epistle reading from Paul or the other apostles is on a separate cycle, and so there is usually no organic connection to the other readings.

The Christian pattern is clearly indebted to the Jewish synagogue practice of reading selections from the Torah and the Prophets, along with other biblical texts. The current Christian approach has been criticized by both Christians and Jews for fostering a promise-and-fulfillment schema that tends to reduce the Hebrew Scriptures to mere preparation for Christ and not taking them on their own terms. (In the Sundays of Lent there is a salvation-history schema that does more justice to the integrity of the Old Testament passages.) That having been said, it is important for Christians to recognize that fulfillment does *not* mean abolition. As we have seen in the stilling of the storm, without recourse to the pertinent texts from the Hebrew Bible the New Testament passage sounds like just another amazing story. Its theological depth is supplied by reading Job 38 and Psalm 107 alongside Mark 4:35–41.

For Reflection and Discussion:

1. Have you ever been caught in a terrible storm like a hurricane or tornado? How did you react?
2. What theological depth do the passages from Job 38 and Psalm 107 add to your understanding of Mark 4:35–41?
3. Do you believe that nature miracles like the stilling of the storm are possible? Why or why not?

7
Mark 7:1–23:
Purity Rules
Cycle B:
Twenty-Second Sunday in Ordinary Time

Due to its length, technical character, and repetitiveness, this passage appears in the Sunday lectionary in an abbreviated form (Mark 7:1–8, 14–15, 21–23). However, because of its relevance to the topic of Mark and Judaism the text is treated here in its full form (7:1–23). The passage appears in a context (6:7–8:21) that describes Jesus' mission to Jews and Gentiles (7:24–37) as well as various sea voyages on the Sea of Galilee, miraculous feedings (6:31–44; 8:1–10), and conflicts with Pharisees and scribes (7:1–23, 8:11–12).

There are three main topics in this conflict with Pharisees and scribes: handwashing and tradition (7:1–8), the practice of dedication, or *qorban* (7:9–13), and things that defile or render someone impure (7:14–23).

The opponents in this dispute are identified as "the Pharisees with some scribes who had come from Jerusalem" (7:1, NAB). The Pharisees were members of a Jewish religious movement that sought to make the holiness of the Jerusalem Temple into the pattern or model for all of Jewish life. They encouraged meals in common as the occasion for sharing wisdom and fellowship. They were serious religious people who were earnestly trying to apply and adapt the precepts of the Torah to the realities of everyday Jewish life. Indeed, they were regarded as progressives among Jewish religious groups of the time. Their more conservative and traditionalist rivals, the Essenes, criticized them bitterly as "seekers after smooth things"—a criticism that probably represents a play on the Hebrew words for "smooth things" *(halaqot)* and religious-legal rulings *(halakot)*. The scribes were experts in the religious laws embodied in the Torah and in their interpretations and applications.

The first topic in the debate is handwashing and tradition (7:1–8). From Mark's account, it appears that some Pharisees and scribes were trying to extend the practice of handwashing involved in Temple activities (such as sacrifices) and in cases of ritual impurity (see Lev 15), and seeking to make it part of the ordinary regimen for all pious Jews—just in case that they might have contacted ritual defilement in some way. In the Mishnah, a large part of the tractate *Yadayim* ("Hands") is devoted to regulations concerning handwashing (1:1–2:4). As in Leviticus 15, the issue in Mark 7:1–8 and *Yadayim* is not so much personal hygiene as it is ritual purity.

The occasion for the debate is the opponents' perception that Jesus' disciples were not observing their rules pertaining to handwashing before meals. The Markan Jesus himself seems to have been somewhat indifferent to traditions about ritual purity, as when he is touched by the woman with the flow of blood (Mark 5:25–34) and when he takes a dead girl (Jairus's daughter) by the hand (5:35–43, especially 5:41).

In an apparently parenthetical comment in 7:3–4, Mark explains Jewish customs about these matters presumably for the benefit of his Gentile readers. His statement that "all Jews" do these things probably should be taken as an example of his rhetorical tendency to universalize (as in 1:5) rather than as a statement of historical fact. What is really at issue in this part of the debate is whether all Jews (including Jesus and his disciples) are bound to follow the interpretations and customs *(halakot)* of the Pharisees and scribes.

According to Mark 7:5, the Pharisees and scribes want to know: "Why do your disciples not follow the tradition of the elders but instead eat a meal with unclean hands?" (NAB). Rather than debating about the specific topic of handwashing, Jesus attacks "the tradition of the elders," that is, the adaptations, extensions, and applications of the Torah developed by the Pharisees and scribes. He does so by appealing to a (somewhat tailored) version of Isaiah 29:13 that accuses the opponents of "teaching as doctrines human precepts" (NAB). Lest anyone miss the point of the biblical quotation, the Markan Jesus provides an application to the opponents: "You disregard God's commandment but cling to human tradition." Rather than setting aside Israel's Scriptures, Jesus uses them to criticize Jewish teachers who in his view seem to be distorting those Scriptures by their human traditions.

The second topic concerns the practice of dedication, or *qorban* (7:9–13). Here Jesus criticizes what seems to have been a custom supported at least by some Jewish teachers according to which someone could take money or property and declare it as dedicated *(qorban)* to God. A problem might arise, however, if a person were to declare something *qorban* for selfish reasons as a way of making sure that his parents might have no access or profit from his money or property. The Markan text portrays this case as in potential conflict with the clear biblical teachings about honoring one's parents (see Exod 20:12; 21:17). In fact, Mishnah *Nedarim* ("Vows") 9:1 allows release from a vow for reasons pertaining to "the honor of his father or mother." The thrust of Jesus' criticism in Mark 7:9–13 is that some Pharisees and scribes were passing off as authentic traditions practices and customs that could have the effect of nullifying the clear teaching of Scripture.

The third topic is what really defiles or renders a person impure (7:14–23). Against the background of many biblical laws pertaining to ritual purity (see Leviticus especially), Jesus proclaims: "Nothing that enters one from outside can defile that person; but the things that come out from within are what defile" (7:15, NAB). Then in private teaching to his disciples, Jesus reiterates his basic principle (7:20, 23) and provides a list of vices (7:21–22) that illustrates his point that moral evils coming from within a person really defile that person. A comparable list of vices appears in the Dead Sea scrolls found at Qumran: "But the ways of the spirit of falsehood are these: greed, and slackness in the search of righteousness, wickedness and lies, haughtiness and pride, falseness and deceit, cruelty and abundant evil, ill-temper and much folly and brazen insolence" (*Rule of the Community* 4:9–11).

In 7:19 the evangelist (or perhaps a predecessor or a later scribe) adds a parenthetical comment that goes far beyond what Jesus says: "Thus he declared all foods clean" (NAB). If Jesus had spoken so clearly on this matter, it would not have been so controversial an issue in the early church. For example, see Galatians 2 and Acts 15, where it is still a matter of debate among early Christians twenty or more years after Jesus' death.

Mark 7:1–23 is a complex and technical passage. In Christian circles it underwent a process of editorial development, as the parenthetical comments in 7:2, 3–4, 11, and 19 show. The Jewish teachings on these matters also underwent a long and complicated process, as the agreement between Mishnah *Nedarim* 9:1 and the Markan Jesus on *qorban* indicates.

In reading Mark 7:1–23 the temptation for Jewish readers is to brand Jesus an apostate and dismiss him entirely as not a Jew. The temptation for Christians is to look upon the Pharisees and scribes as legalists and hypocrites and to extend this judgment to all Jews. However, when the passage is read in its original Jewish context, it places Jesus in the framework of an ongoing debate within Judaism about the value of the Pharisaic-scribal tradition in general and in particular about their traditions that defined ritual handwashing, declared property dedicated to God, and dealt with impurity (ritual or moral?).

It is important also to recognize that Second Temple Judaism was not monolithic. While there was general (but not universal) agreement among Jews about the central importance of the Torah, the Temple, and the land, there were various ways of being a Jew: Apocalyptists, Pharisees, Sadducees, Essenes, Zealots, Samaritans, Christians, and probably several others. In fact, some modern scholars now prefer to speak about Judaisms (in the plural) rather Judaism taken as a uniform phenomenon. Just as Judaism (and Christianity) today comes in many forms, so in Jesus' time there were several ways of living out one's Jewish identity. The Jesus movement offered one such path, and the Pharisees and scribes offered another.

The Markan passage criticizes the Pharisees and scribes for their lack of focus on the essentials, for their failure to distinguish between the important and the accidental, and for their abuse of religion. These are temptations into which many sincerely religious persons—including Christians—have fallen in all ages and still fall today.

For Reflection and Discussion:

1. What do you think of when you think of when you hear the word *Pharisee*? Do you make any connection between Pharisees in antiquity and Jews today?

2. How could the practice of *qorban* be abused in the name of religious observance? Are there any analogues today?

3. What makes someone impure? Is it something internal or external, or both? Is there any relation between ritual and moral purity?

8
Mark 8:27–35:
The Suffering Messiah
Cycle B:
Twenty-Fourth Sunday in Ordinary Time

The question regarding Jesus that runs through the whole of Mark's Gospel is, "Who is this?" The first part of Mark's Gospel (1:1–8:21) establishes that Jesus is a wise teacher and a powerful healer. It also traces a line of misunderstanding of and opposition to Jesus from Pharisees and Herodians (3:6), Jesus' family and the scribes from Jerusalem (3:20–21), the people of Nazareth (6:1–6), and even his disciples (8:14–21).

Mark 8:27–35 serves as the lead text in the Markan journey narrative in 8:22–10:52. That narrative begins and ends with accounts about blind men coming to see (8:22–26; 10:46–52). It features Peter's confession of Jesus as the Messiah (8:27–30) and three passion-resurrection predictions (8:31; 9:31; 10:33–34) followed in each case by a misunderstanding on the part of Jesus' disciples and by his own teachings about himself (Christology) and following him (discipleship).

As mentioned above, the question raised by the Markan journey narrative is, "Who is this?" When Jesus asks that question of his disciples, they first report several popular opinions about Jesus as John the Baptist, Elijah, or one of the prophets (see the same list in 6:14–16). These were reasonable guesses. Jesus had received John's baptism,

111

and to a large extent he was continuing John's mission of proclaiming the coming kingdom of God. In his actions and teachings Jesus (like John) showed affinities to the prophet Elijah, and, according to Malachi 3:23–24, the second coming of Elijah was to precede "the day of the LORD." To many people Jesus looked and acted like a Jewish prophet, and there may well have even been speculation that Jesus was the prophet like Moses promised in Deuteronomy 18:15, 18. Yet when Jesus asks Peter directly "But who do you say that I am?" Peter responds: "You are the Messiah" (8:29, NAB).

The Hebrew word *Messiah* means "anointed." Its Greek equivalent is *Christos*, the origin of the name Christ. In ancient Israel the term *Anointed* (Messiah) was applied to priests, prophets, and (above all) kings. In each case anointing with oil was associated with those taking on these offices. As kings disappeared from Israel's history from the Exile in the sixth century BCE onward, there was a tendency in some (but not all) Jewish circles to look forward to a future king— a Son of David anointed as the Messiah by God. This anointed one would restore the fortunes of Israel as God's people and make Israel into an even more glorious nation than it had ever been.

The first-century BCE Jewish work known as the *Psalms of Solomon* provides a description of what at least some Jews were hoping for. The composition of this book has often been attributed to Pharisees. Its Psalm 17 prays that God will "raise up for them their king, the Son of David, to rule over your servant Israel in the time known to you, O God" (17:21). The psalmist hopes that the Messiah will "purge Jerusalem from Gentiles…and smash the arrogance of sinners" (17:22–23), and that he will "gather a holy people…and judge people and nations" (17:26, 28). Then "their king shall be the Lord Messiah" (17:32).

This religious-political interpretation of the Messiah was not the only understanding of "Messiah" available in Jesus' time, and not all Jews included a Messiah-figure in their eschatological scenarios. However, something like what appears in *Psalms of Solomon* 17 may well be assumed as the context for Peter's identification of Jesus as the Messiah in Mark 8:29. This would also explain the jealousy and suspicion shown to Jesus by the Jewish leaders in Jerusalem as well as the swift action taken by the Roman governor, Pontius Pilate, against him.

From the Christian perspective at least, Peter was correct in recognizing that Jesus was greater than John the Baptist, Elijah, or one of the prophets. He was also correct in identifying Jesus as the anointed one of God, the Messiah/Christ. Where Peter was incorrect, from the Christian perspective at least, concerned what *kind* of Jewish Messiah Jesus was. What Peter fails to see and refuses to see is that Jesus is a *suffering* Messiah. When Jesus outlines the fate that awaits him in Jerusalem (8:31), Peter argues that this cannot be, since the very idea of a suffering Messiah was to him self-contradictory and even nonsensical.

It has become customary to use the expression "messianic secret" in connection with Mark's Gospel. In fact, Mark 8:29–30 provides the only really clear instance of this particular motif, since only here does Jesus tell anyone to be silent precisely about his identity as the Messiah. There are, however, many cases in which Jesus commands silence about himself or his deeds (1:25, 34, 44; 3:12; 5:43; 7:36; etc.). Some interpreters explain the secrecy about Jesus' identity as a way of avoiding political unrest among Jews that might lead to more Roman control and oppression. But at least in the context of Mark's narrative the injunctions to silence may be better viewed as a literary device to allow the unfolding of Jesus' identity as the suffering Messiah as the Gospel proceeds.

Mark's Gospel has been described as a passion narrative with a long introduction. Mark 1 — 13 prepares the reader to appreciate better that Jesus is a suffering Messiah. Only at his trial before the Sanhedrin, at his darkest hour, does Jesus explicitly accept the three christological titles that run through Mark's Gospel: Messiah, Son of God, and Son of man (14:61–62).

Mark 8:31 presents the first of three passion-resurrection prophecies in Mark's Gospel (see also 9:31; 10:33–34). Whether Jesus predicted his death in the precise detail found in these texts is debatable. However, it is very likely that Jesus, as he headed toward Jerusalem, foresaw the possible negative implications of his critique of Temple practices and his proclamation of God's kingdom. In the context of Passover such talk would surely have disturbed both Jewish leaders and Roman officials in Jerusalem.

After proclaiming his own passion and death, Jesus in 8:34–35 warns that following him may well involve suffering. Jesus challenges the crowds and his disciples to deny themselves, take up their crosses, and come after him. The suffering Messiah invites them to share in his suffering. But he also promises that in a paradoxical way embracing the cross and the reality of suffering will bring freedom and life.

If something like the concept of the Messiah found in *Psalms of Solomon* 17 was in the background of Peter's confession, then both Christians and Jews must recognize that the idea of a suffering Messiah that is developed at great length in Mark's Gospel is a dramatic reinterpretation of the notion of Messiah. In view of this innovation it is not surprising that many Jews in Jesus' time could not accept Jesus as their Messiah. Indeed, some of Jesus' own disciples (especially Peter here, but see also John 6:66) found it difficult to embrace such a drastic revision in their own thinking about the Messiah.

For Reflection and Discussion:

1. What do you think of when you hear the words *messiah* and *messianism*?
2. Why was (and is) the idea of a suffering messiah so hard for people to accept?
3. How can anyone save one's life by losing it? Does that make sense to you?

9
Mark 9:2–10:
The Transfiguration
Cycle B:
Second Sunday in Lent

In the church's lectionary the Gospel reading for the Second Sunday of Lent each year concerns the transfiguration of Jesus. The same passage is read on August 6, the feast of the Transfiguration. Lent is forty days of preparation for the celebration of Jesus' death on Good Friday and his resurrection on Easter Sunday. The reading from Mark 9:2–10 looks backward to Moses and Elijah and to the beginning of Jesus' public ministry at his baptism by John. It also looks forward to the glory of Jesus' resurrection, and looks directly at his suffering and death.

In Mark's narrative the transfiguration takes place during the early stages of the journey of Jesus and his disciples to Jerusalem. In this episode an inner core of disciples—Peter, James, and John—go up a mountain and receive a preview or anticipation of the fullness of the risen Jesus' glory. Before their eyes Jesus' appearance changes, and his clothes become dazzling white (9:2–3). They witness the glorified Jesus conversing with two great biblical figures, Elijah and Moses, who were believed to have been taken up into heaven (9:4–6). Then they hear a voice from the heavens that identifies Jesus as the Son of God (9:7). Suddenly the vision is over, and all they see is the human Jesus (9:8). On the way down from the mountain Jesus warns the three disciples not to tell anyone what happened "except when the Son of Man had risen from the dead" (9:9–10, NAB).

The Markan transfiguration account is full of biblical allusions and echoes. In the Bible a high mountain such as Sinai or Zion is often the place where God is revealed most dramatically. If there is a specific biblical model for the transfiguration of Jesus, the most likely candidates are to be found in Moses' experiences of God on Mount Sinai in Exodus 24:12–18 and 34:1–35. Elijah and Moses clearly represent the Prophets and the Law, respectively. And about both there was a mystery surrounding their passing from the earth; see 2 Kings 2:9–12 for the assumption of Elijah ("Elijah went up to heaven in a whirlwind," NAB), and Deuteronomy 34:1–8 for the mystery of where Moses was buried ("to this day no one knows the place of his burial," NAB). In the Holy Land, where people depend on the seasonal rains for their very lives, the cloud is a symbol of hope and life. In Psalm 68:5 the God of Israel is called "the rider of the clouds" (NAB)—a divine epithet found elsewhere in ancient Near Eastern literature. In Exodus 40:34–38 a cloud covers the Tent of Meeting, which is filled with the glory of God. And at the dedication of Solomon's Temple in Jerusalem "the cloud filled the house of the LORD" (1 Kgs 8:10–11, NAB). And it is possible that the three "tents" that Peter proposed to erect have some connection to the Feast of Booths or Tabernacles as described in Leviticus 23:33–36.

Biblical scholars sometimes refer to the transfiguration of Jesus as a christophany. The term takes up the biblical tradition of theophany, as in the manifestations of God's glory to Moses (see Exod 3; 24; 34), Isaiah (Isa 6), and Ezekiel (Ezek 1). In the christophany that is Jesus' transfiguration, the inner circle of the twelve experiences what will be the glorious and eternal state of the risen Jesus, the Messiah/Christ. And they hear a voice from the heavens saying almost the same words that were said at Jesus' baptism: "This is my beloved Son. Listen to him" (9:7; see 1:11, NAB).

Biblical scholars have long debated about the precise nature of the transfiguration account. Was it a historical event, or a resurrection appearance, or an apocalyptic vision? Mark presents it as a historical event witnessed by Peter, James, and John as they journeyed with Jesus from Galilee to Jerusalem. Indeed, it is plausible that Jesus' disciples did gain some extraordinary insight into the glorious character of Jesus as they made their way up to the Holy City, and that their experience has been expressed in the form of a christophany/ theophany and embellished with many biblical touches. Others view the transfiguration narrative as a resurrection appearance account that has been retrojected into Jesus' public ministry. Still others (following the lead of Matt 17:9, where it is called a "vision") take it to be an apocalyptic vision, and interpret it in the context of the dreams and visions found in the Book of Daniel and other Jewish apocalyptic writings.

These debates about the genre and origin of Mark's transfiguration story should not distract attention from the central point of the passage (and the reason for its inclusion in the Lenten lectionary). The transfiguration is intended as a preview or anticipation of Jesus' resurrection. In it Jesus takes on a glorious and dazzling form, the kind of appearance that he will have forever in the kingdom of God. But his way to glory is also his way to the cross (see 8:31, 9:31, 10:33–34), as the disciples are reminded on their way down from the mountain. If Jesus is to rise from the dead, he must die first. And so the disciples are called to join Jesus as they make their way to Jerusalem and to the fate that awaits Jesus there.

The Markan account ends on a peculiar note with the disciples "questioning what rising from the dead meant" (9:10, NAB). As first-century Jews who had contact with the Pharisees (the great proponents of belief in resurrection), the disciples of Jesus were surely familiar with the concept of resurrection. And they presumably were exposed to Jesus' own case for resurrection based on the Scriptures and on the power of God (see Mark 12:18–27). That they knew and believed in the resurrection of the dead is almost beyond debate.

What is unusual, however, about the case of Jesus' resurrection, according to the New Testament, is that it is said to take place for one person only (Jesus) and before the other events in the eschatological scenario (general resurrection, Last Judgment, rewards and punishments, new heavens and new earth). In his warning in Mark 9:9 as in his three passion-resurrection predictions (8:31; 9:31; 10:33–34), Jesus speaks about his own resurrection in isolation from all the other end-time events. This variation from the familiar end-time scenarios of Jewish apocalyptic writings is probably what we are to imagine as puzzling the disciples of Jesus here and prompting their questioning.

The debates about the precise nature of the transfiguration account and about the character of the events underlying it, as well as the recognition of all the biblical motifs woven into it, illustrate that in some Gospel texts it is hard to discern the line between history and theological interpretation. Like other writers in antiquity and like all the other biblical authors, the evangelists do not conform to the nineteenth-century German historiographical ideal of determining and describing events with pure objectivity, as they really happened. Instead, they seek to make links between Jesus and other biblical figures and events (intertextuality) and thus to bring out the deeper theological significance of Jesus' person and activity.

For Reflection and Discussion:

1. Why are mountains so often the settings for profound spiritual experiences?
2. How do you interpret the presence of Moses and Elijah in the transfiguration narrative?
3. What do the cloud and the heavenly voice contribute to the text's claims about Jesus' true identity?

10
Mark 10:2–16:
Marriage and Divorce; Children
Cycle B:
Twenty-Seventh Sunday in Ordinary Time

Jesus the teacher shared an agenda with his Jewish contemporaries, especially the Pharisees. That agenda was not so much concerned with broad theological and philosophical themes (the existence of God, the human condition, the nature of truth, etc.) as it was with practical issues pertaining to Jewish life (the nature of work on the Sabbath, ritual purity rules, marriage and divorce, etc.). On some issues the Markan Jesus is more liberal than the Pharisees are (Sabbath observance, purity regulations), and on others he agrees with them against the Sadducees (on resurrection, as in 12:18–27). But on still other issues, the Markan Jesus shows himself to be more radical or rigorous (depending on one's perspective) than the Pharisees.

According to Mark 10:2, the Pharisees approach Jesus and ask him: "Is it lawful for a husband to divorce his wife?" (NAB). They certainly knew the Scriptures (see Deut 24:1–4, where divorce is taken for granted), and they very likely knew that Jesus' restrictive position seemed to put him in conflict with those Scriptures. And so Mark observes that they "were testing him" (NAB).

Instead of answering them directly, Jesus in good Jewish fashion answers their question with a question of his own: "What did Moses

119

command you?" (10:3, NAB). In fact, in the Torah there is no direct commandment about marriage and divorce. The topic does come up in Deuteronomy 24:1–4, which deals with the case of a man who had divorced his wife who in turn married another man and was divorced by him. Can the first husband remarry his first and now twice-divorced wife? The biblical answer is, No. And the reason is because "she has become defiled" (24:4). In the treatment of this somewhat exotic case, we learn that among Jews divorce was the husband's pre-rogative, and that he could dismiss his wife from his household sim-ply by "handing her a written bill of divorce" (24:1, 3, NAB). That action left both spouses free to marry. But in most cases it also left the woman quite vulnerable, since she was either on her own or had to return to her father's household (perhaps in disgrace).

What was most controversial among Jesus' Jewish contempo-raries was not the fact of divorce (which was taken for granted) but rather the grounds for divorce. The reason for divorce according to Deuteronomy 24:1 is expressed in vague and some mysterious expression: "something indecent" (NAB). In Hebrew this phrase is *'erwat dabar*, which literally means "the shame of the matter." In the Mishnah tractate *Gittin* ("Divorce Decrees") 9:10, we have the opin-ions of three great Jewish teachers roughly contemporary with Jesus on this topic. The House of Shammai interprets Deuteronomy 24:1 to refer to unchastity on the woman's part. The House of Hillel takes it to mean that she is a bad cook. And Rabbi Aqiba allows divorce if the husband found someone more attractive than his wife.

The Markan Jesus bypasses the rabbinic debate about grounds for divorce and questions the institution of divorce itself. And he does so in the form of a scriptural debate. He first acknowledges the pres-ence of Deuteronomy 24:1–4 in the Torah but dismisses it as due only to God's permissiveness with regard to "the hardness of your hearts" (10:5, NAB). Then with quotations from Genesis 1:27 ("God made them male and female," NAB) and Genesis 2:24 ("For this reason a man shall leave his father and mother [and be joined to his wife], and the two shall become one flesh," NAB), Jesus establishes as the origi-nal will of God his own position of "no divorce" and summarizes his main point: "They are no longer two but one flesh" (10:8, NAB).

These same Genesis texts are also used in several of the Dead Sea scrolls (*Damascus Document* and *4Q Instruction*) to prohibit polygamy, if not divorce. Some scholars have found in the Qumran

Temple Scroll 57 a prohibition of divorce at least in the case of the king: "He shall not take another wife in addition to her [his first wife], for she alone shall be with him all the time of her life. But if she dies, he may marry another from his father's house from his family." But most scholars interpret this as forbidding polygamy on the king's part. And besides it belongs to "the law of the king" and is not necessarily applicable to other Israelites.

In private teaching to his disciples in 10:10–12, Jesus restates his teaching in ways much like the sayings quoted in Luke 16:18 (the Q form) and in 1 Corinthians 7:10–11. However, the saying about the case of a woman divorcing her husband and marrying another in Mark 10:12 (something not envisioned by Deut 24:1–14) is generally interpreted as an adaptation made by Mark himself or a predecessor to extend Jesus' teaching to accord with Roman law and custom according to which women could initiate divorce proceedings.

There is wide agreement among biblical scholars that Jesus himself taught "no divorce." This teaching differs from that of his Jewish contemporaries, is attested in several New Testament sources (Mark, Q, Matthew, Luke, Paul), and is coherent with Jesus' radical teachings about the kingdom of God. There is, however, much less consensus about what Jesus meant by it and how he envisioned that it might be put into practice (as a law, as an ideal, as a temporary measure before the full coming of God's kingdom?). And there is also recognition that the New Testament writers introduced some apparent exceptions into Jesus' radical position on divorce. For example, Paul in 1 Corinthians 7:15–16 allows divorce (and remarriage?) in the case where the non-Christian spouse wants to end the marriage to a Christian. And Matthew inserts exceptions in 5:32 and 19:9 for *porneia*, which may refer either to sexual misconduct on the wife's part (thus agreeing with the House of Shammai) or to marriage within the degrees of kinship forbidden by Leviticus 18:6–18 (see Acts 15:20, 29).

After the treatment of marriage, a passage on children (10:13–16) marks a natural progression. However, the primary concern here is the kingdom of God rather than children per se. In the Jewish and Greco-Roman world of Jesus' time children were not regarded so much as innocent and unspoiled, as precious and totally natural. Rather, children were considered as "little adults" who had not as yet attained any power or social status. Little children were viewed as totally dependent on others (mainly their parents), and therefore they necessarily received everything as a gift.

Jesus in Mark 10:15 uses the children coming for his blessing to illustrate something about the kingdom of God: "Whoever does not accept the kingdom of God like a child will not enter it" (NAB). The point here is that it is God's kingdom, it is God's prerogative to give it, and the best we can do is to accept it for what it is—a gift from God. We will enter God's kingdom only when we recognize it as God's gift to us and accept it as such. By dismissing the children as unimportant and bothersome, the disciples show their failure to understand Jesus' teaching about the kingdom of God. Compare Mark 9:36–37, where the social insignificance of children in ancient society is used to illustrate the ideal of leadership as service of others and receiving Jesus and his Father in receiving apparently insignificant persons like children.

For Catholics who preach on this text there are special challenges today. The Catholic tradition has placed Jesus' teaching on "no divorce (and remarriage)" in a legal framework, and does not recognize second marriages without an annulment of the first marriage or the death of the spouse. This causes many problems for otherwise devout Christians. Moreover, revelations about clerical abuse of children have called into question our church's claims to be an advocate for children. These topics must be squarely faced.

Nevertheless, this Markan text conveys a positive message on both issues, one that people today need to hear. Whatever Jesus' precise intentions were with his "no divorce" teaching and whatever negative consequences it has had over the centuries, in its first-century Jewish context it provided some measure of security for women who could not be simply "sent away" or dismissed by their husbands for weak reasons. (Of course, this is not a warrant for forcing women to stay in an abusive relationship.) Moreover, the passage provides a wonderfully positive ideal for married persons—that they really try to become "one flesh."

Likewise, the passage about accepting the kingdom of God as a gift—just as a child must accept everything as a gift—recognizes the child as a real person who counts in society and suggests that adults can learn from children the most important lessons about the nature of Jesus' community and the kingdom of God.

For Reflection and Discussion:

1. How do you regard Jesus' prohibition of divorce? What might its consequences—good or bad—be?
2. Is Jesus' ideal of marriage as the two becoming one flesh possible? Can you point to any examples?
3. What does Jesus' admonition to accept the kingdom of God "like a child" say about the nature of the kingdom and those who may enter it?

11
Mark 12:28–34:
The Great Commandment
Cycle B:
Thirty-First Sunday in
Ordinary Time

With Jesus' arrival in Jerusalem in chapter 11, Mark's narrative reaches its final and climactic location. The chronological framework that Mark provides gives us Passion (or Holy) Week. The first part of Passion Week consists of Jesus' entrance on Palm/Passion Sunday and his prophetic action in the Jerusalem Temple (11:1–25), five controversy or conflict stories with a parable (11:27 — 12:44), and Jesus' eschatological discourse (13:1–37).

The passage about "the great commandment" (12:28–34, NAB) is the fourth among the controversies. In fact, it is more a scholastic dialogue or conversation than a controversy or conflict, since the questioner (a scribe) is sincere in his approach to Jesus and expresses agreement (and more) with Jesus on the matter. The scribe asks Jesus a question: "Which is the first of all the commandments?" (12:28, NAB). Jesus answers in 12:29–31 by quoting two prominent biblical commandments about loving God (Deut 6:4–5) and loving one's neighbor (Lev 19:18). Then the scribe agrees with and approves Jesus' answer, and adds that fulfilling these two commandments is "worth more than all burnt offerings and sacrifices" (12:32–33,

NAB). Finally, Jesus declares that this scribe is "not far from the kingdom of God" (12:34, NAB).

The question raised by the scribe about "the first of all the commandments" was a common question posed to Jewish teachers in Jesus' time. The scribes had counted 613 commandments (248 are positive in form, and 365 negative) in the first five books of the Bible (the Torah). But, of course, the Torah contains rules about all kinds of topics, ranging from murder (Exod 20:13; Deut 5:17) to what one should do on finding a bird's nest on the road (Deut 22:6–7). The question was intended to elicit some basic principle(s) in the Torah and to introduce a hierarchy among the many commandments. It was natural to ask a Jewish teacher like Jesus to supply a summary statement or general principle that would bring together all 613 commandments.

According to the Babylonian Talmud (*Shabbat* 31a), a Gentile approached Shammai and challenged him to "teach me the whole Torah while I stand on one foot." The answer, of course, would have to be short. Shammai refused and chased the Gentile away, presumably because he regarded the request as foolish. However, when the Gentile approached Hillel and asked the same question, he got this answer: "What is hateful to you, do not do to your neighbor." Thus Hillel's response is much like the "Golden Rule" attributed to Jesus in Matthew 7:12 and Luke 6:31 (see also Tobit 4:15). Indeed, because of its somewhat negative formulation, Hillel's answer is sometimes called the "Silver Rule." But the point of the two formulations is much the same.

Jesus' answer here takes the form of two biblical quotations. His response is thus thoroughly traditional in the sense that it consists of two of the 613 commandments in the Torah. The first part of Jesus' answer is taken from Deuteronomy 6:4–5: "You shall love the Lord your God with all your heart" (NAB). Not only is this text taken from the Book of Deuteronomy but it is also one of the Scripture passages recited three times a day by pious Jews in the *Shema* (which takes its name from first Hebrew word in this text, *Shema* = "Hear"). The second part of Jesus' answer is from Leviticus 19:18: "You shall love your neighbor as yourself" (NAB). This text too was well known to the scribe and indeed to all Jews as part of Israel's "Holiness Code." By answering the scribe's question with two familiar biblical quotations, Jesus gives a thoroughly Jewish response.

While Jewish, Jesus' answer is also radical. The word *radical* means going to the "root" of things. Jesus' response to the scribe is radical in the sense that it suggests that the two great principles that underlie or serve as the root of all 613 precepts in the Torah are love of God and love of neighbor. The assumption is that if you love God and love the neighbor, you will naturally do what the Law commands and so do the will of God and be pleasing to God.

It is doubtful that Jesus or Mark believed that the entire Torah could be reduced to these two commandments and that the remaining 611 commandments were thereby abrogated (though Rom 13:8–10 might give this impression). Rather, the idea seems to be that those who let their lives be guided by the double love commandment will naturally do what God wills and what God's Torah requires.

Thus, Jesus' answer to the scribe's question is both traditional and radical. The scribe's positive response to Jesus is surprising, especially in the context of Jesus' Passion Week ministry in Jerusalem where a major theme is opposition to Jesus from all sides (and from the scribes in particular). Not only does the scribe express his agreement with Jesus but he even takes his response a step further by stating that the two love commandments are more important than "all burnt offerings and sacrifices" (12:33, NAB). His statement stands in the tradition of biblical prophets such as Hosea: "For it is love that I desire, not sacrifice, / and knowledge of God rather than holocausts" (Hos 6:6, NAB). For similar sentiments, see 1 Samuel 15:22 and Proverbs 21:3.

This opinion fits well with another major theme in Mark 11 – 13: the opposition between Jesus' proclamation of the kingdom of God and the worship being practiced at the Jerusalem Temple. This theme is further developed in Jesus' evaluation of the scribe: "You are not far from the kingdom of God" (12:34, NAB).

There is no indication that this scribe was already or later became one of Jesus' disciples. Rather, this scribe is one of several Jews in Mark's Gospel who are not disciples of Jesus and are nonetheless praised or at least acknowledged for their pious actions and/or sincerity. They include the "other" exorcist who uses Jesus' name (9:38–40), the rich man who keeps the commandments but rejects the call to discipleship (10:19, 21), the generous widow (12:41–44), and perhaps Joseph of Arimathea who sees to Jesus' burial in accord with Deuteronomy 21:22–23 (15:43–46).

For Reflection and Discussion:

1. How would you characterize the relationship between Jesus and the scribe in this passage? How does it compare with his interactions with other scribes in Mark's Gospel?
2. In what sense is Jesus' response thoroughly Jewish? Could Hillel or Shammai have said the same?
3. How might this episode provide a model for Christian-Jewish dialogue today?

12
Mark 12:38–44:
Scribes and a Widow
Cycle B:
Thirty-Second Sunday in Ordinary Time

Between the Jerusalem controversy stories (11:27 — 12:37) and Jesus' eschatological discourse (13:1–37), Mark develops a contrast of characters between certain ostentatious scribes (12:38–40) and a poor but generous widow (12:41–44). The passage provides the important reminder that we cannot always judge holiness by external appearances. Some surprising and unlikely persons may be the holiest among us. If we look closely at the scribes and the widow in the context of first-century Judaism, we may be able to appreciate the contrast even more fully.

In the most basic sense a scribe was someone who could read and write, which were skills attained by only a small part of the population in the Greco-Roman world. Scribes were needed to write and interpret legal documents (bills of sale, marriage contracts, divorce decrees, etc.), either because their clients could not read and write, or because they had to be sure that their business and personal transactions were legally correct. But scribes were more than copyists.

Scribes were also experts in the Jewish religious tradition. They knew the Scriptures well, and acted as the equivalents of our theologians and professors of religious studies. Scribes were called upon not only to write out legal documents but also to give legal opinions and advice. Remember that to a large extent the Law for Jews in Jesus' time was what is contained in the first five books of the Hebrew Bible (the Torah). The scribes were also the equivalents of our lawyers.

Jesus' critique of the scribes is devastating. Recall, however, that it does not apply to *all* scribes, as the episode in Mark 12:28–34 has just shown. Nevertheless, in Mark's narrative, the scribes are the most persistent and dangerous among the Jewish opponents of Jesus. The scribes criticized in Mark 12:38–40 are said to be very careful about social and religious appearances. They dress in a way ("in long robes," NAB) to draw attention to themselves, like to be greeted in public settings ("glad-handers"), and position themselves in prominent places at synagogue services and banquets (12:38–39) so as to be seen by others. But, according to 12:40, these displays of piety are calculated to improve their business prospects, especially among the more defenseless and credulous members of society: "They devour the houses of widows" (NAB). And they try to disguise their hypocrisy and greed by reciting long prayers.

The scribes caricatured in Mark 12:38–40 are religious professionals. As a Roman Catholic priest, a professor of biblical studies, and a public religious person, I get uncomfortable when reflecting on Jesus' critique of religious professionals such as the scribes. I recognize that my vocation and profession do not guarantee holiness. There is more to holiness than education, ordination, and public position can ensure.

What that "more" is can be seen from the second character in the contrast, the widow. Being a widow in any society is not easy. But being a widow in first-century Palestine was very difficult indeed. It was a male-dominated society. Women were under the authority first of their fathers and then of their husbands for their economic support and social identity. Moreover, there was not much by way of an organized system of assistance for widows (but see Acts 6:1–7). Those in need had to depend either on the extended family or on the kindness of benefactors. Against this social background, the Torah commands special concern for widows: "Cursed be he who violates the rights of the alien, the orphan, or the widow!" (Deut 27:19, NAB; see also 10:17–18, 14:29, 24:17–22).

In such a social setting the most needy and apparently least important person was a childless widow. Presumably her parents were deceased. If she had no children or if her own children were deceased or far away, the widow had no one to whom she could turn. Such seems to be the state of the poor widow sketched in Mark 12:41–44. She was at the opposite end of the social and religious spectrum from the scribes.

The scene constructed in Mark 12:41 takes place in the courtyard of the Jerusalem Temple. According to the Mishnah (*Sheqalim* 6:5), there were thirteen trumpet-shaped chests there, with each one labeled for a specific purpose. The coins made out of copper would reverberate when thrown into the receptacles, thus drawing attention to both the size of the gift and the worth of the giver. The two small coins tossed into the receptacle by the poor widow would not make much noise at all.

There is no indication in the text that the generous widow was a disciple of Jesus or that she even had any contact with Jesus. While women do not belong to Jesus' inner circle (the twelve) in Mark, they *are* prominent at various points in the narrative. One of the first persons healed by Jesus is Peter's mother-in-law (1:29–31). In 5:21–43 Jesus heals a woman with a chronic flow of blood and restores Jairus's daughter to life. In 7:24–30 a Syrophoenician woman (a Gentile) enters into debate with Jesus and convinces him to heal her daughter. Jesus' restrictive position on divorce in 10:2–12 has the effect of providing greater security and stability for married women. According to 12:38–44, the poor widow (and *not* the scribe) is the exemplar of true religion. In 14:1–11 an unnamed woman anoints Jesus as Messiah and in preparation for his burial, and her noble deed stands out in sharp contrast with the plot undertaken by Judas with the chief priests and scribes. Only at the death of Jesus do we learn that many women had been accompanying him throughout his public ministry (15:41). These women see Jesus die; they see where he is buried; and they go to his tomb on Easter Sunday morning (15:40—16:8).

Which figure emerges from the contrast in Mark 12:38–44 as closer to God, more generous, and more holy? It is clearly the poor widow. For her, religious action is not public display, or an occasion to impress others, or an opportunity to improve her economic and social status. For her, as one totally dependent on God, in the hands of God, and without economic or social influence, the Jewish (and Christian) religion was what the Jewish (and Christian) religion should be and is at its best: loving service of God and neighbor. The generous widow in this text reminds us that genuine holiness can be found in some surprising persons and places.

For Reflection and Discussion:

1. What are the points of contrast between the scribes and the poor widow in this text?
2. What does *holiness* mean to you? What are the characteristics of a holy person for you?
3. From the portrayal of the scribes in Mark 12:38–40, what dangers do religious professionals face?

13
Mark 13:24–37:
Eschatology
Cycle B:
Thirty-Third Sunday in Ordinary
Time, and First Sunday in Advent

Mark 13 is sometimes called the Synoptic Apocalypse or the Little Apocalypse, thus differentiating it from the Book of Revelation (also known as the Apocalypse). An apocalypse is a literary form in which a seer, often on the basis of dreams or visions, reports about future events and/or the heavenly realm. Since the content of apocalypses often concerns the end (*eschaton* in Greek) of human history or the world as we know it and the emergence of God's kingdom in its fullness, it is also customary to call Mark 13 Jesus' eschatological discourse, since it pertains to the end, or last things. This passage stands in the apocalyptic tradition of the Book of Daniel and beside the large Jewish apocalypses known as 4 Ezra (2 Esdras 3—14) and 2 Baruch, works roughly contemporary with the Gospels and Revelation. Other versions of the Synoptic Apocalypse appear in Matthew 24—25 and Luke 21 (both of which are revised and expanded versions of Mark 13).

Positioned between the Jerusalem controversies (Mark 11—12) and the passion narrative (Mark 14—15), Jesus' eschatological discourse takes place in the Jerusalem Temple area and has as its starting point Jesus' prophecy of the Temple's destruction: "There will not be one stone left upon another that will not be thrown down" (13:2,

NAB). This prophecy was fulfilled in 70 CE when the Roman armies captured the city and destroyed the Second Temple. The focus moves quickly, however, from Jerusalem's destruction to the future events that will accompany the coming of God's glory in its fullness.

In the first part of the Synoptic Apocalypse (13:5–13) Jesus warns about imposters who will come in his name as well as about wars, earthquakes, and famines, and tells his disciples to expect persecutions and family divisions. These events are labeled "the beginnings of the labor pains" (13:8)—a reference to the Jewish apocalyptic motif of the birthpangs of the Messiah, the painful experiences that must be endured before the Messiah comes in glory. The second part (13:14–23) concerns the "great tribulation" (see Dan 12:1) triggered by the "desolating abomination" (pagan worship in the Jerusalem Temple; see Dan 9:27), and gives warnings against being led astray by false messiahs and false prophets. The third part (13:24–27) describes the cosmic events that will prepare for the appearance of the glorious Son of man and the vindication of the "elect" at the divine judgment. The final part (13:28–37) is an exhortation made up of sayings and parables, urging confidence in God's plan and constant vigilance as this plan unfolds.

The Sunday lectionary uses passages from the third and fourth parts of Mark 13 at the beginning and the end of Cycle B. On the First Sunday of Advent in Cycle B the Gospel text is Mark 13:33–37, while on the Thirty-Third Sunday in Ordinary Time in Cycle B the Gospel reading is Mark 13:24–32. Since these texts overlap and belong together, they are treated here as one unit and in their biblical sequence.

The description of the coming of the glorious Son of man in Mark 13:24–27 is a pastiche of biblical quotations. The "tribulation" mentioned in 13:24a looks backward to 13:19 ("tribulation such as has not been since the beginning of God's creation until now, nor ever will be," NAB), which is in turn rooted in Daniel 12:1 ("a time unsurpassed in distress," NAB). The account of the cosmic portents in 13:24b–25 echoes many biblical texts, most prominently Isaiah 13:10: "The stars and constellations of the heavens / send forth no light; / The sun is dark when it rises, / and the light of the moon does not shine" (NAB). The portrayal of the glorious Son of man in 13:26 alludes to Daniel 7:13: "One like a son of man coming, / on the clouds of heaven" (NAB). And as in Matthew 13:49–50 and 25:31–46, the

Son of man sends out his angels to gather the "elect" (see Mark 13:20, 22) and presides at the judgment where the elect are to be vindicated.

In the Markan context the Son of man is Jesus, and so these biblical and apocalyptic traditions are used in the service of describing the glorious return of the risen Jesus. In Mark's Gospel Son of man is a major title for Jesus. It sometimes refers to Jesus himself or to him as a representative human being (see 2:10, 28; 14:21, 41). It appears in the three passion predictions (8:31; 9:31; 10:33–34) and related passages (9:9, 12; 10:45). But it also occurs in reference to the glorious figure associated with the full coming of God's kingdom (8:38; 14:62), as it does most prominently here in 13:26.

Given the extensive reuse of biblical and other traditional material in Mark 13, it is difficult to say how literally we are expected to take the language employed to describe these future and transcendent events. At any rate, the evangelist's persistent concern throughout his version of Jesus' apocalyptic discourse is to urge caution, patience, and vigilance. One of the most important words running through the discourse is "Watch out!" (*blepete* in Greek; see 13:5, 9, 23, 33). Mark seems to want to cool down apocalyptic enthusiasm and to urge his readers to be patient as God's plan unfolds.

How Mark hoped that his reader would assimilate Jewish and Christian apocalyptic hopes is captured neatly in the final unit in 13:28–37. At the center of the unit is Jesus' saying in 13:31 ("Heaven and earth will pass away, but my words will not pass away," NAB), which is based on Isaiah 51:6 and 40:8 and emphasizes Jesus' authority as a teacher. The central verse is flanked by sayings that suggest both that "all these things" will occur soon in "this generation" (13:30, NAB), and that no one—not even the angels or the Son— knows precisely when they will take place (13:32). Then on either side there are parables that indicate both that "these things" are very close (13:28–29) and that one must always be vigilant because the exact time of their occurrence is uncertain (13:33–37).

This concentric (ABCBA) structure, which is fairly common in the Bible and elsewhere in ancient literature, preserves the tension between lively eschatological expectation and constant vigilance. It affirms that the return of the risen Jesus as the glorious Son of man is certain but leaves open the precise time when it will occur. Thus it promotes an ethical stance according to which people should act always as if the Son of man were to come soon and should conduct themselves always as if they were to face the divine judgment in the very next moment.

Apocalyptic has been called the mother of Christian theology. While that is probably an overstatement, it does at least serve as a reminder that Jewish apocalyptic supplied many of the terms and concepts that the first Christians used in describing Jesus and sketching their concepts of Christian life. In Judaism the apocalyptic trend seemed to have gone underground after the Bar Kokhba Revolt (132–135 CE), resurfacing from time to time in Jewish mystical movements and writings. The rabbis, with their focus on the Torah and their emphasis on *halakhah* ("walking on the way") and general lack of interest in apocalyptic, have constituted the mainstream in Judaism. This historical phenomenon is a reminder that Christianity and Judaism sprang from the same Jewish sources, and that over the centuries they have taken different routes in their theologies. The task facing both faiths today is to understand each other better, and (while acknowledging that our ways have parted) to discern our common roots, to appreciate why our ways did part, and to reflect on how we might respond to those twists and turns within our histories. Apocalyptic is a key topic in that process.

For Reflection and Discussion:

1. What significance do you attribute to the abundant use of biblical phrases in Mark 13:24–32?
2. What is the effect of the repeated use of "watch out" in Mark 13? How might an apocalyptic perspective shape how we live in the present?
3. Why is it appropriate for Christians to read Mark 13:33–37 at the beginning and 13:24–32 at the end of the church's liturgical year?

14
Mark 14:1—15:47:
The Passion and Death of Jesus
Cycle B:
Passion (or Palm) Sunday

Of all the four Gospels, the passion narrative in Mark's Gospel is the shortest and most intensely focused on Jesus. So climactic and important is the passion of Jesus in Mark's overall plan that his Gospel has often been described as a passion narrative (chaps. 14— 15) with a long introduction (chaps. 1—13). According to Mark, Jesus was a great teacher with divine authority and a powerful healer and wonder-worker. But Jesus' identity as a teacher and healer can be properly appreciated only in the light of the cross. That is Mark's most basic concern.

The Markan passion account is a connected narrative that tells the story of the conspiracy against Jesus (14:1–11), his final meal with his disciples (14:12–31), his prayer at the Mount of Olives (14:32–42) and his arrest (14:43–52); his trials before the Jewish Sanhedrin (14:53–72) and before Pontius Pilate (15:1–20); and his crucifixion (15:21–32), death (15:33–41), and burial (15:42–47).

While the basic narrative may be very early, it has also been shaped and retouched by Mark the evangelist. The double climax comes when Jesus before the high priest accepts the titles of Messiah, Son of God, and Son of man (14:61–62), and when at Jesus' death the Roman centurion declares, "Truly this man was the Son of God!" (15:39, NAB). Only in the shadow of the cross does Mark regard it as

appropriate to apply these titles to Jesus. For Mark, Jesus the teacher
and healer is the suffering Messiah.

The entire Markan passion narrative (14:1 — 15:47) is read in
Cycle B of the Sunday lectionary on Passion or Palm Sunday, at the
beginning of Passion Week. The reading takes a relatively long time,
and the content is very rich. And so it happens in many churches that
the homily is greatly abbreviated or even omitted. The result is that
this important text gets less attention from ordinary Christians than it
deserves. But on theological and historical grounds it deserves a great
deal of attention.

The New Testament passion narratives are sensitive (even neuralgic) texts in Christian-Jewish relations. Some passages in them
give the impression that "the Jews" (John, NAB) or "the whole
(Jewish) people" (Matthew, NAB) are responsible for the death of
Jesus. This impression is exacerbated by the way in which the passion
narratives are customarily read in most Catholic parishes. While one
reader takes the words of the narrator-evangelist, the priest-celebrant
reads the words of Jesus and another reader takes the parts of individual figures (Peter, the high priest, Pilate, etc.). This leaves the (usually
negative) words of the Jewish crowds to the congregation, perhaps
reinforcing the impression that "the Jews" or "the whole people" put
Jesus to death.

Rather than treating every part of Mark's passion narrative, I
will focus on three passages that raise issues that have particular significance for Christian-Jewish relations: the character of Jesus' Last
Supper (14:12–26), the responsibility for Jesus' death (14:43—
15:20), and the interpretation of Jesus' last words (15:34).

Jesus' Last Supper (Mark 14:12–26): Was it really a Passover
Seder meal? According to the biblical calendars, Passover—originally
a spring agricultural festival, and later the commemoration of Israel's
liberation from slavery in Egypt—was a pilgrimage festival at which
all Jews were urged to come to the Holy City and its Temple. All the
Gospels say that Jesus and his disciples had come to Jerusalem to celebrate Passover. While Mark (followed by Matthew and Luke)
assumed that the eight-day Passover festival had already begun when
Jesus celebrated his last Supper (and so it was a Passover Seder meal),
John presents another (more historically realistic) chronology according to which Jesus' Last Supper took place on the evening *before* the
first day of Passover and Jesus died while the Passover lambs were

being sacrificed in the Temple, just before the official beginning of Passover at sundown.

Why is John's chronology more realistic on the historical level? Mark provides a clue when he reports that the chief priests and scribes did not want Jesus put to death "during the festival, for fear that there may be a riot among the people" (14:2, NAB). As a pilgrimage festival with thousands of Jews crowding into the city and many with visions of political freedom from Roman hegemony in their heads, Passover was a dangerous time for the Roman officials and their Jewish collaborators. That is why the Roman prefect-governor, Pontius Pilate, had come to Jerusalem from his headquarters at Caesarea Maritima—to oversee the situation, lest it get out of hand. Their plot with Judas (14:10–11) was designed to get Jesus out of the way "not during the festival" (NAB) but *before* it.

What specifically marks Jesus' Last Supper as an official Passover meal is the "odd block" in Mark 14:12–16 about preparations for the Passover meal. It is an odd block because it refers repeatedly to "the disciples" (as opposed to "the Twelve," NAB), because it alone insists that the Last Supper was a Passover meal (compare 14:22–25, where there is no mention of the Passover lamb or any other traditional element of the Seder), and because the two disciples seem to be already present at the site when Jesus comes with "the Twelve" (14:17).

On the historical level it is better to follow John, who presents Jesus' Last Supper as a meal celebrated in the spirit of Passover, something like holding a Christmas party on December 23 or 24. The theological associations between Jesus' death and Passover probably encouraged early Christians like Mark progressively to assimilate Jesus' Last Supper to the Passover Seder meal.

Those associations, however, are not explicit in Mark's account of Jesus' words at the Last Supper (14:22–25). In fact, Mark here very likely relies upon an early church tradition used liturgically in celebrations of the Lord's Supper. What does emerge from Mark 14:22–25 is the picture of a Jewish meal that is set in the Passover season and endowed with theological interpretations pertaining to Jesus' death.

Jesus acts as the *paterfamilias,* or host, at a festive Jewish meal. He takes bread, says a benediction ("Blessed are you, O Lord..."), breaks the bread, and distributes the pieces. When he says, "This is my body" (14:22, NAB), however, he transforms the Jewish meal custom into a prophecy and an interpretation of his own death. And when he repeats the ritual with a cup of wine and declares, "This is my blood of the covenant, which will be shed for many" (14:24, NAB), he again transforms the Jewish meal custom into an interpretation of his death as a covenant sacrifice (see Exod 24:1–8). His final words about the kingdom of God (14:25) place the Last Supper in the context of Jewish hopes about the messianic banquet, according to which life in God's kingdom will be like a great banquet at which the Messiah presides, a motif already glimpsed in Jesus' meals with tax collectors and sinners (see Mark 2:13–17) and the miraculous feedings of the crowds (see 6:34–44 and 8:1–10).

Celebrated in the spirit of Passover but more likely held before Passover officially began, Jesus' Last Supper was a Jewish meal given a Christian theological interpretation with reference to the death of Jesus and in light of various Jewish theological traditions.

Legal Responsibilities (Mark 14:55–66; 15:1–20): Who was responsible for the death of Jesus? The traditional Christian theological response to this question is that our sins were responsible for Jesus' death. That answer echoes the early Christian theological interpretation of Jesus' death as "for us" and "for our sins." Without denying the validity of that theological response, our concern here is more with historical causality in the events of 30 CE and with Mark's presentation of them around 70 CE.

Mark puts most of the blame on the Jewish leaders in Jerusalem ("the chief priests and the entire Sanhedrin," 14:55, NAB) for the death of Jesus. He presents Jesus as undergoing two or perhaps three trials: one before the chief priests and the entire Sanhedrin on the first night of Passover (14:55–66), a second meeting of the same group on the next morning (15:1a), and still another morning session before the Roman prefect-governor, Pontius Pilate (15:1b–20).

The procedure before the Sanhedrin takes the form of a legal trial, though it does seem to have been rigged from the start. However, there does seem to be some historical substance to the two charges made against Jesus at this trial: his threat against the Jerusalem Temple (14:58; see also 11:15–19 and 13:2), and the claims that Jesus was the Messiah/Son of God/Son of man (14:61–62). According to Mark 14:64, the high priest judged the latter claims to be "blasphemy" (NAB) and so "they all condemned him as deserving to die"

(NAB). The proceeding before Pontius Pilate most resembles a (very reluctant) sentencing hearing.

There are many historical problems with Mark's accounts. The first is the timing. It is very unlikely that the Jewish high priest would hold such a legal trial on the first night of Passover. And it is also unlikely that the entire Sanhedrin would appear at the high priest's house on short notice at such a sacred time. A second problem is whether the Jewish Sanhedrin had the legal right to decree and administer capital punishment. That right seems to have been taken over by the Roman officials (see John 18:31). Third, Jesus is executed by crucifixion, which was a punishment typically used by the Romans against political rebels and slaves. The traditional Jewish mode of capital punishment was stoning (see the death of Stephen in Acts 7:58, which is more a lynching than a legal procedure). Finally, the legal charge against Jesus inscribed on his cross was the "King of the Jews" (15:26, NAB). That sounds like a mocking translation of "Messiah" and suggests that Pilate and his Jewish collaborators perceived Jesus as just another in the long line of Jewish rebel leaders who stirred up the people with visions of Israel's return to military and political glory (see Josephus's *Jewish Antiquities* 17:273–85).

On the level of history it appears that the primary legal responsibility for the death of Jesus lay with the Roman prefect-governor, Pontius Pilate. It also appears that Pilate had Jesus crucified with the cooperation (and perhaps the initiative) of Jewish leaders in Jerusalem (chief priests, elders, and scribes) who were probably just as eager as Pilate was to be rid of Jesus (whom they perceived to be just another Galilean troublemaker) and so to preserve the peace of the city especially during the Passover pilgrimage.

On the level of literature it appears that Mark has exaggerated the power and responsibility of the Jewish leaders in Jerusalem and played down the legal responsibility of the Roman governor. For many Christian readers today, Mark's shifting of blame is disappointing and even embarrassing. For Jews, it has been dangerous. Perhaps it can be explained historically in the light of Mark's own situation, especially if the tradition that he composed this Gospel at Rome around 70 CE (the time of the First Jewish Revolt) is correct. In that situation Mark would be eager to place the blame for Jesus' death not on the Roman governor but on the Jewish officials in Jerusalem, and to put some distance between the Jewish rebels of 70 CE and the

Christian movement in Rome. At any rate, Christian teachers and preachers need to explain that the events behind the Markan (and other) passion narratives were very likely more complicated than Mark has made them out to be.

Jesus' Last Words (Mark 15:34): According to Mark 15:34, the last words that Jesus uttered before his death were, "My God, my God, why have you forsaken me?" (NAB). These words are even accompanied by their Aramaic version: *"Eloi, Eloi, lema sabachtani?"* But did Jesus really feel that God had abandoned him at the moment of his death?

Some interpreters have found in these words the portrait of Jesus as a lonely hero facing death without divine or human support. Others have seen in them an indication that Jesus recognized that his hope of bringing about the kingdom of God by his sacrificial death was not going to work out. However, the thrust of Mark's Gospel taken as a whole and the biblical background of these words make such readings of Mark 15:34 very unlikely at any level.

To assume that Jesus did despair at his death contradicts the entire purpose and plot of Mark's Gospel. From the beginning of his Gospel (1:1), Mark identifies Jesus as "the Son of God" (NAB). At Jesus' baptism (1:11) and transfiguration (9:7) a voice from heaven proclaims Jesus to be "my beloved Son" (NAB). And the moment of his death, the Roman centurion overseeing his execution says, "Truly this man was the Son of God" (15:39, NAB). There must be another way to read Jesus' last words according to Mark 15:34.

That other way lies in recognizing them as the first words of Psalm 22, the most famous of the biblical lament psalms. Read in its entirety, Psalm 22 is both a lament over present suffering and an affirmation of trust and hope in God for vindication. The psalm's concern with both suffering and vindication fits well with the dynamic of Jesus' passion, death, and resurrection.

The first part of Psalm 22 presents alternating laments about suffering in the present (22:2–3, 7–9, 13–19) and expressions of confidence in God (22:4–6, 10–12, 20–22). The second part (22:23–32) affirms that God has heard the sufferer's prayer ("he has not spurned or disdained / the misery of the poor wretch," 22:25, NAB), and so he invites others to participate in a thanksgiving sacrifice and the celebration that accompanies it. Without denigrating the intense physical suffering that crucifixion involved, it seems that the key to understanding Jesus' last words according to Mark is the recognition that they are the first words in the great lament that is Psalm 22. For other allusions to Psalm 22 in the Markan passion narrative, see the descriptions of the soldiers dividing Jesus' garments (Mark 15:24 = Ps 22:19) and the mockery of the bystanders at the cross (Mark 15:29 = Ps 22:8). The last words of Jesus according to Mark 15:34 and the other allusions to Psalm 22 place his death (and resurrection) in the context of ancient Israel's laments over present sufferings and hopes for vindication by God in the future.

Mark's story of Jesus' suffering and death constitutes a "dangerous memory" (to use the phrase of the German Catholic theologian, J. B. Metz). The memory of his suffering and death presented in the Markan passion narrative confronts us with the reality of human misunderstanding and injustice, as well as with the mystery of innocent suffering. His memory confronts us also with the struggle that Jesus had to undergo in order to accept as God's will the grim reality made manifest in the cross. His memory also confronts us with the surprising possibility that God can and does work wonders (resurrection) even in the midst of suffering and death. In this sense Jesus suffers as a Jew and recapitulates the experience of Jewish suffering throughout the centuries.

For Reflection and Discussion:

1. What "Passover" dimensions do you find in Mark's account of Jesus' Last Supper?
2. How would you answer the question: Who killed Jesus?
3. What echoes of Psalm 22 do you find in Mark's passion narrative? What happens when you read the full text of Psalm 22?

15

Mark 16:1–8:
Empty Tomb/Resurrection
Cycle B:
Easter Sunday

Jerusalem in Jesus' time has been described as a city ringed about by a huge cemetery. As the religious center for the Jewish people spread all over the Mediterranean world, Jerusalem had become the Holy City and a natural venue for Jews to come and await the resurrection of the dead. According to Zechariah 14:4, Jerusalem is where the Day of the Lord will begin: "That day his feet shall rest upon the Mount of Olives" (NAB).

The soft limestone caves in the Jerusalem area were used extensively as communal tombs for families. The corpse of the deceased person would be laid out on a stone shelf carved out of the cave wall and allowed to decompose for a year. Then the bones would be gathered and placed in a stone receptacle known as an ossuary (bone box), which was usually inscribed with the name(s) of the deceased. This is apparently the kind of burial that we are to envision Joseph of Arimathea providing for Jesus, and that supplies the background for understanding the Markan account of the empty tomb (16:1–8).

Only after narrating the death of Jesus does Mark inform the reader that all through Jesus' public ministry he had women followers (15:41). These women had witnessed his crucifixion and death "from a distance" (15:40, NAB). The great principle of continuity from Good Friday to Easter Sunday is Mary of Magdala (in Galilee). Along with the other women, Mary Magdalene witnessed Jesus' death, knew where he was buried, and came to his tomb on Easter Sunday morning.

According to Mishnah *Shabbat* 23:5 it was customary for Jews to anoint a corpse before burial: "They prepare all that is needed for a corpse. They anoint it and rinse it." But because Jesus had died in the afternoon before sundown on the Sabbath eve, there was no time to attend to these customs. And they could not be carried out on the Sabbath itself, since that presumably would be work. So after they had observed the Sabbath rest, early on Sunday morning the women followers of Jesus (including Mary Magdalene) set out for his tomb in the hope of anointing his corpse and perfuming it (to keep down the stench).

What the women discover is that the stone blocking the entry to the burial cave (to prevent ritual defilement from dead bodies, and to discourage tomb robbers) had been rolled away and the corpse of Jesus was nowhere to be found. The tomb was empty!

The empty tomb could be explained in several different ways. Perhaps the women came to the wrong tomb. Or maybe Jesus' disciples stole his body. Or perhaps Jesus had not died, but revived from a state of shock and left the tomb. These explanations have circulated from New Testament times (see Matt 28:11–15) to the present. However, the Markan (and early Christian) interpretation of the empty tomb was that Jesus had been raised from the dead: "He has been raised; he is not here. Behold, the place where they laid him" (16:6, NAB).

Resurrection was (and is) a Jewish belief. The clearest biblical testimony to it appears in Daniel 12:2: "Many of those who sleep / in the dust of the earth shall awake; / Some shall live forever, / others shall be an everlasting horror and disgrace" (NAB). In this scenario resurrection is a collective or communal event that will take place in connection with the "great tribulation" and the full manifestation of God's kingdom.

The Pharisees were the great proponents of belief in the resurrection of the dead. According to Josephus's *Jewish Antiquities* 18:12–17, the Pharisees believed that "souls have power to survive death and that there are rewards and punishments under the earth for those who have led lives of virtue and vice," while "the Sadducees hold that the soul perishes along with the body." In his Jerusalem controversy with the Sadducees in Mark 12:18–27, Jesus sides with the Pharisees and appeals to the Scriptures (see Exod 3:6, 15, 16; 4:5) and to the power of God as grounds for believing in the resurrection of the dead.

It is possible and indeed likely that Jewish expectations about resurrection were influenced by Greek beliefs concerning the immortality of the soul (just as Josephus's language quoted above was). According to the Book of Wisdom (composed in Greek in the Jewish community at Alexandria in the first century BCE), "the souls of the just are in the hand of God" (3:1, NAB). But belief in the resurrection of the body (that is, the whole person) presents a form of life after death more consistent with the traditional Jewish understanding of the human person as both body and soul/spirit. This holistic anthropology holds that after physical death the whole person is restored to life and lives on forever (see 2 Macc 7). Such a holistic concept of life after death underlies the accounts of the appearances of the risen Jesus in the other Gospels.

What was shocking in the early Christian proclamation about Jesus ("he has been raised," 16:6, NAB) was that resurrection was being predicated of an individual (Jesus of Nazareth) before the other end-time events (general resurrection, Last Judgment, etc.). Or to put the matter more in keeping with early Christian faith, Jesus is "the firstborn from the dead" (Col 1:18, NAB), and his resurrection has inaugurated the series of end-time events that will eventually culminate in the full coming of God's kingdom.

The empty tomb does not prove that Jesus was raised from the dead. Other explanations, as we have seen, are possible. However, the empty tomb is a necessary presupposition for the explanation that Jesus was raised from the dead (unless this is to be taken in purely symbolic terms). If the tomb were not empty, the Christian claim that Jesus had been raised from the dead could easily be falsified or at least spiritualized away.

With their narratives about the appearances of the risen Jesus, the other Gospels and the Acts of the Apostles show how contact with the risen Jesus transformed his fearful disciples into fearless preachers of the gospel. And the epistles sketch how the lives of Christians can be eloquent witnesses to the power of Jesus' resurrection. As Paul wrote to the Corinthians: "If Christ has not been raised, your faith is vain; you are still in your sins" (1 Cor 15:17, NAB).

Resurrection is prominent in the Eighteen Benedictions, or *Amidah,* which are an integral part of the Jewish daily prayer: "You are mighty—humbling the haughty, powerful—calling the arrogant to judgment, eternal—reviving the dead....Blessed are you, O Lord, who revives the dead" (Benediction 2). While not all Jews in Jesus' time believed in resurrection and/or life after death, surely the Pharisees and very likely the Essenes did. And such beliefs were part of the Jewish tradition as seen in the daily prayers and in other writings through the centuries. In some Jewish circles, especially in modern times since the European Enlightenment, there has been a falling off of belief in life after death and resurrection. A similar phenomenon has occurred in Christianity. This may be a historical and theological topic that Jews and Christians today might profitably pursue afresh.

For Reflection and Discussion:

1. Does the empty tomb prove that Jesus was raised from the dead? What does it prove?
2. What is Mary Magdalene's role in the events surrounding Jesus' death?
3. In the context of Jewish beliefs about resurrection, what made early Christian claims about Jesus' resurrection so unusual?

The Gospel of Luke

Part One: Introduction

The Gospel of Luke is a beautiful book. Indeed, it has been called the most beautiful book ever written. For example, what we know as the Christmas story with its wonderful human characters, angels, and shepherds is largely based on Luke 1—2. Luke's Gospel is also an influential book. Millions of people all over the world, regardless of their religious identity, refer to "the good Samaritan," "the prodigal son," "Mary and Martha," and "the good thief."

However, Luke's Gospel can also be a dangerous book in Christian-Jewish relations. The violent reaction of Jews in the synagogue at Nazareth in Luke 4:16–30 becomes the literary model for the accounts in Acts about the treatment that Paul and other missionaries receive in synagogues all over the Mediterranean world. And this literary model has sometimes generated anti-Jewish violence in return throughout history. The stereotype of the Pharisee as self-righteous and legalistic is drawn in large part from and has been propagated by the parable of the Pharisee and the tax collector in Luke 18:9–14 (see also 16:15). And this image has figured significantly in the history of Christian anti-Judaism. Luke describes the execution of Jesus in such a way (see 23:25–26) that it can appear that Jews were more directly involved in Jesus' death than either history or the other Gospels allow. And this portrayal has been at the root of Christian denigrations of Jews as Christ-killers and as a deicide people. Certain elements in Luke's Gospel do have the potential to promote anti-Judaism, and history is full of examples in which this potential has been realized.

Among the many approaches to fostering mutual understanding between Jews and Christians, one of the most successful strategies has been the common study of our sacred and traditional texts. This approach has the advantage of being concrete and specific. Since the study of texts naturally generates questions, it also engages participants in active dialogue. And it helps Christians and Jews to discover

149

and appreciate better what they have in common and where they differ. It is in this spirit that I present this guide to Luke's Gospel.

WHO, WHEN, WHERE?

The early Christian writing whose texts we will study here is commonly known as "the Gospel according to Luke." The word *Gospel* (*euangelion* in Greek) means "good news" and was used frequently by Paul (in the earliest Christian writings that we have) as a shorthand description of Jesus' life, death, and resurrection and their effects in relating to God. Mark (the first evangelist) used the term at the start of his story of Jesus ("the beginning of the gospel of Jesus Christ"), and so *Gospel* came to describe a literary genre or kind of book that told the story of Jesus. The New Testament contains four Gospels: Matthew, Mark, Luke, and John.

Our four Gospels are traditionally associated with famous (and not so famous) figures in early Christian history. Matthew and John were among the twelve apostles, and Mark was associated with Peter and Luke with Paul. But from a strict textual perspective all four Gospels are anonymous compositions, since in none of them does the author step forward and identify himself by name (as Paul does in his letters and John does in Revelation). The ascriptions of the Gospels to the various famous figures entered the manuscript tradition sometime in the second century CE.

The ascription "According to Luke" points to the author as the figure mentioned several times in the New Testament in connection with the apostle Paul. Someone named Luke is described as Paul's co-worker (Phlm 24), "the beloved physician " (Col 4:14, NAB), and Paul's faithful companion (2 Tim 4:11). It is generally acknowledged that the person who wrote Luke's Gospel also wrote the Acts of Apostles (see Acts 1:1–2). There are several passages in Acts (16:11–16; 20:5–16; 21:1–17; 27:1—28:16) that use first-person plural language ("we") in describing Paul's journeys especially on the Mediterranean Sea. On the basis of these references there developed the tradition that the author of "Luke's Gospel" was Luke the companion of Paul.

The historical accuracy of this tradition is a matter of longstanding debate, and deciding it is more important for interpreting Acts than it is for interpreting the Gospel. However one decides, it is important to recognize that "Luke" (as we will call him) has his own theological perspective and does *not* merely repeat or echo what he might have heard from Paul. In fact, Luke is one of the most important theological voices within the New Testament.

Most modern scholarly discussions of Luke–Acts assert that the author was a Gentile Christian who wrote primarily for other Gentile Christians. That may be correct. But none of the Pauline references denies that Luke was a Jew. It is true that in his two-volume work Luke wants to portray Jesus as "a light for revelation to the Gentiles" (Luke 2:32a, NAB), and so he traces the spread of the gospel from Jerusalem to Rome. But the same verse (2:32b, NAB) also refers to Jesus as "glory for your people Israel," which is an apt description of Luke's Gospel taken by itself.

While Luke may have been a Gentile, he clearly knew a great deal about Judaism and expects his readers to be conversant with the Jewish Scriptures and Jewish life in the Holy Land. Some scholars explain this fact by suggesting that Luke was a God-fearer, that is, a Gentile who frequented the synagogue and learned much about Judaism but never fully converted to the point of undergoing circumcision and taking on the observance of the food laws and the Sabbath. However, perhaps the simplest explanation may be that Luke was a Christian Jew (like Paul and almost all the first followers of Jesus) who believed that Jesus of Nazareth was both the glory of Israel and a light for revelation to the Gentiles.

When did Luke write his Gospel? Because Acts 28 leaves off before Paul's death, it has often been asserted that Luke–Acts was composed in the early to mid-60s of the first century CE. But some passages in the Gospel (19:43–44; 21:20, 24) seem to allude to the siege and destruction of Jerusalem in 70 CE. And so the composition of Luke–Acts is today commonly placed around 85 or 90 CE.

Where was Luke's Gospel written? Its composition has been associated with almost every area in the Mediterranean world: Palestine, Syria, various cities in Asia Minor (present-day Turkey) and Greece, and Rome. Good cases have been made for Antioch in Syria and Caesarea Maritima in the land of Israel. But there is no consensus about where Luke wrote.

WHY, WHAT, HOW?

It is easier to answer these three questions because Luke has provided a preface or prologue at the beginning of his work. That preface consists of one long and complicated sentence written in elegant Greek. Its vocabulary and style stand in marked contrast to the "Bible Greek" in which the infancy narrative (1:5—2:52) is written. With this sentence Luke establishes himself as a learned and sophisticated writer who, according to the criteria of the Greco-Roman world, would be regarded as a historian (like Tacitus, Suetonius, and Josephus) in the root sense of the word as one who "searches" or "inquires."

This Gospel is dedicated, according to 1:3, to "most excellent Theophilus" (NAB). It was common in antiquity for elite authors to dedicate their works to the wealthy patrons who supported them in carrying out their projects. The Greek name *Theophilus* means "lover of God." Whether this name refers to Luke's actual patron or is a symbol for the ideal reader whom Luke hopes to reach, we will probably never know.

The subject matter of Luke's Gospel is described as "the events that have been fulfilled among us" (1:1, NAB). These "events" include Jesus' life, death, and resurrection as well as the spread of the gospel in Acts. Luke does not claim to have been an eyewitness to the events treated in his Gospel. But he does state that he has consulted "eyewitnesses" and "ministers of the word" (1:2, NAB). He also claims to have carried out careful research on his own ("after investigating everything accurately anew," NAB), and that he sought to write everything down in "an orderly sequence" (1:3, NAB). The "order" need not be understood only in chronological terms. It may also refer to whatever might facilitate the readers' grasp of the material and foster their embrace of the gospel. Luke's ultimate purpose is that the reader (Theophilus) might find in his story of Jesus and the early church a confirmation and deepening of what he previously received in whatever instruction he underwent in the process of becoming a Christian: "that you may realize the certainty of the teachings you have received" (1:4, NAB).

So in his one-sentence preface, Luke tells us that he wanted to write a connected narrative about Jesus (What?), on the basis of traditional sources and his own research (How?), in order to inspire greater confidence about the Christian faith among his readers (Why?).

SOURCES AND STRUCTURE

Luke's Gospel is a revised and expanded version of Mark's Gospel. Luke used material from Mark mainly in three large blocks: Luke 3:1—6:19; 8:4—9:50; and 18:15—24:11. He omitted about 30 percent of Mark, much of it in what is called "the great omission" of material in Mark 6:45—8:26 between Luke 9:17 and 9:18. In between the Markan blocks there are two large Lukan blocks known as "the small insertion" (6:20—8:3) and "the large insertion" (9:51—18:14).

The material for these insertions is taken largely from the Sayings Source Q and from Luke's special traditions. The Sayings Source Q (from *Quelle*, the German word for "source") was a collection of sayings attributed to Jesus that Matthew and Luke used independently in their rewritings of Mark's Gospel. Luke's special material (designated L for Luke) refers to traditions found in neither Mark nor Q, though it is often difficult to distinguish between what was traditional (L) and what was composed directly by Luke.

Besides including material not present in Mark's Gospel, Luke smoothed out awkward points, improved on Mark's Greek style and vocabulary, and tightened up the structure of Mark's narrative. In general, Luke followed Mark's geographical-theological outline: Jesus' public ministry in Galilee and environs, his journey from Galilee to Jerusalem, and his passion and death in Jerusalem. He has, however, prefaced Jesus' adult career with accounts about his birth and infancy (1:5—2:52). He has also considerably expanded the journey narrative (9:51—19:44) to make it four times as long as Mark's journey narrative (8:22—10:52) is. And he solved the problem of the abrupt ending of Mark (16:8) by adding accounts of appearances by the risen Jesus (24:12–53).

Luke's editorial activity has resulted in the following "orderly sequence." After the preface (1:1–4), Luke's Gospel describes how Jesus prepared himself among the faithful in Israel in accord with the Scriptures (1:5—4:13). Then in 4:14—21:38 it recounts the public ministry of Jesus as a teacher and healer in Galilee (4:14—9:50), on the great journey (9:51—19:44), and at Jerusalem and its Temple (19:45—21:38). The passion narrative (22:1—24:53) takes place in Jerusalem, and includes Jesus' Last Supper, arrest, crucifixion, death, resurrection, and ascension. Luke's Gospel is about a Jewish teacher who was born, lived, and died in the land of Israel among his own people.

MAJOR LUKAN THEMES

There is a tradition that Luke was an artist, indeed a painter. While the tradition's historical reliability is doubtful, it does express nicely Luke's love of details and his ability to communicate in apparently simple but subtle ways. Those who read his Gospel need to be sensitive both to the details in his carefully etched literary portraits and to the larger surface on which he presents his tapestry of Jesus' life and the early church's history. As the following expositions of particular texts will show, Luke weaves throughout his Gospel (and Acts) many motifs and themes. The following list may help readers to see where particular passages fit within Luke's overall vision and to make connections among the themes. This list is a retouched version of what appeared in my book *The Church According to the New Testament: What the Wisdom and Witness of Early Christianity Teach Us Today* (Sheed & Ward, 2001), 109–12.

Holy Spirit: In the infancy narrative Jesus is conceived through the Holy Spirit (1:35), and Zechariah and Simeon prophesy under the inspiration of the Holy Spirit. The Spirit descends upon Jesus at his baptism (3:21–22), and his public ministry is defined in terms of the coming of the Spirit upon him (4:18–19). Throughout his ministry of teaching and healing, Jesus is the bearer of the Holy Spirit, and he promises to send the Spirit upon his disciples after his ascension (24:49). In Acts, the Spirit is the great principle of continuity between the time of Jesus and the time of the church.

Salvation History: Luke's dominant concern is the integration of the story of Jesus in God's plan of redemptive history. That history is divided into three great periods: the time of preparation up to and including John the Baptist (3:15–20; 16:16), the presence of salvation in Jesus ("today," "now"), and the age of the church under the guidance of the Holy Spirit (Acts). Jesus inaugurates a movement that is an outgrowth of Judaism (2:21–40), includes Gentiles (4:16–30), and poses no political threat to the Roman empire (23:1–16, 25–26).

Jesus the Prophet: The theme of Jesus the prophet is one of Luke's most important christological contributions. At the beginning of his public ministry (4:16–30) Jesus is presented as a prophet after the patterns of Isaiah 61:1–3 and of Elijah and Elisha. He not only acts as a prophet (7:16) but he also dies as a prophet (13:33; 24:25–27). At

Pentecost (Acts 2) the Holy Spirit passes on to Jesus' followers in a kind of prophetic succession.

The Twelve Apostles: More than any other evangelist, Luke is most responsible for bringing together the terms *twelve* and *apostles*. The key sentence is Luke 6:13: "he called his disciples and chose twelve of them, whom he also named apostles" (NRSV). Whereas in 9:1–2 Jesus sends out the twelve, in 9:10 those who return are called "apostles." These texts (see also Luke 11:49; 17:5; 22:14; 24:10) suggest an identity between the twelve and the apostles. They also prepare for the many references to the twelve apostles in Acts (see 1:2, 26; 2:37, 42, 43; 4:33, 35, 36; 5:2, 12, 18, 29, 34, 40, etc.). In Luke–Acts the twelve apostles also function as a principle of continuity between the time of Jesus and the time of the church. From this Lukan theme, we get the concept of apostolic succession.

Prayer: Luke is sometimes called the Gospel of prayer because in it Jesus is portrayed as praying at the decisive moments in his life: his baptism (3:21), the healing of the leper (5:16), the choice of the twelve (6:12), Peter's confession of faith (9:18), the transfiguration (9:28–29), his arrest (22:40–46), and his death (23:34, 46). It also contains two large instructions about prayer: its content (the Lord's Prayer) and the value of persistence (11:1–13), and the need for persistence and humility in prayer (18:1–14).

Rich and Poor: Among the several passages that concern relations between rich and poor, the most important are the blessings and woes (6:20–26), the parable of the rich fool (12:13–21), planning the guest list for the banquet (14:12–14), the rich man and Lazarus (16:19–31), and the story of Zacchaeus (19:1–10). These texts suggest that Luke's community included both rich and poor members, and that one of his purposes in writing the Gospel was to warn the wealthy members about relying too much on riches.

Meals/Banquets: The Hebrew Bible attaches special significance to meals in various contexts: covenant, sacrifices, wisdom, and eschatology. One of the most certain and controversial matters in Jesus' ministry was his custom of sharing meals with tax collectors and sinners. Luke gives great prominence to banquet scenes: the sinful woman with the ointment (7:36–50), the discourse against the Pharisees (11:37–52), the teachings about etiquette and the kingdom of God (14:1–24), the Last Supper (22:1–38), and the appearances of the risen Lord (24:13–49). These banquets are occasions for Jesus' teachings and for fellowship with him, and point toward the banquet that will constitute the kingdom of God.

Women: In the infancy narratives Elizabeth, Mary, and Anna represent the best of Israel's traditions. The episode of the sinful woman in 7:36–50 illustrates the close relationship between love and forgiveness. Women accompany Jesus during his public ministry (8:1–3), and Mary and Martha provide hospitality to him along the way (10:38–42). Women feature in the parables of the lost coin (15:8–10) and the persistent widow (18:1–8). There are women at the cross (23:49) and at Jesus' tomb (24:10–11). Whether Luke promotes the cause of women or keeps them in their place is a matter of dispute among scholars today.

Jerusalem: Luke's story of Jesus begins in the Jerusalem Temple (1:5–25), and as a boy he displays his wisdom there (2:41–52). His journey ends with his taking possession of the Temple area and exercising a ministry there (19:45 — 21:38). After his resurrection Jesus appears to his disciples in Judea (on the road to Emmaus) and in Jerusalem (24:13–49), and the gospel is to go forth from Jerusalem (24:47).

Eschatology: The future coming of the Son of man is certain in fact but indefinite in time. The proper attitude in the present is watchfulness (12:35–48). Even though the kingdom of God is "among us" (17:20–21, NAB), its future fullness will be so sudden and obvious that the search for signs is futile (17:22–37). The events surrounding the coming of the glorious Son of man (21:5–36) call for patient endurance (21:19) but are ultimately an occasion for rejoicing since "your redemption is at hand" (21:28, NAB).

Parallel Lives: In keeping with his emphasis on Jesus as an example for others, Luke draws many parallels between Jesus in his Gospel and Paul in Acts: the prophecy about suffering (Luke 2:29–35; Acts 9:15–16), the preface to the ministry (Luke 4:16–30; Acts 13:14–52), the way to Jerusalem (Luke 9:51; Acts 19:21), the passion predictions (Luke 9:22, 44–45; Acts 20:22–24; 21:10–12), the farewell speech (Luke 22:21–38; Acts 20:18–35), heroism in the face of death (Luke 22:39–46; Acts 20:36–38), and the trial narratives (Luke 22:47 — 23:25; Acts 21:27 — 26:32). The way of Jesus provides the model for his followers.

IS LUKE ANTI-JEWISH?

In many respects Luke's Gospel is a deceptive book. On the surface everything seems simple and straightforward. But when one scratches the surface, what emerges is often more complex and ambiguous. Of course, this is an aspect of Luke's literary artistry. He makes it look easy at first, but then pushes the reader to go deeper.

Even the language of Luke's Gospel appears at first glance to be rather elementary Greek. But students soon find themselves puzzled by little points that they had not seen or mastered in their introductory Greek course. Likewise, on major Lukan themes there are learned monographs, studying the same texts and using the same scholarly methods, which come to very different conclusions. For example, some scholars regard Luke as friendly toward women, while others claim that he only keeps women in their place and subordinates them to men. Some scholars view Luke as the champion of the economically poor, but others see him as primarily concerned with guiding the rich members of his own community. And on the question of Luke's attitude toward Jews and Judaism, some scholars consider him as positively disposed, while others contend that he is an implacable and dangerous enemy.

On the surface it appears that Luke is well disposed toward Jews and Judaism. He clearly knows a great deal about them. He may well have been a Jew himself, or perhaps he belonged to the shadowy company of God-fearers who attached themselves to local synagogues.

Furthermore, the story that Luke tells is dominated by characters who are Jews. Jesus of Nazareth, Zechariah and Elizabeth, Mary, Simeon and Anna, the twelve apostles, the other disciples, the recipients of Jesus' healings, and the audiences for his teachings are almost all Jews who live in the land of Israel. Luke describes Jesus' birth and infancy with allusions to Samson and Samuel, and to various texts in the Hebrew Scriptures. During Jesus' ministry of healing and teaching there are strong echoes of the narratives about the Jewish prophets Elijah and Elisha in the Books of Kings. And Jesus' last words ("into your hands I commend my spirit," NAB) in Luke 23:46 are a quotation from a biblical lament psalm (Ps 31:5a). Only well into the Acts of the Apostles does a Gentile (the Roman centurion, Cornelius, in Acts 10—11) become part of the Jesus movement. And this development is a great surprise to all the Christian Jews who constitute the church in the land of Israel.

The question of Luke and Judaism gets more complicated and pressing in the Acts of Apostles. This short treatment of Luke's Gospel is hardly the place to explore that matter in any depth. However, looking at the opposing conclusions reached by two reputable New Testament scholars can illustrate the clash of scholarly opinions on this issue.

In *The Jews in Luke–Acts*, Jack T. Sanders contends that Luke "comes to the opinion that all Jews are equally, in principle at least, perverse; and he turns his attack on all together, without distinction" (317). Sanders also notes that "in Luke's opinion, the world will be much better off when 'the Jews' get what they deserve and the world is rid of them" (317). These statements, of course, represent Sanders's interpretation of Luke, not Sanders's own views. In fact, Sanders laments that Luke's polemic against the Jews has become all too common within Christianity and Western society and urges vigilance in combating it.

A very different approach can be found in Robert L. Brawley's *Luke–Acts and the Jews: Conflict, Apology, and Conciliation*. He argues that Luke–Acts was the product of the struggle (that involved all Jews) for the legacy of Israel as the people of God in the late first century CE. In this context Luke tried to show how Jesus qualifies as the Messiah despite being rejected by a large and influential segment of Judaism, and how the early church's missionary outreach to and acceptance of non-Jews was appropriate for the fulfillment of Israel's destiny ("a light for revelation to the Gentiles"). Brawley concludes that "rather than setting gentile Christianity free, Luke ties it to Judaism. And rather than rejecting the Jews, Luke appeals to them" (159).

Sanders and Brawley are only two voices in a larger academic debate. They are, however, representative. In the expositions that follow I am generally in agreement with the irenic and positive approach taken by Brawley. Nevertheless, what I do ought to be evaluated by raising the kinds of questions that led Sanders to his conclusion that Luke is hostile to Jews and Judaism.

Part Two: Lectionary Commentary

1
Luke 1:5—2:52:
The Infancy Narrative
Cycle A, B, and C:
Advent and Christmas Seasons

Luke begins his story of Jesus with a full account of Jesus' birth, infancy, and youth. In the church's lectionary these texts are spread over the Sundays and feast days from Advent through the Christmas season and even into early February, and occur in the various yearly cycles. Moreover, in the popular imagination the Lukan texts tend to get mixed in with Matthew's infancy narrative to form a hybrid Christmas story. The goal here is to look at the Lukan infancy narrative in its own right and to let its distinctiveness shine forth. What emerges is a recognition of Luke's concerted effort at placing Jesus' origins within the Jewish tradition.

Rather than treating every passage in Luke 1—2 or focusing on only one or two of them, here we try to view the Lukan infancy narrative as a whole. After the long and sophisticated Greek sentence that constitutes Luke's prologue (1:1—4), there is a dramatic shift in literary style at 1:5 to a simple, straightforward, Semitic kind of Greek found in the Greek version of the Hebrew Bible (the Septuagint), especially in its rendering of the Books of Samuel and Kings. This sudden change has the effect of placing Luke's readers (and us) back in time into the world of the Bible and in first-century Palestinian Judaism (rather than in elite circles in Greek culture as in the prologue).

159

The gross structure of Luke's infancy narrative highlights a comparison between John the Baptist and Jesus. The point is while John is great, Jesus is even greater. The comparison begins with the announcements of the births of John (1:5–25) and of Jesus (1:26–38), followed by Mary's visit to Elizabeth (1:39–56). Then there are accounts about John's birth and circumcision (1:57–80) and about Jesus' birth and presentation (2:1–40), followed by the episode about Jesus in the Temple (2:41–52). In contrast to Matthew 1—2, where there is a good deal of danger, violence, and suffering, the tone of the Lukan infancy narrative is thoroughly positive and joyous, with everything proceeding according to the divine plan.

The Lukan infancy narrative breathes the air of the biblical infancy narratives about Samson in Judges 13 and Samuel in 1 Samuel 1—2. These birth stories along with those of Isaac in Genesis 17—18 and Moses in Exodus 1 were quite popular among Jews in the first century. They were repeated, embroidered, and contaminated often, and their hybrid versions found their way into Jewish writings current in New Testament times (*Jubilees*, Pseudo-Philo's *Biblical Antiquities,* Josephus's *Jewish Antiquities,* etc.). These Jewish birth stories surely influenced Luke 1—2 in literary style, content, and theology.

Luke 1—2 is best understood as a blend of historical, haggadic, and theological elements, all focused on the person of Jesus. The places (the Jerusalem Temple, Nazareth in Galilee, Bethlehem, etc.) and the characters (John the Baptist, Jesus, the emperor Augustus, etc.) are certainly historical. While the term *midrash* should probably be avoided if it is taken in its strict sense as commentary literature about Scripture, it is fair to use the word *haggadic* with reference to Luke's infancy narrative in the sense of its imaginative developments of biblical texts with regard to Jesus. And the Lukan texts make many theological claims about Jesus and suggest that what can be said about Jesus as an adult was true of him even as a child. The critical problem, of course, is discerning where history leaves off and imaginative biblical interpretation *(haggadah)* and/or Christian theology begins.

Jewish Characters: All the main characters in Luke's infancy narratives are observant and exemplary Jews. They represent the best in the biblical tradition. It is from such pious Jews that the Lukan Jesus emerges onto the stage of world history (see Luke 3:1–2). Luke's story begins in the Jerusalem Temple (1:5–25), where Zechariah is taking his annual turn at performing his priestly duties.

Both Zechariah and Elizabeth come from priestly families. According to Luke 1:6, they are exemplary Jews: "Both were righteous in the eyes of God, observing all the commandments and ordinances of the Lord blamelessly" (NAB). The surprising birth of their son John is announced to Zechariah while the people are at prayer. The angel promises that John will follow the patterns set by the Nazarite Samson (1:15) and the prophet Elijah (1:17).

The announcement of Jesus' birth in Luke 1:26–38 follows the model of the biblical call stories (see Exod 3—4; Isa 6; Jer 1) and describes Jesus in terms of his ancestry from King David (1:32) and with reference to Israel's hopes for an ideal descendant of David (1:32–33). When Mary visits Elizabeth (1:39–45, NAB) she is greeted as "the mother of my Lord"—a title used in Israel's monarchical times when the king's mother was a more prominent figure at the royal court than the queen was (especially when the king might have several wives). Mary's song in 1:46–55 is a paraphrase and expansion of Hannah's song in 1 Samuel 2:1–10.

According to Luke 1:57–66, the child John was circumcised and named on the eighth day after his birth, in keeping with Jewish Law. Zechariah's song (1:68–79) is a pastiche of biblical phrases in celebration of God visiting his people. The note that John spent time "in the desert" until he began his public activity (1:80) is often taken as the link between John (and Jesus) and the Jewish sect that gave us the Dead Sea scrolls discovered in the late 1940s in the Judean Desert. At least they were in the same vicinity.

According to Luke 2:1–20, Jesus the Son of David came to be born in Bethlehem, the city of David, because of a census ordered by the Roman emperor Augustus and a decree forcing Jews like Joseph to be enrolled in their ancestral city. Jesus is "her firstborn son" (2:7, NAB), which in Jewish tradition gave him certain privileges and social position. The humble circumstances of Jesus' birth leads most people to ignore him. Nevertheless, this child is said to be a source of "peace to those on whom his [God's] favor rests" (NAB)—a translation of 2:14 confirmed by several texts found among the Dead Sea scrolls.

In Luke 2:21–40 the elderly Simeon and Anna represent those faithful Israelites who looked forward to the consolation and redemption of Israel (2:25, 38). The occasion for their prophecies about Jesus (cast in the language of Isa 40—55) is the fidelity of Joseph and Mary in performing the Jewish rituals of the mother's purification after giving birth (see Lev 13) and the presentation of the child (see Exod 13:2, 12, 15). These rituals had been preceded by the circumcision and naming of Jesus on the eighth day after his birth (2:21). And Luke rounds off his account of the infancy of Jesus by noting that "when they had fulfilled all the prescriptions of the law of the Lord, they returned to Galilee" (2:39, NAB).

The only account in the Gospels about Jesus' life between his birth and the beginning of his public ministry is set in the context of a family pilgrimage from Nazareth in Galilee to Jerusalem. We are undoubtedly supposed to imagine one of the three annual pilgrimage feasts (see Exod 23:14) in the Jewish calendar—Passover, Pentecost, or Tabernacles. In this episode recounted only in Luke 2:41–52 the twelve-year-old Jesus enters into discussion with the sages at the Temple Mount and astonishes everyone by his brilliance (2:46–47). Presumably the topic of their conversations is the Torah and issues related to it. When confronted by his parents about his absence, Jesus explains that he had to be "in my Father's house" (2:49, NAB). This vague expression (which is even vaguer in Greek—literally, "in the things of my Father") is usually taken to refer to the Jerusalem Temple. Thus the Lukan infancy narrative begins and ends at the Jerusalem Temple.

Jewish Canticles: Luke's infancy narrative is punctuated by several hymns (1:46–55; 1:68–79) or fragments of hymns (2:14; 2:29–32). These all stand in the tradition of Jewish religious poetry. They are constructed on the basis of parallelism of members, according to which one statement (or stich) is matched by another cast in slightly different words that are either similar (synonymous) or opposite (antithetical) in content. The hymns are made up of biblical phrases and expressions put together in new combinations and new contexts (the anthological style). They celebrate the saving power of God on behalf of God's people and made manifest in history. Their content is generally more Jewish than it is explicitly Christian, though the context in which Luke has placed them has certainly made them Christian.

These hymns or hymnic fragments appear in a Semitic style of Greek, like that of the Septuagint and the rest of Luke 1:5—2:52. Many scholars have argued that they were composed in Hebrew or Aramaic, and then translated into biblical Greek. Some have attributed them to the early Jewish Christian community in Jerusalem, while others regard them as basically pre-Christian products emanating from Jewish groups back as far as the second century BCE (Maccabean times).

The hymn in Luke 1:46–55 is traditionally called the Magnificat. This title is taken from the first word in the Latin translation: *Magnificat anima mea Dominum* ("My soul magnifies the Lord," NRSV). After proclaiming in synonymous parallelism the intent to praise God (1:46b–47), the hymn presents interlocking antithetical (1:48a, 49) and synonymous (1:48b, 50) statements to explain why God should be praised in all ages for exalting this lowly woman. Then it takes her case as an example of how God deals with the proud (1:51), the powerful (1:52), and the rich (1:53). The final verses (1:54–55) suggest that this is how God also deals with Israel as his covenant people. In the Lukan context the Magnificat celebrates the birth of Mary's child as God's way of bringing about a great reversal in human society and fulfilling his promises to Israel.

The song in Luke 1:68–79 is widely known as the Benedictus ("blessed"), from the first word in its Latin version. This hymn celebrates God's saving visitation on Israel's behalf. The three basic themes or motifs appear first with reference to God in 1:68–70: God's visitation or intervention for Israel (1:68), God's raising up a horn of salvation from the house of David (1:69), and God's word spoken through his prophets (1:70). These same three motifs occur in the center of the hymn (1:71–75) with reference to Israel as God's covenant people. Then in 1:76–79 the child is addressed with reference to the prophetic word (1:76), salvation for God's people (1:77), and God's visitation or intervention (1:78–79). In the Lukan context Zechariah celebrates the birth of Jesus as God's saving visitation on Israel's behalf and the fulfillment of God's promises. He also makes clear the subordination of his own son John to Jesus.

The angels' song in Luke 2:14 is called the Gloria, from its first Latin word *(gloria)*. The first line ("glory to God in the highest," NRSV) echoes the angelic proclamation in Isaiah 6:3a ("Holy, holy, holy is the LORD of hosts," NRSV). The second line ("and on earth peace…," NAB) takes up what is said in Isaiah 6:3b ("All the earth is filled with his glory!" NAB). In the Lukan context the angels proclaim that God's presence (the *Shekinah* in Hebrew) resides in the newborn child Jesus.

Simeon's song in Luke 2:29–32 is commonly entitled *Nunc Dimittis,* again from its first two Latin words ("Now dismiss"). In

2:25 Simeon is described as "awaiting the consolation of Israel" (NAB). The key phrases in his song are taken from various passages in Isaiah 40—55: seeing salvation (40:5), in the sight of all the peoples (52:10), and a light of revelation to the Gentiles and glory for Israel (42:6, 46:13, 52:10). In the Lukan context the elderly prophet Simeon, under the guidance of the Holy Spirit, identifies the child Jesus as the consolation of Israel.

Looking Backward and Forward: Luke's infancy narrative is meant to be read while looking in two directions—backward to Jesus' roots in Israel's history and Israel's Scriptures; and forward to Jesus' public ministry as an adult, his death and resurrection (in Luke's Gospel), and the spread of the movement that he began (in Acts). Luke 1:5—2:52 places Jesus' birth and infancy within Israel as God's people. The vocabulary, theological concepts, and literary style all create a biblical atmosphere for what follows. The adult characters— Zechariah and Elizabeth, Mary and Joseph, and Simeon and Anna— are devout Jews who remain faithful to the Torah and await the consolation of Israel. The children—John and Jesus—are described in terms of biblical figures such as Samson, Samuel, David, and Elijah. These characters live in a society structured by Jewish rituals (circumcision and naming on the eighth day, purification for women after giving birth, presentation of the male child to God) and Jewish customs (annual Temple service for men from priestly families, pilgrimages to Jerusalem on certain feasts).

Luke's account of Jesus' origins also makes us look forward. It shows that what Jesus was as an adult, he already was as a child. He is a prophet and a Son of David. He is the "Son of the Most High" (1:32, NAB). He is Savior, Messiah, and Lord (2:11). Many of the great themes that are developed in the body of the Gospel and in Acts are anticipated in the infancy narrative: the prominence of women, the activity of the Holy Spirit with regard to Jesus, the importance of prayer at decisive moments, Jesus' identification with the poor in Israel, and the Jerusalem Temple as the home of Jesus. The words of the prophet Simeon taken over from the Book of Isaiah in Luke 2:32 aptly summarize the content of Luke's two-volume work: "glory for your people Israel" (Luke's Gospel, NAB) and "a light for revelation to the Gentiles" (Acts of the Apostles, NAB).

Mary the mother of Jesus can be a model for all readers of Luke's Gospel. This young Jewish woman trusts in God's word (1:38), believes that God's word to her will be fulfilled (1:45), and continues to reflect on what God is doing in her life and in that of her son (2:19). Mary fits perfectly Jesus' own definition of his disciples as those who "hear the word of God and act upon it" (8:21, NAB; see 11:28).

For Reflection and Discussion:

1. In what ways does Luke situate the birth and infancy of Jesus within Judaism? Why did he do so?
2. Could an observant Jew in antiquity or today sing the hymns in Luke's infancy narrative? What might be problematic?
3. What effect does Luke's emphasis on the Jewish identity of Jesus have on you as a reader of the Gospels today?

2
Luke 4:16–30:
Jesus in the Synagogue at Nazareth
Cycle C:
Third and Fourth Sundays in
Ordinary Time

Luke's account of Jesus' inaugural sermon in the synagogue at Nazareth is generally understood to be a revised and expanded version of Mark 6:1–6. Luke's narrative appears at the beginning of Jesus' public activity, whereas Mark places it in the middle of Jesus' ministry in Galilee. Moreover, Luke's account is much fuller, with many themes and motifs that become prominent as his Gospel (and Acts) unfolds. It is entirely plausible on the historical level that Jesus read the Hebrew Scriptures and preached in the synagogue at Nazareth, and that he experienced some rejection in his own hometown. But it is equally likely that Luke has taken the tradition about this incident and developed it into what is now often called Luke's programmatic preface to Jesus' public ministry. Luke both hands on tradition and adapts it.

The narrative begins by noting Jesus' arrival in Nazareth (4:16a) and ends with his departure (4:30). The body of the text describes first Jesus' reading of and comment on the Isaiah text (4:16b–21) and the people's initial mixed reaction to him (4:22), and then Jesus' explanations about his prophetic ministry (4:23–27) and the people's negative reaction (4:28–29).

The Scripture reading takes place in the synagogue at Nazareth. In Jesus' time the synagogue (based on the Greek word for "gathering" or "assembly") was the local center of Jewish life, education, and prayer. Whether there was a distinct and substantial building designated as "the synagogue" in Nazareth in the early first century is not certain. At least no such building has yet been discovered. But the primary purposes of the synagogue were cultural, educational, social, and religious. The gathering may have taken place at a large private home or in some public building.

It is also hard to know precisely what Sabbath lectionary cycle was in force in the early first century. But there is no doubt that there were readings from the Law and the Prophets, along with homiletic comments and communal prayers. Anyone of sufficient learning could be invited to read the biblical text and comment on it. Luke tells us that it was Jesus' custom to go to the synagogue on the Sabbath. This then is the scene for Jesus' inaugural sermon. With this scene Luke emphasizes once more Jesus' roots in first-century Judaism.

The Scripture text that Jesus reads, according to Luke 4:18–19, is basically Isaiah 61:1–2a (with some allusion to 58:6): "The Spirit of the Lord GOD...a year of favor from the LORD" (NAB). The choice of this passage serves to link Jesus back to Israel's hopes for the future after the return from exile in the sixth century. It also anticipates themes that will shape Luke's presentation of Jesus' public ministry: the power of the Holy Spirit in Jesus' life; his identity as the anointed one, or Messiah; his mission to marginal persons; his gospel of freedom; his healing power; and his proclamation of divine forgiveness cast in terms of the biblical Jubilee year. The mention of God's vindication or vengeance in Isaiah 61:2 is omitted.

According to Luke 4:20, Jesus had been reading from a scroll. Among the earliest discoveries in the Dead Sea manuscripts at Qumran was an almost completely preserved scroll of the Book of Isaiah (now on exhibit at the Shrine of the Book in Jerusalem). Jesus rolls up the scroll, hands it to the synagogue attendant *(hazzan)*, sits down, and begins to speak. Luke's description of the synagogue service seems accurate enough—at least to approach verisimilitude. Indeed, it is the earliest description of a synagogue service that we have, and it is often used by historians of early Judaism to reconstruct the Jewish Sabbath liturgy in the first century.

After reading the text from Isaiah, Jesus offers what is perhaps the shortest sermon ever given: "Today this scripture passage is fulfilled in your hearing" (4:21, NAB). In Luke's Gospel *today* is an important word. It refers to what Luke regards as the special time of Jesus, indeed, a unique time. The time of Jesus' public ministry and passion is the middle or center of time, the pivotal moment in which Jesus is the unique bearer, agent, and vehicle of the Holy Spirit. It is as if all the energies of the Holy Spirit are focused and concentrated in the person of Jesus. The claim is that Isaiah's prophecy is being fulfilled (not abolished) in the time of Jesus. All the teachings and actions of Jesus are empowered by the Holy Spirit. The Spirit's power active in Jesus marks him as the prophet par excellence.

The initial reaction (4:22) to Jesus is mixed. On the one hand, the people are impressed by his eloquence. On the other hand, they find it hard to understand where his eloquence came from. They know him only as the son of Joseph. They are unaware of the many extraordinary things said about Jesus thus far in Luke's Gospel (such as "Son of God"). Their measured admiration will turn to hostility in 4:28–29.

From Jesus' words in Luke 4:23–24 one can surmise that the people of Nazareth had heard about Jesus' activities elsewhere in Galilee (see 4:14–15). And they seem to have been annoyed on two fronts: They wonder (cynically) where all his power came from, and they want it (selfishly) for themselves and for their own benefit. Their reaction allows Jesus to make two points about his role as a prophet: He is a rejected prophet, because no prophet gains acceptance in his native place; and Jesus as a prophet ministering to outsiders stands in the tradition of Elijah and Elisha.

In the Scriptures a prophet is sent from God to proclaim God's will and God's judgment upon the people. Since they tell hard truths, prophets are seldom popular figures. The power of the prophet comes from God, from the Holy Spirit, not from popular opinion or popular acceptance. The saying is generally true: "No prophet is accepted in his own native place" (4:24, NAB). This proverb is used to explain why Jesus does not confine his activity to Nazareth.

According to 4:25–27, Jesus' ministry to outsiders stands in line with those of the biblical prophets Elijah and Elisha. These ninth-century prophets taught through parables and symbolic actions, healed the sick and restored dead persons to life, and suffered rejection and persecution for proclaiming God's will and judgment. And they exercised a ministry to outsiders.

In 1 Kings 17:7–24 God sends Elijah to an outsider—a widow of Zarephath of Sidon, clearly outside the land of Israel. There he first miraculously provides food for the widow and her son, and then miraculously restores the son to life. In 2 Kings 5 Elisha heals the leprosy of the Syrian army commander, Naaman. He is clearly a Gentile. But it is important to attend to Naaman's profession of faith after his healing: "Now I know that there is no God in all the earth, except in Israel" (5:15, NAB).

The programmatic preface establishes Jesus as a prophet after the pattern of Elijah and Elisha. Indeed, the best biblical models for the Gospels' portrayals of Jesus are the texts about Elijah and Elisha in 1 and 2 Kings. Luke's interest in Jesus' prophetic identity extends to his followers. When, according to Acts 2, the spirit of prophecy is poured out on the first Christians assembled in Jerusalem at Pentecost (Weeks), they come to stand in the prophetic succession reaching back to Elijah and Elisha.

Luke's programmatic preface ends on a note of rejection. According to Luke 4:28–29, the people in the synagogue become outraged and try to kill Jesus. This anticipates the theme of the rejection of Jesus and his apostles that runs through Luke–Acts. But not all Jews reject Jesus. In fact, all his disciples and other followers up to Cornelius in Acts 10–11 are Jews. Moreover, as in the case of Naaman, the mission of Jesus and his disciples is to promote among outsiders the recognition that "there is no God in all the earth, except in Israel."

The programmatic preface in 4:16–30 introduces many of the great themes to be developed in Luke's two volumes: the fulfillment of Scripture and its promises, Jesus as the agent of the Holy Spirit, good news for the poor, the proclamation of freedom and forgiveness, "today" as the time of Jesus and the center of salvation history, Jesus' ministry to outsiders, prophetic succession, and rejection by some of his own people.

If the function of a preface is to provide a preview of what will be set forth in the body of a book, Luke 4:16–30 is a precious resource for readers of Luke–Acts. But Christian preachers and teachers need to be careful about going beyond what Luke says. In particular, the fulfillment of the Jewish Scriptures does not mean their abolition.

And the rejection of Jesus by some Jews in Nazareth does not mean that all Israel rejected Jesus or that all Israel is rejected by him. Indeed, the thrust of Jesus' mission and that of the movement begun by him is to bear witness and lead all nations to recognize (as Naaman did) that "there is no God in all the earth, except in Israel."

For Reflection and Discussion:

1. From Luke's account, how do you imagine the synagogue service? What do you see? What do you hear?
2. What does the fulfillment of Scripture mean to you? What might it have meant to Luke?
3. What picture of Jesus' relationship to Judaism emerges from Luke's version of the incident at the synagogue in Nazareth?

3
Luke 5:1–11:
The Call of the Fishermen
Cycle C:
Fifth Sunday in Ordinary Time

The first disciples of Jesus were Jewish fishermen from Galilee. Commercial fishing has long been a major business enterprise at the Sea of Galilee. And Capernaum, which served as Jesus' base of operation for much of his public activity in Galilee, is on the western shore of the Sea of Galilee and may be described as a fishing village. Simon (also known as Peter) and his brother Andrew, as well as two sons of Zebedee (James and John), made their living from fishing there. These men had nets and boats, were very likely able to read and write (at least enough to conduct their businesses), and were apparently successful in their work. Thus they had the prospect of a relatively safe and secure life in their future. But, according to all the Gospels, these small businessmen left their occupations and families in order to become companions of a wandering Jewish preacher of God's kingdom.

In Mark 1:16–20 and Matthew 4:18–22, Jesus approaches first Peter and Andrew, and then James and John. He simply says "Follow me" (NRSV), and they come after him. There is no indication that these men had known Jesus beforehand or even knew anything about him. Rather, on Jesus' word alone ("Follow me") they leave everything and become part of his movement. Luke, however, tells the story of Jesus' call of his first disciples in both a more realistic and a more miraculous way.

The Lukan call story is placed only after several accounts of Jesus' healing and preaching activity (4:31–44), including the healing of Simon Peter's mother-in-law (4:38–39). The scene is set in Luke 5:1–3 with Jesus teaching the crowds on the shore while he sits in a boat offshore. It is like that for "the day of parables" in Mark 4:1–2. The heart of the narrative — the call of fishermen to be Jesus' first disciples — is dependent to a large extent on the account in Mark 1:16–20 (and Matt 4:18–22). The miraculous catch of fish is somehow related to the post-resurrection narrative in John 21:1–14. Scholars have long debated whether John has moved a miracle story into the post-Easter period, or Luke has moved an Easter appearance story back into the beginning of Jesus' public ministry. At any rate, Luke takes some of the mystery out of the Markan and Matthean accounts by establishing a history between Jesus and the fishermen (see 4:38–39), and by presenting their positive response to Jesus' call as in part motivated by their experience of their miraculous catch of fish under Jesus' direction.

In the rabbinic tradition it was customary for prospective sages to seek out a master teacher or rabbi, to apprentice themselves to him, and eventually to become sages in their own right. The rabbinic curriculum included human wisdom, the Scriptures of Israel, traditions surrounding them, the sayings of great Jewish teachers, and applications or actualizations of them to new or unforeseen situations. In the Gospels, however, Jesus seeks out his own followers, summons them personally, and offers them a curriculum centered on the kingdom of God. The first followers of Jesus are fishermen by trade, and Jesus plays on their profession and promises to make them "fishers of men" (Mark 1:17; Matt 4:19, NAB).

In the Lukan account Jesus not only alludes to their profession (5:10) but even gives them lessons about how to fish more effectively. Having used their boat as a platform for teaching in 5:1–3, Jesus in 5:4–7 instructs them to "put out into deep water and lower your nets for a catch" (5:4, NAB). Despite his professional misgivings, Simon obeys Jesus' word. And they get such an abundant catch that their nets begin to tear, and they have to call for help from other fishermen.

In the church's lectionary Luke 5:1–11 is paired with the call of the prophet in Isaiah 6. In the Jerusalem Temple Isaiah receives a vision of God's glory expressed in a remarkably vivid way. Isaiah's response is a confession of his own unworthiness and sinfulness: "I am a man of unclean lips, living among a people of unclean lips" (Isa 6:5, NAB). But God reassures the prophet and sends him on a mission to preach repentance to his people Israel.

This biblical pattern of divine revelation, human confession of unworthiness, and commissioning appears also in Luke's account of Jesus' call of his first disciples. The revelation in this case is in the miraculous catch of fish. Although Peter and his companions were professional fishermen, on their own they were catching nothing. When Jesus appears and tells them what to do, they make a huge catch of fish. This surprising (even miraculous) event is taken to be a revelation of Jesus' identity as someone sent by God.

As Isaiah does, so Simon Peter confesses his personal unworthiness: "Depart from me, Lord, for I am a sinful man" (Luke 5:8, NAB). In the presence of God's miraculous action in Jesus and in the presence of Jesus as the agent and vehicle of the Holy Spirit, Peter faces up to his own sinfulness and unworthiness.

Nevertheless, as with Isaiah, God has other plans for Simon Peter. Instead of rejecting Peter, Jesus gives him a mission: "Do not be afraid; from now on you will be catching men" (5:10, NAB). Peter, who had earned his living as a fisherman, is now called to bring life—spiritual and eternal life—to other human beings. Accepting his commission means leaving behind his family and his fishing business in Capernaum. The story ends with the statement: "When they brought their boats to the shore, they left everything and followed him" (5:11, NAB).

The image of Jesus' first followers as "fishers of men" apparently created a subtle problem for Luke. In the fishing process the fish do not come away alive and well. Rather, either the fish are killed immediately by a hook, or at some later stage they lose their life and are eaten. And so the biblical prophets often use the image of fishermen in warning Israel about punishments to come: "Look! I will send many fishermen, says the LORD, to catch them" (Jer 16:16, NAB; see also Ezek 29:4–5; Amos 4:2; Hab 1:14–15).

Luke seems embarrassed by the fact that catching fish generally involves killing them . And so Luke alone among the evangelists uses the verb *zogrein*, which contains the Greek roots for "life" *(zoe)* and "catch" *(agrein)* and means "to catch alive." This rare word conveys the idea that the mission to which Peter and the others are called consists in giving life to people and keeping them alive. In this way Jesus invites his first followers to join in his mission of proclaiming God's kingdom and inviting people to right relationship with God and eternal happiness.

Whereas Mark and Matthew based the first disciples' response to Jesus on the power of his word alone, Luke has added the notions of their prior knowledge of Jesus and of Jesus' miraculous display of power on the lake. Whereas the people of Jesus' hometown had reacted to Jesus in a hostile manner (see 4:29–30), these Jewish fishermen respond to Jesus with reverence and awe (as Isaiah responded to his encounter with the glory of God). Moreover, Luke makes the call of Simon and his companions into a dramatic moment and so establishes them as essential figures in a life-giving ministry, as witnesses to Jesus' life-giving ministry and miraculous power from the beginning of his public ministry, and as principles of continuity between the time of Jesus and the time of the Holy Spirit/the church. For other texts relevant to the theme of discipleship, see Luke 6:12–16, 9:1–6, 10:1–12, 14:25–33.

For Reflection and Discussion:

1. Have you been to the Sea of Galilee, or have you seen a photograph of it? How do you imagine Luke's scene of Jesus and the fishermen?
2. How would the miraculous catch of fish have served as an incentive for Simon Peter and others to follow Jesus?
3. Does the biblical pattern of divine revelation, confession of unworthiness, and commissioning correspond to your own religious experience?

4
Luke 6:17, 20–26:
Blessings and Woes
Cycle C:
Sixth Sunday in Ordinary Time

In the early twenty-first century we in the West live in a materialistic society where it seems that almost everything is for sale. We are bombarded by advertising whose goal is to convince us to buy things that we really do not need. The assumption of much of this advertising is that such and such a product will satisfy our desires, amuse us, and make other persons admire or even love us. In this framework it appears that happiness consists in having money and other possessions, having our desires and appetites satisfied, having "a good time," and avoiding all conflict and embarrassment.

What is happiness? How and where do we expect to find it? By his blessings and woes in Luke 6:20–26, Jesus challenges common assumptions about the nature of human happiness, and proclaims that it is to be found in right relationship with God and in the kingdom of God.

The Lukan blessings and woes constitute the introduction to Jesus' first substantial block of teaching in the Gospel. The passage as a whole (6:20–49) is known as the Sermon on the Plain. In Luke's theological geography the plain is where Jesus meets the crowds (6:17–19), and so in his Gospel the first sermon is situated on the plain. The sermon is generally regarded as having been taken over almost entirely from the Sayings Source Q that Matthew and Luke used independently in revising and expanding Mark's Gospel. Matthew took over the Q ser-

175

mon and greatly expanded it into his Sermon on the Mount in Matthew 5—7. Luke, however, seems to have merely inserted the basic Q form, added a few features (especially the woes), and presented it as a sample or summary of Jesus' teaching.

The Lukan sermon has three parts. First, Jesus issues blessings and woes that reverse ordinary human assumptions and raise questions about the nature of happiness (6:20–26). Then he offers short sayings about loving one's enemies, and proposes as the criterion not human self-interest but rather God's inclusive love for all humans (6:27–38). Finally, in 6:39–49 he warns about judging others rashly, affirms that wisdom is proved by deeds, and urges that one's life be built on the firm foundation of genuine wisdom.

The sermon begins with four blessings, or beatitudes (6:20–23). They declare "happy" or "blessed" in turn the poor (6:20), the hungry (6:21), the weeping (6:22), and the persecuted (6:23). The beatitude is a common literary form in the psalms and biblical wisdom books. For example, the first sentence in the first psalm is a beatitude: "Blessed the man who follows not / the counsel of the wicked... / but delights in the law of the LORD" (Ps 1:1–2, Lectionary). Likewise, Psalm 32 begins with a beatitude: "Happy the sinner whose fault is removed, / whose sin is forgiven" (Ps 32:1, NAB).

The Lukan Beatitudes differ from the earlier biblical beatitudes on two counts. They are cast in the second-person plural ("you"), not in the third person. Moreover, they are oriented not so much to human happiness in the present world but rather to the kingdom of God.

It is generally assumed that Luke took over these Beatitudes in their present form from his source Q, and that they echo the voice of Jesus. Matthew in 5:3–12 of his Sermon on the Mount has expanded the list of Beatitudes from four to eight or nine, and reverted to the more usual Jewish third-person style. While maintaining the orientation of Jesus' Beatitudes toward the kingdom of God, Matthew at some points tends to spiritualize their content: "the poor in spirit" (5:3, NAB), and "hunger and thirst for righteousness" (5:6, NAB). Luke, however, retains the concreteness and even economic harshness of his source. The poor, the hungry, the weeping, and the persecuted are declared to be "blessed" or "happy." At the beginning of his epitome of Jesus' teachings, Luke introduces the theme of the "great reversal" associated with the kingdom of God. That theme was raised already in Mary's Magnificat: "The hungry he has filled with good things; / the rich he has sent away empty" (Luke 1:53, NAB). It will be illustrated in a graphic and even terrifying way in the parable of the rich man and Lazarus (16:19–31).

The four beatitudes are accompanied by four woes in 6:24–26. The woe is also a biblical literary form found most prominently in the prophetic books of the Bible. Thus Isaiah 5:8–10 threatens divine judgment on those who gobble up the property of others for themselves: "Woe to you who join house to house" (NAB). And Micah 2:1–5 warns those who show no social consciousness: "Woe to those who plan iniquity.... / They covet fields, and seize them" (NAB).

There is no indication that Luke took over the four woes from his Q source. At least, they are nowhere to be found in Matthew 5—7. Rather, it appears that Luke composed them to underline by way of contrast the content of the four beatitudes. The four woes warn the wealthy (6:24), those who are filled now (6:25a), those who laugh now (6:25b), and those with good reputations (6:26) that their fortunes also will be reversed in the fullness of God's kingdom.

Luke's addition of the four woes in 6:24–26 is often taken as a sign of his special interest in relations between rich and poor, perhaps even within his own community. He encourages the economically poor to recognize that true happiness resides in right relationship with God and God's kingdom rather than in material possessions, and Jesus invites the poor to the banquet of God's kingdom (see the discussion of Luke 14:7–14). And at the same time he warns the rich that material wealth is no guarantee of happiness, and that now is the time to share one's possessions with those in need (see the discussion of Luke 16:19–31).

Jesus' blessings and woes turn common assumptions about life upside down. They challenge us—Christians and Jews alike—to define the core of our existence, and to make choices about our ultimate values and about the nature of happiness and about where and how it is to be found.

For Reflection and Discussion:

1. Can the economically poor really be happy? Can the rich be really unhappy?
2. How do the Lukan Beatitudes turn common assumptions about happiness upside down? Does this ring true to you?
3. What impact might the Beatitudes have on the way you live in the present?

5
Luke 9:51–62:
The Journey Begins
Cycle C:
Thirteenth Sunday in
Ordinary Time

The most striking structural feature in Luke's Gospel is the large amount of space devoted to the journey of Jesus and his disciples from Galilee (their home area) to Jerusalem (where Jesus is to die). The journey takes up about ten chapters (9:51 — 19:44) out of the twenty-four chapters in Luke's Gospel. While the journey reflects the historical practice of Jesus, who went from place to place in carrying out his ministry (see 9:58), Luke seems to have taken over the specific idea of Jesus' last journey from Mark 8:22 — 10:52. But Luke has greatly expanded Mark's journey account by giving it four times more space than Mark did.

On the way Jesus teaches his disciples about who he is (Christology) and what it means to follow him (discipleship). The Lukan journey narrative contains many of the most famous passages in the New Testament: the good Samaritan (10:25–37), Mary and Martha (10:38–42), the prodigal son (15:11–32), the rich man and Lazarus (16:19–31), and the ten lepers (17:11–19).

The goal of the journey is Jerusalem. Luke keeps the journey motif going by punctuating the narrative with "travel notices" (see 9:57; 10:1, 38; 13:22, 31–33; 14:25; 17:11; 18:31, 35; 19:1, 11, 28,

41). However, it is hard to follow the journey on a map or grasp exactly how Luke conceived of the geography of the Holy Land. Rather, the journey appears to be primarily a literary framework into which Luke fits many of the traditions about Jesus to which he had access.

The purpose of the journey is made clear in Luke 13:31–33 when some Pharisees (in a friendly gesture) warn Jesus that Herod Antipas wants to kill him. At this point Jesus reveals that by divine necessity he as a prophet must go to Jerusalem and meet his fate: "Yet I must continue on my way today, tomorrow, and the following day, for it is impossible that a prophet should die outside of Jerusalem" (13:33, NAB).

That sense of destiny or fate is clear from the start of the journey in Luke 9:51. The expression "the days for his being taken up" (NAB) refers to the whole complex of events comprising Jesus' suffering, death, resurrection, and ascension. It may also allude to the "taking up" of the prophet Elijah in 2 Kings 2. The connection between Jesus and the prophets Elijah and Elisha signaled in Luke 4:25–27 is reinforced at several points in Luke 9:51–62. While Jesus' journey may seem to end with his death, in fact from Luke's perspective his death is one part of his being taken up after the pattern of Elijah. The way is which Jesus is said to have approached the journey (literally, "he set his face") suggests that he consciously and willingly undertook the journey that he knew might well involve his death and his exaltation.

According to Luke 9:52–56, Jesus immediately encounters two sets of opponents, one from the Samaritans (9:52–53) and the other from his own disciples (9:54–56). The Samaritans refuse to accept Jesus in their village when they learn that Jerusalem is his destination. (For tensions between Samaritans and Jews, see the discussion of Luke 10:25–37.) The Samaritans had their own sanctuary on Mount Gerizim and did not regard Jerusalem as their holy city. They perceived Galileans like Jesus and his companions to be allied with the Judeans and so against them. Their rejection of Jesus, who is apparently on a pilgrimage to the Jerusalem Temple, provides an interesting case of Jesus being a victim of anti-Jewish (Galilean-Judean) prejudice.

His own disciples also oppose Jesus when they suggest calling down "fire from heaven to consume them [Samaritan villagers]" (9:54, NAB). Their suggestion alludes to Elijah's action in 2 Kings 1:9–12 in calling down fire from heaven to consume his pursuers. The disciples share the hostility of their fellow Jews toward Samaritans and want Jesus to show that he is a man of God after the model of the prophet Elijah. But Jesus, though he is like Elijah in many respects, is not a destructive prophet and has no need to prove his identity as a prophet by a destructive action. So at the start of their journey Jesus warns his disciples against false notions of what it means to be followers of a suffering prophet (see 13:33).

Jesus' correction of his disciples leads into a brief presentation on the cost of discipleship in 9:57–62, which in turn prepares for the instruction that Jesus gives when he sends seventy-two of his disciples out on a mission (10:1–24; see also 9:1–6). The cost of discipleship is high, since it may involve disregard of physical stability (9:58) and of family obligations (9:59–60, 61–62).

Even in his home area of Galilee, Jesus seems to have often been on the road while carrying out his ministry of teaching and healing. Modern scholars sometimes characterize him as a wandering (or, itinerant) radical. And his various missionary discourses (such as Luke 9:1–6 and 10:1–24) indicate that he expected his first followers to do likewise. In fact, throughout the Greco-Roman world philosophies and religions were spread largely by traveling missionaries. And so at the very beginning of the climactic journey of his life, Jesus warns his followers in 9:57–58 that although foxes and birds may have stable abodes, "the Son of Man [Jesus] has nowhere to rest his head" (NAB).

When in 9:57–60 a prospective disciple proclaims "I will follow you wherever you go" (NAB), Jesus challenges him to choose between carrying out the sacred family obligation of burying one's father and proclaiming the kingdom of God by joining in Jesus' mission. In any culture attending to the burial of one's parents is an important human duty. In first-century Judaism, where family ties were much more significant than they are today in the modern West, neglecting the burial of one's parent would be regarded as shocking behavior. And that is Jesus' point. His extreme example takes a negative route in order to drive home a positive statement about the overwhelming importance of proclaiming God's kingdom and becoming part of the new family of Jesus defined as those "who hear the word of God and observe it" (8:21; see 11:27–28, NAB).

The third example pertaining to the cost of discipleship (9:61–62) also alludes to Elijah and Elisha. According to 1 Kings 19:19–21, when Elijah chose Elisha to become his disciple and successor, Elisha made this request: "Please, let me kiss my father and mother goodbye, and I will follow you" (19:20, NAB). But Jesus, when faced with a similar request from a prospective disciple, is even more rigorous than Elijah was and declares that "no one who sets a hand to the plow and looks to what was left behind is fit for the kingdom of God" (9:62, NAB).

The three short units in Luke 9:57–62 illustrate the high cost of following Jesus. They also suggest the supreme value of joining in his mission of proclaiming the kingdom of God. The several allusions to Elijah and Elisha throughout Luke 9:51–62 highlight the nonviolent (9:54–56) and demanding (9:61–62) character of Jesus, even as he embarks on the journey that will lead to his "being taken up" (9:51, NAB) and in being raised up in the glory of resurrection and ascension.

For Reflection and Discussion:

1. How does Luke bring out the idea that Jesus went willingly to his death? In what sense is to be an "exodus"?
2. How do you react to Jesus' instructions about dealing with one's parents? Are they insensitive or even inhuman?
3. What effect does placing the sayings about the cost of discipleship at the beginning of the journey narrative have?

6
Luke 10:25–37:
The Good Samaritan
Cycle C:
Fifteenth Sunday in Ordinary Time

According to rabbinic tradition, the Torah (the first five books in the Bible) contains 613 commandments, 248 of them positive in form and 365 negative in form. It is not surprising that Jewish teachers would be asked to provide a summary of the Torah or to name the "greatest" commandment. According to the Babylonian Talmud (*b. Shabbat* 31a), a Gentile asked the Jewish teacher Shammai to "teach me the whole Torah while I stand on one foot." Shammai refused to answer and chased the man away. But Hillel, when given the same request, gave an answer that sounds like the "Golden Rule" attributed to Jesus in Matthew 7:12 and Luke 6:31: "What is hateful to you, do not do to your neighbor; that is the whole Torah, while the rest is commentary; go and learn it."

In Mark 12:28–34, Matthew 22:34–40, and Luke 10:25–28, Jesus' response to the question about the greatest commandment consists of two of the 613 commandments in the Torah: love God with your whole heart (Deut 6:4–5) and love your neighbor as yourself (Lev 19:18b). According to Matthew 22:40, observance of these commandments will ensure observance of all the commandments: "The whole law and the prophets depend on these two commandments" (NAB).

While the Lukan version of the episode (Luke 10:25–28) agrees with its parallels in their basic content, it does have some distinctive features. The "scholar of the law" (NAB, a loose rendering of "lawyer") asks Jesus a more general question—about what he needs to do "to inherit eternal life" (10:25, NAB). Then in 10:26–27 Jesus gets him to answer his own question. His answer joins Deuteronomy 6:4–5 and Leviticus 19:18 into one commandment, leaving out the first/second gradation found in the parallel passages. Finally, in 10:28 Jesus challenges the lawyer to act upon his own summary of the Torah: "do this and you will live" (NAB).

The parable of the good Samaritan in Luke 10:29–37 serves as a commentary or illustration of the commandment to love one's neighbor. The instruction about prayer in 11:1–13 concerns the love of God, while the Mary-and-Martha episode in 10:38–42 provides bridge between passages about love of neighbor and love of God.

The parable is introduced or occasioned by the lawyer's question in 10:29: "And who is my neighbor?" (NAB). It is often said that wise lawyers ask only questions whose answers they already know. But the answer that this lawyer got from Jesus very likely came as a great surprise.

The parable presented in Luke 10:30–35 is usually called "the good Samaritan." It is one of the most famous stories in the Christian Bible. And almost everyone understands and uses the expression "good Samaritan" in everyday speech. Nevertheless, this familiar title may obscure a very important point about the parable. In fact, from a literary perspective, the central character, the one character who is present from beginning to end, is not the good Samaritan but rather the man who was robbed, beaten, and left to die. Given the context, we may safely assume that the victim is a Jew. If we focus first on the injured man, we may see the parable in a new light.

The parable begins with a report (10:30) about what happened to a man traveling on the road from Jerusalem to Jericho. This is a long, winding, mountainous road well suited to bandits. The man is robbed, beaten, and left to die. The parable leads us to imagine ourselves in his position. If you have ever been robbed or been the victim of a violent crime or been stranded on a dangerous highway, you know the feeling. You need help, and are not particular about from whom it may come.

Three persons come upon the injured man. The first passerby is a Jewish priest, and the second is a Levite (10:31–32). Both belonged to Jewish families that could trace their ancestry back to Aaron and the patriarch Levi. We may imagine that they were returning home from serving their annual turns in ministering at the Jerusalem temple (see Luke 1:5–25). We are not told why they passed by. Perhaps they were in a hurry to get home. Perhaps they did not want to get involved. Perhaps they feared ritual defilement from having contact with a corpse (see Num 19:11–22). All we really do know is that a priest and a Levite passed by the injured man and went on their way.

The third person does not pass by. Rather, according to 10:33–35, he stops, attends to the injured man, takes him to an inn, and pays all his expenses. He is truly a friend in need. Again, imagine that you are the victim. How would you feel toward the man who showed such compassion to you? How would you respond to him? Would you refuse his help?

The surprise is that the third passerby is a Samaritan. The structure of the story—first a priest, then a Levite—leads one to expect that the third passerby would be a lay Israelite. This would make the parable into a kind of Jewish anticlerical joke. But instead the third passerby turns out to be a Samaritan.

Among Jews in Judea and Galilee, Samaritans were regarded with suspicion. Some Jews considered them as not Jews at all, while others looked on them as at best second-class Jews. Their temple on Mount Gerizim and their acceptance of only the Pentateuch as Scripture set them apart from other Jews. And there was the long-standing suspicion that the Samaritans descended from non-Jews settled in Samaria by the Assyrians. Here then is the real challenge of the parable. Those with impeccable credentials as Jews—the priest and the Levite—pass by the victim, while the only one who stops and ministers to the injured man is a Samaritan.

The occasion for the parable, according to Luke, was the lawyer's question: "And who is my neighbor?" In Luke 10:36–37 the focus shifts back to the question: "Who showed himself to be the neighbor to the injured man?" It was the Samaritan. When we read the parable from the perspective of the victim, from the vantage point of the man who had been robbed, beaten, and left to die, we can appreciate the challenge. It was only the stranger, the outsider, the foreigner who acted as a neighbor. And so when Jesus asks the lawyer, "Which of these three, in your opinion, was neighbor to the robber's victim?" (NAB) the only possible answer is: "The one who treated him with mercy" (NAB).

But the story does not end simply with a widening of the definition of "neighbor." Rather, the parable is transformed into an example story when Jesus says: "Go and do likewise" (NAB). The parable in which the victim is the central character suddenly becomes a story about the good example shown by the Samaritan who ministered to the man who had been robbed and left for dead. The entire passage then becomes a case or illustration of Jesus' teaching that we know as the "Golden Rule": "Do to others as you would have them do to you" (NAB).

Teachers and preachers need to be cautious about letting this text project an anti-Jewish message. In the Luke's context it is a story told by a Jewish teacher to a fellow Jew to raise the possibility that someone whose Jewish credentials were marginal (the Samaritan) might act more compassionately toward a Jewish victim than persons whose Jewish credentials (a priest and a Levite) were impeccable and indisputable. The point that both Jews and Christians need to hear flows from identifying with the injured man. Then my neighbor is anyone who is willing to help me in my time of need. In thinking about the neighbor in Leviticus 19:18, we must be willing to abandon our prejudices, accept help from whoever offers it, and be willing to help others in their time of need (whoever or whatever they may be).

For Reflection and Discussion:

1. What is gained by the reader first identifying with the man in the ditch and only later with the good Samaritan?
2. How does the parable of the good Samaritan illustrate the biblical commandment to love one's neighbor as oneself (Lev 19:18)?
3. How would you answer the lawyer's question, "What must I do to inherit eternal life?"

7
Luke 10:38–42:
Women in Jesus' Circle
Cycle C:
Sixteenth Sunday in Ordinary Time

In their long journey from Galilee to Jerusalem, Jesus and his disciples rely upon the kindness of people along the way. Their reception by two sisters—Mary and Martha—serves as a literary and theological hinge between the parable of the good Samaritan with its theme of love of neighbor (10:29–37) and the instruction about prayer as a way of showing love of God (11:1–13). These passages illustrate various dimensions of the summary of the Torah in 10:25–28. The episode in Luke 10:38–42 seeks to strike a balance between love of God and love of neighbor. It suggests that while serving the neighbor is necessary and important, it should not preclude or interfere with the service of God.

Contrast of characters is a prominent feature in Luke's Gospel. The practice of providing hospitality to itinerant philosophers and religious teachers was a custom in first-century Palestine. One sister (Mary) is eager to take in Jesus' teaching by sitting at his feet (10:39). The other sister (Martha) is duly attentive to her role as hostess. She welcomes Jesus (10:38) and is occupied with serving her guests (10:40). She is doing what a good woman in that time and place was expected to do. And she resents what she perceives as the laziness and inattentiveness shown by Mary. Martha appears to be the practical one. She is organized, hardworking, and sensitive to the obligations of hospitality. Mary, however, seems more interested in what Jesus has to say than in what needs to be done around the house. It is only natural that Martha should lose patience and ask Jesus to tell Mary to help her in serving the guests.

What is surprising is that in Luke 10:41–42 Jesus sides not with the hardworking and responsible Martha but rather with Mary. Instead of affirming Martha, Jesus suggests that the comfort of the guests should not prevent the hosts from hearing what the teacher has to say. Only a few things are really necessary for the guests, and there is no need for superfluities. The women of the household in particular should not be deprived of the opportunity to participate in the instruction being conducted by the Jewish teacher known as Jesus of Nazareth.

In the context of the ancient world and of first-century Palestine, Jesus' response to Martha in Luke 10:41–42 ("Mary has chosen the better part," NAB) was surprising. In that context women were not expected to participate with men in study groups and in discussions about religious and philosophical matters.

A rabbinic text that is often cited in this context appears in Mishnah *Abot* 1:5: "Yose ben Yohanan of Jerusalem says: 'Let your house be wide open. And seat the poor at your table. And do not talk too much with women.'" While Yose's saying may be defensible or at least understandable, the parenthetical comment in the same mishnah goes much further in its negative attitude about women: "He spoke of a man's wife; all the more so is the rule to be applied to the wife of one's fellow. In this regard did sages say, 'So long as a man talks too much with a woman, he brings trouble on himself, wastes time better spent on studying Torah, and ends up an heir of Gehenna.'"

First-century Jewish culture like many cultures in our world today had sharply defined roles for men and women. When a great teacher like Jesus came to the house for a visit, the local men gathered to hear him and to ask him questions. Women were expected to absent themselves, and occupy themselves in women's work. What is surprising in Luke 10:38–42 is that Mary becomes part of the discussion and that Jesus approves of her participation as "the better part." The circle of Jesus is open and inclusive. It embraces all kinds of persons, and involves men and women.

One message of Luke 10:38–42 is that the early Jesus movement was relatively open and welcoming to the participation of women.

This seems to reflect historical reality. Nevertheless, Christian teachers and preachers need to be cautious about proclaiming Jesus as the first feminist. Jesus as a first-century Jewish male must have been a man of his time, and it is probably an exaggeration or wishful thinking to make too much out his alleged egalitarianism. And it is a historical and sociological fact that in the early stages of religious movements there is a blurring of gender (and social and economic) differences. But as time goes on, there is also a gradual reversion to cultural norms as the movement settles down and finds its place in the wider society (see the Pastoral Epistles).

Besides misreading first-century Jewish history, there is also a danger of drawing too sharply the contrast between Jesus and his Jewish contemporaries (with too much emphasis on texts like Mishnah *Abot* 1:5). While enlightening to some extent, such comparisons can easily become invidious and serve to propagate negative stereotypes about Jews and Judaism. Meanwhile, Christians have enough to do in explaining New Testament texts like Colossians 3:18 ("Wives, be subordinate to your husbands," NAB) and 1 Timothy 2:11–12 ("A woman must receive instruction silently and under complete control. I do not permit a woman to teach or have authority over a man. She must be quiet," NAB).

Luke's Gospel is sometimes called the Gospel of women because it features women characters far more prominently than the other three Gospels do. In the infancy narrative Elizabeth, Mary, and Anna all appear as models of genuine biblical piety. In Luke 7:36–50 the anointing of Jesus' feet by "a sinful woman" (NAB) is the occasion for his teachings about the close relationship between love and forgiveness. In 8:1–3 we learn that some women were regularly providing for Jesus and the twelve, and even accompanying them: "Mary, called Magdalene...Joanna, the wife of Herod's steward Chuza, Susanna, and many others" (NAB).

There is nothing against assuming that these same women accompanied Jesus and the twelve on the Lukan journey from Galilee to Jerusalem. As we have seen in 10:38–42, women like Mary and Martha provided hospitality for Jesus along the way. Jesus manifests his healing power first by curing a crippled woman on the Sabbath (13:10–17) and then by healing a man with dropsy on the Sabbath (14:1–6). Jesus also tells parables in pairs. The parable of the lost sheep (15:4–7) features a male character, while the parable of the lost coin (15:8–10) focuses on a woman. And the parable of the persistent widow (18:1–8) illustrates an attitude of persistence in prayer that Jesus encourages several times.

In the passion narrative Jesus' women followers are present at his death and burial. They observe him being crucified (23:49), and know exactly where he was buried (23:50–56). On Easter Sunday morning these women go to the tomb, find it empty, and relay the message to the male disciples that Jesus has been raised from the dead (24:1–12).

Not all interpreters, however, are confident that Luke is really the friend of women. Some contend that while Luke does give special prominence to women characters, at the same time he reinforces their subordination to males and leaves them in their place within the patriarchal framework of first-century society. Indeed, one distinguished New Testament scholar, Elisabeth Schüssler Fiorenza, views Luke 10:38–42 as the product not of Jesus' earthly ministry but rather of a struggle within the early church. She takes Martha as a symbol for powerful and independent Christian women who presided over house churches, and views the praise of Mary's passivity and subordination that is attributed to Jesus as "the better part" to be a political strategy on the part of Christian men to force women back into a male-dominated social context and to snuff out those house churches over which women exercised authority. While I do not agree with this reading of Luke 10:38–42, it does illustrate that on the topic of women as on many other topics there is some ambiguity in Luke's presentation (or at least in our understanding of it).

For Reflection and Discussion:

1. With which character—Mary or Martha—do you identify more easily?
2. What impression would Jesus' openness to women's participation in his movement have made on his contemporaries?
3. Is Luke a friend or a foe of women? Or is that the wrong question?

8
Luke 11:1–13:
Prayer
Cycle C:
Seventeenth Sunday in Ordinary Time

Luke is sometimes also called the Gospel of prayer because in it Jesus prays at key points in his life and gives two substantial instructions about prayer. The first of these instructions (11:1–13) features a sample prayer (which we know as the Lord's Prayer or the Our Father) that contains many Jewish phrases and themes (11:2–4), along with a parable encouraging persistence in prayer (11:5–8) and sayings about God's eagerness to answer prayers (11:9–13).

The sample prayer (11:2–4) comes in response to the disciples' request that Jesus teach them "to pray just as John taught his disciples" (11:1, NAB). The occasion is marked as especially important by the notice that the request was preceded by Jesus' own prayer ("he was praying in a certain place," NAB). Given how Luke described John the Baptist in 3:1–20, one can guess that John's prayer concerned the coming of God's kingdom and the proper preparation for it. And so does the prayer offered by Jesus.

The prayer of Jesus is often called the Lord's Prayer in keeping with one of the titles (*Kyrios*/Lord) given to Jesus in some New Testament texts or the Our Father from the first words in the version presented in Matthew 6:9–13. The Lukan version is generally regarded as the earlier form, though Jesus presumably composed the prayer in Aramaic (and it is easy enough to translate both Greek versions back in the Aramaic).

The fuller and more familiar Matthean version can be explained as a typical Jewish Christian expansion of something like the Lukan form. It contains a more usual Jewish title for God in prayer ("Our Father in heaven," NAB) and the addition of parallel phrases ("your will be done, on earth as in heaven" and "deliver us from the evil one," NAB) in keeping with the Jewish practice of prolonging prayer in the name of *kawanah* (greater attention to God in prayer). The concluding "seal" found in many later manuscripts ("for yours is the kingdom, the power, and the glory...") corresponds in function to the common Jewish technique of rounding off and summarizing the body of a prayer.

The Lukan version of the Lord's Prayer (11:2–4) consists of a direct address to God ("Father"), two "you" petitions ("hallowed be your name" and "your kingdom come," NAB), and three "we" petitions (for daily bread, for forgiveness of sins, and for protection in the final testing or trial).

The direct address to God as "Father," while not unique in Second Temple Judaism, is sometimes regarded as a sign of Jesus' distinctive approach to God. It suggests a certain intimacy with God on Jesus' part that was pivotal in developing the understanding of Jesus as "the Son of God." With this prayer Jesus invites his followers to share in that same relationship of intimacy with God. However, the simple address plays off the more common Jewish epithet "Our Father in heaven," and apparently Matthew (and other Jewish Christians) did not find a sharp contrast between the two modes of addressing God in prayer.

The body of the sample prayer consists of five short petitions, two with "you" and three with "we" language. Petition is at the heart of Jewish prayer. In many of the psalms the speaker addresses God directly, and this posture carries over in most Jewish and Christian prayers. To make a petition in prayer assumes that God is present (not absent or distant), hears prayers, and is willing to act upon them. Petition is also a confession of human limitation. It admits that humans need help from outside, and affirms that God can and does supply that help when asked to do so. The two "you" petitions concern the coming of God's kingdom, and the three "we" petitions ask God to sustain us in the process.

The content of the Lukan (and Matthean) Lord's Prayer is greatly illumined by two famous and important Jewish prayers. The *Kaddish,* often called the mourner's prayer, is in fact a prayer for the coming of God's kingdom. It asks first for the hallowing of God's name: "May his [God's] great name be magnified and sanctified in the world that is to be created anew." It goes on to pray for the coming of God's kingdom: "May the Holy One, blessed be he, establish his kingdom and his glory during your life…speedily and at a near time."

The *Amidah,* or Eighteen Benedictions, which is the Jewish daily prayer par excellence, consists mainly of petitions with "you" (God) and "we" language. It contains prayers for material sustenance in the face of the coming kingdom ("may its [this year's] harvest be abundant; hasten the time of our deliverance") and for divine forgiveness ("Forgive us, our Father, for we have sinned against you"). The late first-century work known as the *Didache* directs Christians to recite the Lord's Prayer "three times in the day" (8:3), thus suggesting that the Lord's Prayer functioned as an early Christian abbreviation of and alternative to the Jewish Eighteen Benedictions.

The sample prayer that Jesus gives is a prayer of petition. The material accompanying it in Luke 11:5–13 approaches the dynamic of petition from both human and divine perspectives. The parable of the friend at midnight (11:5–8) tells the story of a persistent neighbor who will not take no for an answer to his request for bread with which to feed an unexpected guest. The neighbor's persistence reaches the level of even "boldness" or "shamelessness" *(anaideia).* The point is that we should be that persistent in prayers of petition.

The sayings gathered in Luke 11:9–13 stress that God is very eager to answer our prayers. The block of sayings in 11:9–10 ("ask and you will receive…," NAB) envisions an almost automatic process, with no qualifications. This may well be an overstatement, but it does place a very high value on the efficacy of prayers of petition. The next block (11:11–13) uses the analogy of a father giving gifts to his son. No father would give a snake or a scorpion to his son when asked for a fish or an egg. Arguing from the lesser to the greater *(qal wahomer),* Jesus suggests that more than any human father God is willing and eager to give us good things when we make our petitions. And the very best thing that God can give to us is "the Holy Spirit" (compare Matt 7:11, which has simply "good gifts," NAB).

The second substantial Lukan instruction on prayer (18:1–14) takes the form of two parables. The parable of the persistent widow (18:1–8) shows how the widow can wear down even an unjust judge and force him to render for her a just decision. The point is that if a harsh and unjust judge will eventually give into a persistent widow, will not God *(qal wahomer)* answer the prayers of his righteous elect?

The parable of the Pharisee and the tax collector (18:9–14) encourages humility in prayer. Here the Pharisee is the model of the pious person, but his prayer consists in counting up his own spiritual accomplishments. By contrast, the tax collector because of his profession was suspected of cheating his fellow Jews and of collaborating with the Romans. Nevertheless, his prayer is heard because he simply acknowledges his unworthiness and prays: "O God, be merciful to me a sinner" (NAB).

A further aspect in Luke's theology of prayer is that at the most decisive moments in Jesus' career he prays: at his baptism (3:21), in the early stages of his healing activity (5:16), before choosing the twelve (6:12), before Peter's confession of Jesus as the Messiah (9:18), before the transfiguration (9:28–29), in the garden before his arrest (22:42), and at his death on the cross (23:34, 46). In many of these passages Jesus calls upon God as his "Father."

Both Jews and Christians can learn from Jesus' teaching and example regarding prayer, according to Luke. Jews can come to recognize that in form and content Jesus' prayer (and Christian prayer) has deep roots in Judaism, and that we both pray especially for the full coming of God's kingdom. Christians can grow in appreciation of petition as an essential element in Jewish prayer and theology. Moreover, by observing Jews at prayer they may be challenged to cultivate greater reverence in prayer and to understand the creative tension between individual and group in Jewish prayer. Both of us need to take to heart the need for persistence and humility in prayer, the value of prayer at decisive moments in our lives, and above all the recognition that the one to whom we pray is like a loving parent who hears our prayers and wants to respond generously to them.

For Reflection and Discussion:

1. Is there anything in the Lord's Prayer that a Jew could not say with complete sincerity and integrity?

2. Why is the prayer of petition so important for Jews and Christians? What understandings of God and the human condition underlie this emphasis?

3. Why does Jesus place such emphasis on persistence in the prayer of petition?

9
Luke 14:1, 7–14:
At the Pharisees' Banquet
Cycle C:
Twenty-Second Sunday in
Ordinary Time

In every culture, sharing a meal establishes a special bond between humans. In the ancient Near East and especially in ancient Israel, meals were important social occasions, signs of hospitality and respect. Meals were (and are) also associated with central moments in Israel's religious life. The system of sacrifices in the Jerusalem Temple was based on the notion of the people sharing a meal with God and eating in God's presence. As Proverbs 9 shows, meals were also occasions for dispensing and sharing wisdom. Passages like Isaiah 25:6–10 envision the future pilgrimage of all the nations to Jerusalem on the Day of the Lord as culminating in a great banquet. Passover was (and is) celebrated every year with a ritual family meal, and the Sabbath meal is a high point in the weekly rhythm of Jewish life today.

When Jews in Jesus' time came to express their hopes concerning the coming kingdom of God, they often evoked the image of a great feast at which God and/or his Messiah presides. The Qumran community apparently celebrated their common meals according to a hierarchical seating plan that highlighted the roles of the priests and of the Messiah(s) of Israel and of Aaron at the coming heavenly banquet.

They were conscious of the symbolic significance of these meals as anticipations of life in God's kingdom.

One of the most striking and controversial features of Jesus' public activity was his practice of sharing meals with socially and religiously marginal persons ("tax collectors and sinners"). These meals function as enacted parables of Jesus' message of reconciliation with God against the horizon of the coming kingdom. They provide important perspectives on Jesus' Last Supper and the Christian practice of the Eucharist.

The Pharisees were also well known for their fellowship *(haburah)* meals. These meals were means of building community identity among the members of the group, and were occasions for developing and sharing the distinctive traditions of the Pharisaic movement.

According to Luke, Jesus often participated in meals organized by Pharisees. According to Luke 7:36–50, it was at the house of Simon the Pharisee that a sinful woman anointed Jesus' feet and Jesus delivered his teachings about love and forgiveness. In Luke 11:37–52 the invitation to dine at the house of a Pharisee serves as the occasion for Jesus' denunciation of certain Pharisaic practices. And in Luke 14:1–24 Jesus' teaching about the kingdom of God takes place while he is dining "at the home of one of the leading Pharisees" (14:1, NAB).

The banquet teachings in Luke 14 consist of the healing of a man with dropsy (14:2–6), two statements about banquets (14:7–14), and the parable of the great banquet (14:15–24). The key to interpreting the whole passage is supplied by the guest who says: "Blessed is the one who will dine in the kingdom of God" (14:15, NAB). The background or horizon of everything in Luke 14:1–24 is the kingdom of God.

On one level, Jesus' teaching about places of honor in Luke 14:7–11 is commonsense advice, typical of what one finds in wisdom books like Proverbs and Sirach. If on entering a wedding banquet hall you proceed uninvited to the head table, it is likely that you will be asked to move down and sent away (for all to see!) in shame to a table assigned to persons of lower importance on this occasion. But if you first take the lower place and then are invited to the head table (for all to see!), you will be honored in the eyes of the other guests as somebody who is truly important.

Besides conveying wise teaching especially in a society in which honor and shame were very significant values, Jesus may well be criticizing the emphasis that Jews like the Qumran people and probably the Pharisees too placed on symbols of status at their meals (which were understood as anticipations of life in the coming kingdom of God). His wise teaching is clinched with a general saying about the "great reversal" that will characterize the full coming of God's kingdom: "For everyone who exalts himself will be humbled, but the one who humbles himself will be exalted" (14:11, NAB).

The second banquet teaching (14:12–14) concerns the kinds of people that Pharisees should invite to their banquets. The usual human practice is to invite social equals or superiors to share a meal, whether they be relatives, friends, or business associates. Behind this custom is the concept of mutual benefit, of doing a favor to get a favor in return, what we call *quid pro quo* ("something in return for something"). When I do something good or beneficial for you, you are generally expected to do something good or beneficial for me. When I invite you to dinner, I may expect you to invite me on another occasion. And on goes the cycle of doing favors and mutual benefit. There is nothing wrong with this. In fact, one might say that the sense of mutual benefit and obligation keeps human societies running quite well.

In this context Jesus' advice about inviting guests does not seem very wise. He tells the Pharisees not to invite friends, family, relatives, or wealthy neighbors to their banquets. Instead, he tells them to invite persons who were regarded as the most marginal in their society: "invite the poor, the crippled, the lame, the blind" (14:13, NAB). It is precisely "because of their inability to repay you" (NAB) that you should invite them. This is surprising and even paradoxical teaching from a wisdom teacher.

The effect of Jesus' surprising teaching pushes the Pharisees beyond commonsense wisdom into their most deeply held religious beliefs about resurrection of the dead and about rewards and punishments after death. Not all Jews in Jesus' day believed in life after death. But the Pharisees did. According to the first-century Jewish historian Flavius Josephus, the Pharisees "believe that souls have power to survive death and that there are rewards and punishments under the earth for those who have led lives of virtue or vice" (*Jewish Antiquities* 18:14).

According to Luke 18:14, Jesus challenges the Pharisees to invite socially marginal persons to their banquets precisely because they cannot offer anything in return. In doing so the Pharisees would be affirming in a practical way their beliefs in resurrection and in rewards and punishments after death: "you will be repaid at the resurrection of the righteous" (NAB).

Jesus' banquet teachings challenge Jews and Christians today to take seriously and act upon our traditional beliefs in resurrection and divine judgment. If we believe that the best and most important rewards come from God, then we are freed to do good not merely for the sake of some calculated gain or perceived benefit from other humans but rather because we want to serve God and other persons in doing so. If we are confident that God will take care of us in the Last Judgment, we are freed to imitate God as the greatest benefactor of all and to share the benefactions of God with others. Thus belief in resurrection and divine judgment can shape every aspect of our lives if we act upon what we profess to believe.

It is interesting to note how, according to Luke, the Pharisees keep inviting Jesus to their banquets. They seem to regard him as a wise teacher who shares their concerns and as someone who might teach them something important. Of course, Luke presents Jesus as generally criticizing and correcting the Pharisees. But they do keep inviting him! Of all the Jewish groups in his day, Jesus seems to have had most in common with the Pharisees.

For Reflection and Discussion:

1. Why do you think that Pharisees kept inviting Jesus to dinner? What does that say about their relationship?
2. How might inviting marginal persons to dinner express belief in resurrection?
3. How can the Lukan banquet teachings contribute to a better appreciation of Jewish Sabbath and holiday meals and to the Christian celebration of the Eucharist?

10
Luke 15:11–32:
The Prodigal Son
Cycle C:
Twenty-Fourth Sunday in
Ordinary Time

The Bible has a strong sense of both sin and repentance. In the Bible, sin is failure to love God, the neighbor, and the self. Sinners miss the mark, transgress, err, wander, rebel, refuse, profane, and/or act treacherously. They are evil, bad, worthless, twisted, and/or guilty. Sinful actions are symptoms of a general sinful orientation. Repentance involves turning back to God and to a virtuous way of life in relation to others.

The dynamic of sin, repentance, and forgiveness is most obvious in the annual Jewish observance of the Day of Atonement (Yom Kippur). Leviticus 16 describes in detail the ancient rituals of sacrifice and sprinkling of blood associated first with the tabernacle and then with the Temple. Since the destruction of the Second Temple in 70 CE, the Jewish Day of Atonement has taken other liturgical forms. But the purpose and message remain the same as in the Bible: "on this day atonement is made for you to make you clean, so that you may be cleansed of all your sins before the LORD" (Lev 16:30, NAB).

The biblical themes of sin, repentance, and forgiveness are well displayed in the lament contained in Daniel 9. The dynamic there rests on the basic biblical convictions about the justice and the mercy of God.

It also rests on the Jewish notion of the individual as part of the community of God's people. Daniel is the sage par excellence, primarily because he is the recipient of revelations from God. While he is part of the Jewish exilic community in Babylon, there is no hint of any personal sin on his part. Indeed, his greatness resides in steadfastly resisting temptations to engage in idolatry or act against the Torah in order to save his life and improve his status at the royal court. Nevertheless, Daniel proclaims: "We have sinned, been wicked and done evil; we have rebelled and departed from your commandments and your laws" (9:5, NAB). While acknowledging repeatedly the people's unfaithfulness and injustice, Daniel throws himself and his people upon the mercy of God: "Justice, O LORD, is on your side....But yours, O Lord, our God, are compassion and forgiveness" (9:7, 9, NAB).

The parable of the prodigal son in Luke 15:11–32 is a paradigm of the biblical dynamic of sin, repentance, and forgiveness. Sin involves turning aside from God and God's will. Meanwhile, God patiently and lovingly awaits our repentance and return. Repentance means acknowledging our sin and throwing ourselves on the mercy of God. And forgiveness and reconciliation are possible only because of God's mercy.

The parable of the prodigal son is part of a set of three parables about "the lost": lost sheep (15:4–7), lost coin (15:8–10), and lost son (15:11–32). They are placed in the context of complaints by Pharisees and scribes about the company that Jesus keeps (15:1–3). Their complaint is that "this man welcomes sinners and eats with them" (15:2, NAB). The "sinners" were those Jews who paid little or no attention to the Torah, while the tax collectors were regarded as dishonest Jews in the service of the Romans. By way of contrast, the Pharisees were serious religious persons dedicated to observing the Torah, and the scribes were thoroughly conversant with the Torah and its interpretation. These latter groups were puzzled as to why an apparently serious Jewish religious teacher like Jesus of Nazareth would spend so much time and effort on hopeless cases like tax collectors and sinners.

Jesus' response to their complaints first takes the form of two short "twin" parables—the lost sheep (15:4–7) and the lost coin (15:8–10), which have the same basic structure. There is a substantial possession (a large flock of sheep, ten coins); one small part (one sheep, one coin) becomes lost; there is an intensive search; what was lost is found; and there is great rejoicing over what is found again. These parables are intended to describe God's joy over the sinner who repents (15:7, 10). The point in the context of Jesus' own ministry is that since God's mercy is so great and since God takes great joy in the repentance and rescue of sinners, Jesus' practice of associating with tax collectors and sinners is in keeping with his role as God's representative.

The parable known commonly as "the prodigal son" in fact focuses on the father's love and joy over the return of his lost son. The adjective *prodigal* can mean "lavish," "extravagant," or "wasteful." The son is prodigal in wasting his inheritance and ending up in misery. But the father is also prodigal in his extravagant display of mercy and in putting on a lavish banquet to welcome back his lost son.

The parable concerns a father and his two sons. It illustrates God's willingness to accept the repentance of those who sin and to restore them to full membership in God's household. At the same time it offers a justification for Jesus' association with certain disreputable persons.

Early in the Christian tradition there developed an interpretation that equates the younger son with the Gentile church and the older son with the Jewish people. But it is unlikely that either Jesus or Luke had such a potentially anti-Jewish reading in mind. The parable is told within a completely Jewish context. Jesus the Jewish teacher defends himself and his practice before other Jewish teachers. He explains why he spends time with marginal Jews and suggests that other learned and pious Jews who ought to know better (scribes and Pharisees) fail to understand the ways of God and of Jesus his agent in proclaiming and inaugurating God's kingdom.

The story of the younger son (15:12–24) illustrates the biblical dynamic of sin, repentance, and forgiveness. When the younger son requests his share of his father's estate, his request is granted. While biblical scholars tend to focus on the legal procedures pertaining to inheritance in ancient Israel, the more important theological point is that the prodigal father gives his prodigal son the freedom to do what he wants. The prodigal son quickly spends all his assets foolishly, and when a famine occurs he is reduced to the depth of degradation for Jews: feeding pigs (unclean animals), and feeding himself on food meant for pigs. Finally he comes to his senses (15:17–19) and reasons that he would be better off even as a slave on his father's estate. But in 15:20–24 his father's joy is so great (prodigal) that at his prodigal son's return he accepts him as an honored guest and a full member of his household. The first part of the parable describes what God is like—abounding in goodness, mercy, and love, like the father who prepares the feast and offers a welcome to his wayward son.

The story of the elder son (15:25–32) addresses good people like the Pharisees and scribes (and many of us today) who are offended by Jesus' offer of divine forgiveness to tax collectors and sinners. The elder son is angry about the apparent injustice of the father in accepting the younger son back and celebrating his return. The tone adopted by the elder son is impolite (no mention of "father" in direct address) and harsh ("your son"). Nevertheless, the father remains positive and conciliatory: "But now we must celebrate and rejoice, because your brother was dead and has come to life again" (15:32, NAB).

We are not told whether the elder son accepted the father's explanation. And that is the point. The ending of the parable is left open, and it is up to the Pharisees and scribes (and us) to accept or reject Jesus' defense of God's ways and of his own practice in cultivating religiously marginal persons.

Repentance and forgiveness are essential parts of biblical spirituality. We can turn our lives around. We can go home again. God wants us to take responsibility for our lives and to repent, and God wants to forgive us. God never gives up on us, and so we need never give up on God.

The seriously religious among us—the Pharisees and scribes, you and I—can also learn important lessons from the elder son. He fails to recognize that the sincere repentance of sinners is an occasion for joy for us all. He is jealous and bitter instead of being generous and joyful over the return of a lost brother. The elder son refuses to enter into the communal process of repentance and forgiveness. He fails to recognize that repentance and forgiveness go together, are possibilities for us all, are part of our spiritual heritage, and are causes for joy and celebration among us all.

For Reflection and Discussion:

1. Imagine yourself as the younger (prodigal) son. What would you do if you were in his situation? What might you expect from God?
2. Do Jews and Christians worship the same God? What are the characteristics or attributes of that God?
3. Can you understand the reaction of the older son? Have you ever had similar thoughts about converts or repentant sinners?

11
Luke 16:1–13:
Money Matters
Cycle C:
Twenty-Fifth Sunday in
Ordinary Time

The words *spirituality* and *money* seldom appear in the same sentence. Yet Luke, that master of Christian spirituality, gives a good deal of attention to money and material possessions throughout his two-volume work, but especially in chapter 16 of his Gospel. Wisdom teachers in the ancient Near East and in Israel in particular took money matters as a major topic, and Jesus as a Jewish wisdom teacher was no exception. Some scholars argue that in Luke's community there were special problems between rich and poor members, and so Luke took great interest in addressing money matters. For Jews and Christians today who are serious about spirituality, money and possessions are important issues in everyone's life and raise challenging questions: What should we do with our money? What are proper attitudes toward wealth? Is there any relation between economics and spirituality?

Jesus was a wisdom teacher, not an economist. We cannot expect from Luke's Gospel economic master plans applicable to twenty-first-century conditions. But we can expect wise principles that are usually correct and that can help us in thinking about the proper uses of money and material possessions.

Ancient Jewish wisdom books like Proverbs, Sirach (Ben Sira), and the Qumran wisdom text known as *4QInstruction* pay a lot of attention to money matters. And it is not at all surprising that Luke's Gospel should give a prominent place to Jesus' wise teachings about money and material possessions. The parable about "the dishonest steward" (16:1–8) challenges people of faith to be more creative and enterprising about spiritual matters than even the clever estate manager was about material things. The three subsequent short teachings go in several directions: why you should be generous to those in need (16:9); the positive value of being trustworthy, faithful, and honest in the use of money (16:10–12); and not making money into a god (16:13). The ultimate question of all these teachings is, Whom do you trust—God or money?

The parable in Luke 16:1–8 is usually called "the dishonest steward." What is surprising and even shocking is that Jesus appears to condone and even praise an apparently dishonest action. Some have suggested that the parable was based on an actual incident that had been brought to Jesus' attention. In that setting it was expected that Jesus' reaction would be negative and condemnatory. However, Jesus surprises his interlocutors by praising the steward's cleverness and challenging them to be even more clever in matters of spirituality.

According to Luke 16:1–2, a steward or manager had been overseeing the property of an owner. In the Greco-Roman world (including Palestine) it was common for wealthy absentee landlords to put their estates in the hands of local property managers. This particular manager was apparently doing a bad job and reportedly squandering the owner's property. And so the owner summons the manager, tells him to get his accounts in order, and suggests that he look for another position.

The manager recognizes that he is in trouble and must find some way to save his skin. He says to himself: "I am not strong enough to dig and I am ashamed to beg" (16:3, NAB). He needs to find a way of getting out of his present dilemma and of ingratiating himself with someone who can give him a new job and allow him to carry on with his accustomed lifestyle.

His strategy as described in Luke 16:5–7 is to have his master's debtors rewrite their promissory notes at a lesser rate—fifty measures of olive oil instead of a hundred, and eighty kors of wheat instead of a hundred. By having the debtors rewrite their own notes in their own hands, the steward avoids committing forgery and makes the debtors accomplices in his scheme. Then he might also be able to use their cooperation as a lever to get a new job.

There are two ways to interpret what the manager did. In one reading the manager is simply dishonest. He cheats his boss and makes the other businessmen part of his dishonesty, thus setting them up for blackmail in the future. In another reading the manager is simply shrewd. The assumption is that the manager has been working on a commission basis. And in having the promissory notes rewritten, the manager is deliberately forgoing his own commission, thus sacrificing a short-term gain in the hope of a long-term gain. In this reading, the steward, after squandering his master's goods, redeems himself by giving to the owner what was owed him and ingratiates himself with other businessmen by lowering their debts.

However one interprets the manager's strategy, what the boss praises is the shrewdness, cleverness, and enterprise of the manager. In the ancient world (and much more so today) an enormous amount of intelligence, energy, and cleverness goes into the accumulation, management, and increase of money. What if the same kind of intelligence, energy, and cleverness went into serving God, clarifying and promoting moral values, and helping poor and defenseless persons in our society? This is the thrust of Jesus' comment in 16:8b about the superior cleverness of "the children of this world" (NAB) in comparison with "the children of light" (NAB). If the former can be so enterprising in money matters, why cannot the latter be even more enterprising in religious, moral, and social matters?

The three short teachings in Luke 16:9–13 about money matters are held together to some extent by the keyword *trust*. The Hebrew verb for "trust, believe" is *'aman*. From this root we derive our word *Amen*, by which we affirm that we trust or believe what was just said. The noun *Mammon*, which literally means something in which we place trust, became a synonym for money and other material goods as something in which people often place their trust.

The first short teaching (16:9) concerns almsgiving or giving to the poor. The expression translated as "dishonest wealth" is literally "the mammon of iniquity." The idea seems to be that by giving to the poor now you will make friends who might speak or act on your behalf at the time of your death or even during your life when your fortunes may be reversed and you find yourself in need. The logic seems to be that when we give money to others in need, we may build up spiritual capital that is more deserving of our trust than material possessions are, and so we may enlist a host of people who may help us in our own spiritual or even material need.

The second short teaching (16:10–12) concerns trustworthiness and stewardship. The logic seems to be that how well we deal with money and material possessions can be indicative of how we approach spiritual matters. If we are trustworthy and faithful and honest in dealing with our possessions and those of others, we will most likely be trustworthy and faithful and honest in dealing with God and with other persons. There is no flat rejection here of money or material possessions. Rather, they are assumed to be part of our ordinary lives. The virtues of trustworthiness, fidelity, and honesty, which are necessary for the good stewardship of material goods, are the kinds of virtues that are also needed in our relationships with God and with one another.

The third short teaching (16:13) asserts that no one can serve two masters, in this case, God and wealth (Mammon). The logic seems to be that many people make the choice for wealth and so effectively make money (Mammon) into a god or at least their ultimate reality. Their lives often end in frustration and unhappiness. Believers affirm that God, and not Mammon, is their ultimate reality.

For Reflection and Discussion:

1. Do you regard financial matters as part of your spirituality?
2. In what ways does the "dishonest" steward show himself to be wise in money matters?
3. U.S. currency bears the motto "In God We Trust." In what or in whom do you trust?

12
Luke 16:19–31:
The Rich Man and Lazarus
Cycle C:
Twenty-Sixth Sunday in
Ordinary Time

The parable of the rich man and Lazarus in Luke 16:19–31 treats money matters in a memorable and somewhat frightening way. We all need a good scare from time to time, and this narrative fits that description well. The basic message is that now (before it is too late) is the time to share your money and material goods with those in need.

The story features two characters (16:19–21). The rich man is splendidly dressed and feasts sumptuously every day. The other man is poor. His name is Lazarus, which is a Greek form of the Hebrew name *Eleazar* (meaning "God helps"). He is a beggar at the rich man's door, desiring nothing more than to eat from the scraps from the rich man's table. The two men could not be more different. And the rich man seems to be unaware of Lazarus's existence.

Both men die, and their fortunes are totally reversed (16:22–23). The poor man Lazarus ends up in perfect bliss, in Abraham's bosom, which we might call "heaven." The rich man ends up in the "netherworld," in what may be called Hades in Greek, Sheol (or even Gehenna) in Hebrew, and hell in English. Their respective fates reflect the beatitude in Luke 6:20 ("Blessed are you who are poor, / for the kingdom of God is yours," NAB) and the woe in 6:24 ("But woe to you who are rich, / for you have received your consolation," NAB).

The rest of the parable (16:24–31) is a dialogue between the rich man and "Father Abraham." While the rich man seems to be sincere in his requests, his tone remains imperious and demanding, what one might expect from someone accustomed to getting his own way.

The first request from the rich man (16:24–26) involves sending Lazarus to bring some water to him to relieve his physical suffering. Only at this point does he acknowledge the existence of Lazarus. But Abraham explains that it is now too late. The rich man had it good during his lifetime on earth, while the poor man did not. Now things are reversed. And there is no reversing the reversal, since "between us and you a great chasm is established" (16:26, NAB).

The second request from the rich man (16:27–29) involves sending Lazarus to warn the rich man's five brothers about what might happen to them unless they change their ways. Again he is still giving orders to some extent. Abraham answers that "they have Moses and the prophets" (16:29, NAB). In other words, they (and we) can know about sharing goods with the poor from the Hebrew Scriptures. Indeed, the Hebrew Bible is full of texts that demand special care for the weakest members of society. For example, Deuteronomy 24:17 teaches: "You shall not violate the rights of the alien or of the orphan, nor take the clothing of a widow as a pledge" (NAB). And Isaiah 58:7 describes the kind of fasting that is most acceptable to God as including "sharing your bread with the hungry, / sheltering the oppressed and the homeless" (NAB).

The third request from the rich man (16:30–31) is that "someone from the dead" (NAB) should go to his brothers and tell them about the reversal of fates for rich and poor after death. Abraham tells him that it would make no difference. If they will not listen to Moses and the prophets, they will not listen to someone from the dead.

The point of the parable is that now (after death) is too late for the rich man to share his goods. He should have done so when he was alive on earth. While the parable does concern life after death, it is also about social justice in the present. After death it is too late to share one's goods. When he was on earth, the rich man was too occupied with himself and took no notice of poor persons such as Lazarus.

The parable of the rich man and Lazarus is part of the larger Lukan theme of sharing material possessions. This theme owes more to the Hebrew Scriptures and their insistence on social justice than it does to the ideologies of socialism or communism.

The parable of the rich fool in Luke 12:16–21 carries a message similar to that of Luke 16:19–31. There was a rich man whose land provided a bountiful harvest. Instead of enjoying his bounty and sharing it with others, he turns all his energy and resources into building more and bigger barns to store all his surplus. His hope is that one day in the future he will "rest, eat, drink, be merry" (12:19, NAB). But that day never comes. His life is cut short by death, and he has to leave all his earthly possessions behind. A recurrent theme in Jewish wisdom literature is the folly of the man who spends his life amassing great wealth, only to leave it all to foolish heirs who will squander it. The challenge of this parable is to become "rich in what matters to God" (12:21, NAB) and to view life in the present as a gift from God.

In the early chapters of Luke's Acts of the Apostles the theme of sharing material goods within the Christian community is prominent. According to Acts 2:44, the earliest Jewish Christians at Jerusalem practiced a kind of community of material goods: "All who believed were together and had all things in common" (NAB). And, according to Acts 4:32, "no one claimed that any of his possessions was his own, but they had everything in common" (NAB).

However, the Lukan ideal of community of goods does not seem exactly the same as the practice of another Jewish group known as the Essenes as they are described by Josephus and Philo. The Essenes were the Jewish religious movement generally understood to be behind the Dead Sea scrolls. They lived a communal life both in isolated places like Qumran and in more populated places such as the Essene Quarter in Jerusalem. They ate together, had a common purse, and held property in common. They wore white garments taken from common stock. Their earnings were turned over to the administrator of their common fund. New members were expected to hand over all their worldly possessions to the community. Their lifestyle was much like that of later Christian religious orders and may well have provided the model for them.

The early Christians' model of sharing goods as it is described by Luke was different. According to Acts 2:45, "they would sell their property and possessions and divide them among all according to each one's need" (NAB). The idea is that whenever one Christian was in need, some other one was expected to sell off some property and through the mediation of the apostles was to meet the need of the first person. This process is illustrated positively by the example of Barnabas (Acts 4:36–37), who sells his field and turns over the proceeds to the apostles, and negatively by the terrifying case of Ananias and Sapphira (5:1–11), who hold back from the proceeds of their sale for themselves.

According to the Lukan model of sharing, Christians do not renounce their right to private property (as the Essenes did and as Christian religious do). Rather, they freely place their property at the disposal of church officers, who in turn meet the needs of the poor. Moreover, their charity seems to have been limited to members of the Christian community. And also there is a historical dispute about how accurately these Lukan texts reflect the actual practice of the early Christians in Jerusalem. Is Luke's portrait based on the exceptional instance of Barnabas (Acts 4:36–37)? Or does it reflect the general custom of the Jewish Christians at Jerusalem?

In either case, however, Luke's position is clear. *Now* is the time to share your money and material goods with those in need, since spiritual riches before God are more important and lasting than material possessions are.

For Reflection and Discussion:

1. Does the parable's portrayal of the rich man ring true to your experience? In what ways?
2. How might you apply this parable to relations between rich and poor nations today?
3. How do you share your possessions with those in need? Why do you do so?

13
Luke 17:11–19:
Healing and Thanksgiving
Cycle C:
Twenty-Eighth Sunday in
Ordinary Time

Thanksgiving is a very popular holiday in the United States. It is a fall harvest festival. It is a day of enjoyment, a day of special foods, visits with family and friends, and relaxation from work and other pressures. Almost everyone likes Thanksgiving Day. Yet most everyone loses sight of what the day is supposed to be. Indeed, someone once told me that of all the holidays he especially likes Thanksgiving because "it's not religious." Of course, the original purpose of Thanksgiving—to thank God for all the good (and not so good) things in our lives—was very religious. The problem is that few people today understand the biblical notion of thanksgiving.

Luke's account of the cleansing of ten lepers in 17:11–19 can help people today to enter into the biblical concept of thanksgiving. While there are many themes and motifs in this passage, here the focus will be on Jesus healing the ten lepers (17:11–14) and the thanksgiving offered by one of those who were healed (17:15–19).

The healing takes place as Jesus and his companions make their way through Samaria and Galilee on their journey to Jerusalem (17:11). As he approaches a village, ten lepers come to meet him. Keeping their distance from him, they cry out: "Jesus, Master! Have pity on us!" (17:12–13, NAB). We are to assume that the lepers had heard about Jesus' success as a healer, and perhaps they even knew about the healing of a leper early in Jesus' public ministry (see Luke 5:12–16). Jesus responds to their request simply by directing them to show themselves to the priests (17:14). Only as they have started on their way do they realize that they have been healed from their leprosy.

The topic of leprosy is treated in great detail in Leviticus 13– 14. Most biblical scholars agree that what is called *sara'at* there and elsewhere in the Hebrew Bible is *not* what today is called leprosy (Hansen's disease). Rather, the term refers to various skin diseases that were thought to be infectious and rendered persons ritually impure or unclean. Those who suffered from these conditions were supposed to identify themselves to those with whom they came in contact by shouting "Unclean, unclean!" (Lev 13:45, NAB) lest the latter be contaminated physically and/or ritually. And they were to separate themselves from the community and live on the outskirts of their village or city: "He shall dwell apart, making his abode outside the camp" (Lev 13:46, NAB). The only way in which *sara'at* sufferers could return to human society was to have themselves examined by the priests according to the detailed instructions in Leviticus and be declared by them to be free from the disease.

The Lukan narrative reflects the stipulations of Leviticus 13– 14. The lepers are on the outskirts of the village. They stand at a distance from Jesus. They seek healing from Jesus: "Have pity on us!" And Jesus instructs them to go to the priests and presumably have themselves declared clean once more. Jesus observes the precepts of the Torah.

There is no description of the actual healing. In Luke 5:12–16 Jesus heals a leper by touching him (and so rendering himself unclean?) and saying: "I do will it. Be made clean" (5:13a, NAB). And there the healing was immediate and complete: "And the leprosy left him immediately" (5:13b, NAB). But in 17:11–14, Jesus simply tells the lepers to go to the priests and they do so. The healing apparently takes place on their way to the priests. The lepers' faith in the word of Jesus is made manifest by their setting out to visit the priests and is rewarded by their healing.

For his part Jesus shows himself to be powerful in word and deed. On the strength of his word (in this case a word in full accord with the Torah), ten men suffering from leprosy are restored to physical health, ritual purity, and human community. And the pairing of Luke 17:11–19 with the Naaman story in 2 Kings 5 in the church's lectionary affirms once more Jesus' identity as a prophet after the pattern of Elisha and Elijah (see Luke 4:27). That pairing reminds us that those two ninth-century prophets are far better models for understanding the Jesus of the Gospels than the "divine men" of the Greco-Roman world are.

The biblical theme of thanksgiving comes to the fore in the second part of the story (17:15–19), when one of the healed lepers returns to praise God and to thank Jesus. That man is a Samaritan, a person regarded by some Jews as a foreigner and not a real Jew (see the discussion of Luke 10:25–37 above), one who was perhaps the least expected to come back and give thanks for his healing by Jesus the Jew. And so Jesus asks: "Has none but this foreigner returned to give thanks to God?" (17:18, NAB). Then he says to the Samaritan: "Your faith has saved you" (17:19, NAB). The verb *save* (*sozo* in Greek) has the double sense of "heal" in the physical sense and "save" in the spiritual sense. That the man's faith brought about his physical healing has already been suggested in 17:14. But here in 17:19 there is probably also an allusion to the more spiritual aspect of salvation.

The Hebrew word for "giving thanks" is *hodah*, the causative form of the root *yadah*. The same word can also mean "to confess, proclaim, or recite." This wide range of meaning is the key to understanding what the Bible means by thanksgiving. In the biblical context, to give thanks means to confess, proclaim, and recite what God has done in our world and in our lives. Thanksgiving in the biblical sense begins from the mighty acts of God. It focuses on God's work in creating the universe and ourselves within it, on God's liberating his people from slavery in Egypt and on God's continuing care for this people, and on God as the ultimate sovereign and goal of all creation. Thanksgiving in the Bible begins and ends with God.

In our modern secular society, thanksgiving can easily degenerate into self-congratulation and smugness. While ostensibly thanking God, we may fall into admiring our own accomplishments and into imagining that we have earned all our own good fortune. The biblical approach to thanksgiving is very different from that. It focuses on God. It congratulates God, not ourselves. It sees clearly the greatness of God and how dependent we are on God. It is God-focused and not self-absorbed. It proclaims the mighty acts of God, not our own puny achievements.

The theme of thanksgiving is at the heart of both Jewish and Christian worship. There are many thanksgiving psalms in the biblical Book of Psalms. One of the most extensive and important texts discovered among the Dead Sea scrolls is known as the *Hodayot*, or *Thanksgiving Hymns*. The Jewish prayer-book is filled with expressions of thanks and praise directed to God. One of the traditional names for the ongoing sacrament of Christian life is the Eucharist, which derives from the Greek word for "thanksgiving." The Eucharistic prayers are essentially prayers of thanksgiving in which Christians recall the mighty acts of the God of the Bible and proclaim what God has done in the history of our salvation. Jews and Christians share a very rich concept of thanksgiving.

For Reflection and Discussion:

1. How do you understand thanksgiving? How does your concept compare with the biblical concept?
2. What do you make out of the fact that Jesus appears to be very conscious and observant of the regulations pertaining to leprosy in Leviticus 13—14?
3. What significance does the fact that the only healed leper who gave thanks was a Samaritan?

14

Luke 23:34, 43, 46:
The Last Words of Jesus
Cycle C:
Passion (or Palm) Sunday

In Luke's narrative of Jesus' crucifixion and death (23:33–49), there are three sayings attributed to Jesus as he is dying on the cross. In each case, even in death, Jesus shows himself to be faithful to the principles and ideals that he taught and practiced during his public ministry. In death as in life, Jesus is a person of complete integrity and provides a good example. Analysis of these three sayings can help us to appreciate better Luke's distinctive approach to Jesus' passion and death in Luke 22—23.

As Jesus was being crucified, he says (Luke 23:34), "Father, forgive them, they know not what they do" (NAB). In his public ministry Jesus addresses God as "Father" (10:21) and teaches his followers to do so too when saying the Lord's Prayer (11:2–4). In his struggle to accept God's will in the garden at Gethsemane he calls upon God as "Father" (22:42). In his very last words (23:46) he introduces the quotation of Psalm 31:5 with the direct address "Father." In 6:27–28 Jesus challenges his disciples to love their enemies, and in 17:4 he goes so far as to urge them to forgive someone even seven times in the course of one day. Here in 23:34 he forgives those who are responsible for his death. The idea that these persons acted out of ignorance appears several times also in Acts (see 3:17; 13:27; 17:34). At the time of his crucifixion and death, the Lukan Jesus reaffirms his intimate relationship with God as his "Father," forgives his enemies, and even makes an excuse for them.

The second of Jesus' three "last words" in 23:43 is directed to the so-called good thief, one of the two criminals (literally, "evildoers") with whom he is crucified. According to Luke, one of them affirmed Jesus' innocence in 23:41: "this man has done nothing criminal" (NAB). When the good thief asks Jesus to remember him when he comes into his kingdom, Jesus promises in 23:43: "Amen, I say to you, today you will be with me in Paradise" (NAB). The introductory "Amen" formula that begins the statement is common in Jesus' sayings in the Gospels (though rare elsewhere in Jewish texts) and adds solemnity to what follows. The word *today* occurs eleven times in Luke's Gospel, and at several key points (2:11; 4:21; 19:9) it affirms the presence of salvation in the person of Jesus. The term *Paradise* recalls the expulsion of Adam and Eve from the earthly Paradise in Genesis 3, and suggests that Jesus as the New Adam has opened up the heavenly Paradise. But the most important aspect of Luke 23:43 is that with it Jesus carries on his mission to the lost, in this case an evildoer.

According to Luke 23:46, the third and very last words of Jesus are a quotation from Psalm 31:5a: "Father, into your hands I commend my spirit" (NAB). At the decisive moments in his life, the Lukan Jesus turns to prayer. And these prayers generally allude to his identity as God's Son and his relationship to God as Father. So in his very last words he prefaces his quotation of Psalm 31:5a with the address "Father" and makes it into his own prayer. Psalm 31 is a lament, one of a very large number of lament psalms in the Bible. In the laments, the speaker typically addresses God directly ("O God"), describes the present suffering and complains about it, reminds God about what God has done in the past and needs to do in the present, asks God to relieve the suffering and make things right again, and alludes to a thanksgiving sacrifice. For thousands of years the biblical laments have provided suffering persons with the vocabulary to address God in their pain, to have the courage to shake off their religious inhibitions and to show genuine human emotions (especially anger), and to experience the sense of community that enables them to recognize that they are not alone.

The first part of Psalm 31 (NAB) consists of a petition in verses 2–5 ("in your justice deliver me"), an expression of trust in God in verses 6–9 ("Into your hands I commend my spirit"), a lament in

verses 10–14 ("my life is worn out by sorrow, / my years by sighing...
/ I am like a shattered dish"), another expression of trust in verse 15
("But I trust in you, LORD; / I say, 'You are my God'"), and another
petition in verses 16–19 ("rescue me... / save me in your kindness").
The second part offers praise to God in verses 20–23 ("how great is
your goodness, LORD") and addresses the faithful in verses 24–25
("love the LORD... / Be strong and take heart").

In suffering a shameful death on the cross Jesus stands in solidarity with all sufferers in the past and present. To appreciate properly
why the Lukan Jesus recites Psalm 31:5a, it is necessary to read the
whole psalm and so enter into the dynamics of the biblical laments.
Death by crucifixion was both physically painful and socially shameful. It was inflicted by the Romans on rebels and slaves. One ancient
author called it "the cruelest way to die."

The physical dimension of Jesus' suffering echoes what is said
in Psalm 31:11 (NAB): "My strength fails in affliction; / my bones are
consumed." The element of shame is highlighted in 31:12: "To all my
foes I am a thing of scorn, / to my neighbors, a dreaded sight, / a horror to my friends." And the fact that Jesus finds himself the victim of
various plots among the political and religious leaders—Jews and
Gentiles both—and abandoned even by his closest followers is captured well by Psalm 31:14: "I hear the whispers of the crowd; / terrors
are all around me. / They conspire together against me; / they plot to
take my life." The Lukan passion narrative in general and Luke 23:46
in particular place Jesus within the tradition of the biblical laments.

With Psalm 31:5a Jesus entrusts himself into the hands of God
as his Father. Throughout his public ministry, according to Luke,
Jesus encouraged his followers to trust in God. He taught them not to
be anxious about what they are to eat or wear. He declared "blessed"
or "happy" those who have nothing or no one else to rely upon or to
support them. And he now shows exemplary trust in God at this most
decisive moment.

At the same time Jesus the righteous sufferer expects vindication from God. This is another recurrent theme in the biblical laments.
The words immediately following Psalm 31:5a are full of trust in
God's power to bring good out of evil and life out of death: "you will
redeem me, LORD, faithful God" (31:6, NAB). In Christian faith the
resurrection of Jesus is the vindication of his life, teaching, healing,
suffering, and death. He trusted in God, and God vindicated him in the

resurrection. He hoped in his Father, and God gave him life again. This is the basis of Christian hope for resurrection.

For Reflection and Discussion:

1. How are various elements in Psalm 31 echoed in Luke's passion narrative?
2. In what sense is Jesus in his passion and death an example for us all?
3. How do each of Jesus' last words according to Luke illustrate a major concern in Jesus' public ministry?

15
Luke 24:13–35:
The Appearance on the Road to Emmaus
Cycles A, B, C:
Easter Afternoon/Cycle A:
Third Sunday in Easter

Luke 24:13–35 tells a story about the afternoon of the first Easter Sunday. It concerns two discouraged disciples who were ready to give up on Jesus and his movement. It features a mysterious stranger who accompanies these two "sad sacks" on the road and who turns out to be the risen Jesus. The two move from the deep discouragement of "we were hoping" (24:21, NAB) to burning hearts (24:32) and shouts of joy. The text has been described as everyone's favorite Easter story.

In Luke's Gospel, as in the other Gospels, there are two kinds of Easter accounts: stories about the empty tomb of Jesus and stories about appearances of the risen Jesus to his followers. Luke's empty tomb narrative (24:1–12) follows the basic outline of Mark 16:1–8, but emphasizes in 24:5–7 the continuity between what Jesus taught in Galilee and his resurrection ("that the Son of Man must…rise on the third day"). It also makes clear in 24:11–12 that the women who found the tomb empty conveyed the message to Peter and the other apostles (something left ambiguous by Mark 16:8).

The two appearance stories in Luke 24:13–35 and 24:36–49 explain how Jesus' followers came to recognize him in his risen state.

In both cases the recognition comes through reflecting on the Scriptures (24:27, 45) and sharing a meal (24:29–31, 41–43) with the risen Jesus. The story of Jesus' ascension in Luke 24:50–53 ("he parted from them and was taken up to heaven," NAB) evokes memories of Enoch (Gen 5:21) and Elijah (2 Kings 2), and is told at greater length in Acts 1:9–12.

Luke 24:13–35 is the longest and most elegant appearance account in the New Testament. While the story is probably rooted in early Christian tradition, its language, style, and themes are thoroughly Lukan. It seeks to underscore the continuing presence of the risen Jesus within the Christian community through the witness of Scripture and the shared meal.

The narrative begins in Luke 24:13–16 with the two disciples (not members of the twelve) on the road from Jerusalem to Emmaus, a village in Judea whose exact location remains disputed. They encounter the risen Jesus on the way but fail to recognize him.

In 24:17–27 they enter into conversation with the mysterious stranger and explain the reasons for their discouragement to him. They thought that Jesus was "the prophet" and that he was going to restore Israel to its rightful place in the world. But they saw him condemned and crucified by "our chief priests and rulers" (24:20, NAB). To add to their discouragement Jesus' body had disappeared. Their assumption seems to have been that his body had been stolen. The mysterious stranger, however, claims in 24:25–27 that Jesus' suffering and death were in accord with God's will made manifest in Israel's Scriptures, and that it was necessary for the Messiah to suffer before entering into his glory.

Then in 24:28–32 the mysterious stranger shares a meal with the two discouraged disciples. At this point the stranger acts in way that reminds them of what Jesus did in feeding the five thousand (9:16) and at the Last Supper (22:19): "he took bread, said the blessing, broke it, and gave it to them" (24:30, NAB). Then the disciples' eyes were opened and they recognized that the mysterious stranger was the risen Jesus. Finally, in 24:33–35 the two disciples return to Jerusalem and share their good news with the eleven apostles (the twelve minus Judas) at a common meal ("the breaking of the bread").

This passage brings up three major themes that have appeared throughout Luke's Gospel: Jesus as a prophet, the fulfillment of Scripture, and shared meals. The two disciples describe Jesus as "a prophet mighty in deed and word before God and all the people" (24:19, NAB). In many respects their description is accurate. Jesus surely exhibited the characteristics of a Jewish prophet. He taught in words and deeds (symbolic actions, miracles), called the people to repent, offered predictions about the future, and suffered hostility and opposition. In his programmatic preface in 4:16–30, Luke portrayed Jesus' mission in terms of Isaiah 61:1–3 and placed Jesus in line with Elijah and Elisha. The people proclaim Jesus as a prophet ("a great prophet has arisen in our midst," 7:16, NAB), while Simon the Pharisee in 7:39 expresses (a mistaken) skepticism about Jesus' identity as a prophet ("if this man were a prophet," NAB). The purpose of Jesus' last journey becomes clear in 13:33 when Jesus faces the fact that prophets customarily die in Jerusalem. While designating Jesus as a prophet is accurate enough, Luke wants also to insist that in his death and resurrection Jesus fulfills the Law, Prophets, and the Writings ("David").

In the infancy narrative the prophet Simeon not only described Jesus in terms of Isaiah 40—55 but also warned that he would be "a sign that will be contradicted" (2:34, NAB). One the problems associated with New Testament claims that it was "necessary that the Messiah [or Son of Man] should suffer these things" (24:26, NAB) is that it is hard to find any such texts in the Hebrew Bible. In Acts 8:26–39, however, Luke gives us a clue as to what he had in mind. There the Ethiopian eunuch, while reading about the Suffering Servant in Isaiah 53, encounters the evangelist Philip. After quoting Isaiah ("like a sheep he was led to the slaughter," NAB), the Ethiopian asks, "About whom is the prophet saying this?" (8:34, NAB). In response, Philip began with the Scripture passage and "proclaimed Jesus to him" (NAB). The Ethiopian then requests baptism from Philip. The structural parallels between Luke 24:13–35 and Acts 8:26–39 (the exposition of Scripture and the meal/baptism) are striking. The point is that in 24:25–27 Luke very likely expects readers to think in terms of Isaiah 53 and the Suffering Servant.

The encounter between Jesus and the two disciples on the road to Emmaus issues in a meal at which they come to recognize the mysterious stranger as the risen Jesus. This evokes the banquet theme that runs through Luke's Gospel. Banquets given by Pharisees serve as the occasions for wise teachings by Jesus in 7:36–50, 11:37–54, and 14:1–24. One of the accusations made against Jesus is that "this man welcomes sinners and eats with them" (15:2, NAB), which provides Jesus with the opportunity to defend his inclusive ministry in terms of God's care for the lost. It is in the context of the theme of Jesus' meals that we must interpret not only his feeding of the five thousand (9:10–17) but also his Last Supper (22:15–20) and his post-Easter meals with the disciples (24:13–35, 24:36–49).

In Luke's Gospel the reflection on Israel's Scriptures and the sharing of the meal with the risen Jesus provide the pattern for the disciples' experience on the first Easter Sunday afternoon in both 24:13–35 and 24:36–49. Both elements have deep roots within the Jewish tradition and make little sense without recourse to it. The same structure remains essential today to the Christian celebration of the Eucharist as the sacrament of ongoing Christian life. In the Eucharist Christians repeat the experience of the disciples on the road to Emmaus and come to know the risen Jesus in the Scriptures and "the breaking of the bread" (NAB).

For Reflection and Discussion:

1. Is resurrection a Jewish belief? How and when did Jews of Jesus' time expect the resurrection to take place?
2. What does the risen Jesus sharing meals with his disciples say about the nature of his resurrection?
3. In what sense is Jesus a prophet and the fulfillment of the prophecies in the Scriptures?

Epilogue:
Reading the Gospels in Context

Christianity is an incarnational religion. With John the evangelist we profess that "the Word became flesh / and made his dwelling among us" (John 1:14, NAB). Where the incarnation took place was the land of Israel, among the Jewish people. The time was over two thousand years ago. Then that land was part of the Roman Empire, and many people there hoped that God's promises to his chosen people might somehow be fulfilled so that they might find peace and freedom in accord with their dignity as God's people.)

The introductions and textual studies in this volume have tried to illustrate the positive value of reading Gospel texts in their original Jewish contexts. While the three Synoptic Gospels present a common vision of Jesus, they also present distinctive portraits of him. By attending to their Jewish settings and roots as well as their literary and theological individuality, this volume has attempted to present a positive and constructive approach toward reducing the anti-Jewish potential in certain Gospel texts. The paradox on which this book has been based is that the more we study the Gospels in their original Jewish contexts, the less we view them as anti-Jewish and the more we appreciate their richness and allow the word of God within them to speak to us.)

I have written as a Catholic Christian and more specifically as an American Jesuit priest and a biblical scholar who preaches regularly. I am aware that other readers, Christians and Jews alike, might see and say things differently. However, I am fully convinced that the key to understanding both Testaments in the Christian Bible appears in what has long been one of my favorite biblical texts and an inspiration for my own work on Second Temple Judaism and the New Testament: "In those days ten men of every nationality, speaking different tongues, shall take hold, yes, take hold of every Jew by the edge of his garment and say, 'Let us go with you, for we have heard that God is with you'" (Zech 8:23, NAB).

Glossary

Apocalypse—a narrative recounting a dream or vision about the future or the heavenly realm.

Beatitude—a declaration of someone as happy, fortunate, or blessed.

Eighteen Benedictions – the traditional Jewish daily prayer consisting of praises and petitions.

Eschatology—teachings about resurrection, divine judgment, and rewards and punishments.

Essenes—a Jewish religious movement contemporary with Jesus, most likely the group behind the Dead Sea scrolls.

Gospels—the "good news" about Jesus and the narratives about him.

Herod Antipas—the son of Herod the Great, who ruled Galilee in Jesus' time.

Herodians—supporters of Herod the Great and his dynasty.

Hillel—a Jewish teacher around Jesus' time, known for his liberal views in comparison with those of Shammai.

Hodayot—the book of thanksgiving hymns found among the Dead Sea scrolls.

Josephus—A Jewish historian who in the late first century wrote accounts of Israel's history *(Jewish Antiquities)* and the revolt against Rome *(Jewish War)*.

Kaddish—the Jewish prayer for the full coming of God's kingdom, also used as a prayer for the dead.

L—the symbol used to designate traditional material used only by Luke.

Laments—psalms that feature complaints about suffering and affirmations of trust in God.

Lectionary—a book that contains the biblical readings used in liturgical celebrations.

M—the symbol used to designate traditional material used only by Matthew.

Midrash—Jewish interpretations of Scripture, often collected in commentary format.

Mishnah—the collection of Jewish traditions made around 200 CE on various matters in the Torah.

Nostra aetate—the 1965 document from Vatican II about the relationship of the Catholic Church to other religions (including Judaism).

Ossuary—a box made out of stone for storing the bones of a deceased person.

Passover Seder—rituals and prayers associated with the Jewish celebration of Passover.

Pharisees—a Jewish religious movement contemporary with Jesus that emphasized observance of the Jewish Law and priestly spirituality.

Q—the symbols used to designate the collection of Jesus' sayings used independently by Matthew and Luke.

Qumran—the site near the Dead Sea where many ancient Jewish texts were discovered in the late 1940s and early 1950s.

Rule of the Community—a Dead Sea text that may have served as the rulebook for an ancient Jewish monastic community.

Sabbath—the seventh day of the week (our Saturday), set apart by Jews for prayer, rest, and fellowship.

Sadducees—a conservative Jewish group, contemporary with Jesus, noted for its opposition to the doctrine of resurrection.

Samaritans—the inhabitants of the territory between Galilee to the north and Judea to the south.

Scribes—experts in matters of Jewish Law and religious practice.

Septuagint— the ancient Greek translation of the Hebrew Scriptures used also by early Christians.

Shammai— a Jewish teacher around Jesus' time, known for his conservative views in comparison with those of Hillel.

Supersessionism—the belief that Christians have completely replaced Jews as the chosen people of God.

Synagogue —the gathering place for Jewish prayer and fellowship.

Synoptics—the term applied to the Gospels of Matthew, Mark, and Luke because they share a common view of Jesus and his public activity.

Talmuds—the collections of traditions and interpretations of the Mishnah, made in Palestine (fourth century) and Babylonia (fifth century).

Torah—the Hebrew term for the laws in the Bible and for the first five books of the Hebrew Bible.

For Further Study

THE GOSPEL OF MATTHEW

Davies, William D., and Dale C. Allison. *A Critical and Exegetical Commentary on the Gospel According to Matthew*. 3 vols. International Critical Commentary. Edinburgh: T&T Clark, 1988, 1991, 1997.

Goldsmith, Martin. *Matthew and Mission: The Gospel Through Jewish Eyes*. Carlisle, UK: Paternoster, 2003.

Harrington, Daniel J. *The Gospel of Matthew*. Sacra Pagina 1. Collegeville: Liturgical Press, 1991.

Luz, Ulrich. *Matthew: A Commentary*. 3 vols. Hermeneia. Minneapolis: Fortress, 1989, 2001, 2005.

Neusner, Jacob. *A Rabbi Talks with Jesus*. New York: Doubleday, 1993.

Overman, J. Andrew. *Matthew's Gospel and Formative Judaism: The Social World of the Matthean Community*. Minneapolis: Fortress, 1990.

————. *The Gospel of Matthew. Church and Community in Crisis*. *New Testament in Context*. Valley Forge, PA: Trinity Press International, 1996.

Saldarini, Anthony J. *Matthew's Christian-Jewish Community*. Chicago: University of Chicago Press, 1994.

Senior, Donald. *Matthew*. Abingdon New Testament Commentaries. Nashville: Abingdon, 1998.

Sim, David C. *The Gospel of Matthew and Christian Judaism: The History and Social Setting of the Matthean Community*. Edinburgh: T&T Clark, 1998.

Westerholm, Stephen. *Understanding Matthew: The Early Christian Worldview of the First Gospel*. Grand Rapids: Baker, 2004.

THE GOSPEL OF MARK

Brown, Raymond E. *The Death of the Messiah. From Gethsemane to the Grave. A Commentary on the Passion Narratives in the Four Gospels*. New York: Doubleday, 1994.

Cook, Michael. *Mark's Treatment of the Jewish Leaders*. Leiden: Brill, 1978.

Donahue, John R., and Daniel J. Harrington. *The Gospel of Mark*. Sacra Pagina 2. Collegeville, MN: Liturgical Press, 2002.

Harrington, Daniel J. *What Are They Saying About Mark?* Mahwah, NJ, and New York: Paulist, 2005.

Heil, John P. *The Gospel of Mark as a Model for Action*. Mahwah, NJ, and New York: Paulist, 1992.

Hooker, Morna D. *The Gospel According to St Mark*. Peabody, MA: Hendrickson, 1991.

Horsley, Richard A. *Hearing the Whole Story: The Politics of Plot in Mark's Gospel*. Louisville: Westminster John Knox, 2001.

Marcus, Joel. *Mark 1–8*. Anchor Bible. New York: Doubleday, 2000.

———. *The Way of the Lord: Christological Exegesis of the Old Testament in the Gospel of Mark*. Louisville: Westminster John Knox, 1992.

Moloney, Francis J. *The Gospel of Mark: A Commentary*. Peabody, MA; Hendrickson, 2002.

———. *Mark: Storyteller, Interpreter, Evangelist*. Peabody, MA: Hendrickson, 2004.

Telford, William R. *The Theology of the Gospel of Mark*. Cambridge: Cambridge University Press, 1999.

THE GOSPEL OF LUKE

Bovon, François. *Luke 1: A Commentary on the Gospel of Luke 1:1–9:50*. Hermeneia. Minneapolis: Fortress, 2002.

Brawley, Robert L. *Luke–Acts and the Jews: Conflict, Apology, and Conciliation*. Atlanta: Scholars Press, 1987.

Chance, J. Bradley. *Jerusalem, the Temple, and the New Age in Luke–Acts*. Macon, GA: Mercer University Press, 1988.

Fitzmyer, Joseph A. *The Gospel According to Luke*. Anchor Bible. New York: Doubleday, 1981, 1985.

Jervell, Jacob. *Luke and the People of God: A New Look at Luke–Acts*. Minneapolis: Augsburg, 1972.

Johnson, Luke T. *The Gospel of Luke*. Sacra Pagina 3. Collegeville, MN: Liturgical Press, 1991.

Moessner, Donald P. (ed.). *Jesus and the Heritage of Israel: Luke's Narrative Claim Upon Israel's Legacy*. Harrisburg, PA: Trinity Press International, 1999.

Sanders, Jack T. *The Jews in Luke-Acts*. Philadelphia: Fortress, 1987.

Tannehill, Robert C. *Luke*. Abingdon New Testament Commentaries. Nashville: Abingdon, 1996.

Tiede, David. *Prophecy and History in Luke–Acts*. Philadelphia: Fortress, 1980.

Tyson, Joseph. *Images of Judaism in Luke–Acts*. Columbia: University of South Carolina Press, 1992.

———. *Luke, Judaism, and the Scholars: Critical Approaches to Luke–Acts*. Columbia: University of South Carolina Press, 1999.

Nov. 30